On Understanding Buddhists

SUNY Series in Buddhist Studies
Matthew Kapstein, Editor

ON UNDERSTANDING

Buddhists

Essays on the Theravāda Tradition in Sri Lanka

John Ross Carter

STATE UNIVERSITY OF NEW YORK PRESS

Published by
State University of New York Press, Albany

Printed in the United States of America

For information, address State University of New York
Press, State University Plaza, Albany, NY 12246

Production by Bernadine Dawes
Marketing by Bernadette LaManna

Library of Congress Cataloging-in-Publication Data

Carter, John Ross.
On understanding Buddhists : essays on the Theravāda tradition in
Sri Lanka / John Ross Carter.
p. cm. — (SUNY series in Buddhist studies)
Includes bibliographical references and index.
ISBN 0–7914–1413–2 (acid-free paper) : $49.50. — ISBN
0–7914–1414–0 (pbk.: acid-free paper) : $16.95
1. Theravāda Buddhism—Sri Lanka. 2. Buddhism—Doctrines.
I. Title. II. Series.
BQ360.C38 1993
294.3'91'095493—dc20 92–10830
CIP

1 2 3 4 5 6 7 8 9 10

To
Wilfred Cantwell Smith
Teacher,
Virtuous Friend

CONTENTS

PREFACE

This is a study about friends of old and of today, a study offered in response to their friendship. It is an attempt to glimpse what they beheld, to come to understand a little, perhaps, of what undergirds their lives.

I speak of friends of old, having in mind those Buddhists who have gone on before us, who speak to us through their recorded words, words shared by them and remembered by countless others through the centuries, words that have come before the eyes of a person living today. And by writing of friends of today I mean the numberous men and women who are Buddhists who have been faithful and caring in enduring friendship.

It takes time for friendship to form and hold. It also has taken time to develop the observations occurring in the chapters that follow because of the demands and delights of undergraduate teaching and the recurring responsibilities and challenges of administrative tasks. I am grateful to the Fund for the Study of the Great Religions of the World, Colgate University, for the exhilarating opportunities for sabbatical leaves to study abroad, a necessity comparable to the need among some of our colleagues to work in their laboratories.

The anonymous donor who, in consultation with Kenneth W. Morgan, established this Fund at Colgate also initially established the funding for the Center for the Study of World Religions at Harvard University. There I first met Wilfred Smith, in 1965; and I continued to be affiliated with that program, then administered by the committee on Advanced Degrees in the Study of Religion of the Graduate School of Arts and Sciences, until 1972, when I came to Colgate to attempt to carry on the program launched by Kenneth Morgan.

At the Center at Harvard it soon became clear to the small but growing band of men and women in the graduate program that Wilfred Smith, supported by the quiet, community-building, resolute enthusiasm of his wife, Muriel, placed primary importance on the qualitative significance of the person in the context of learning and trust. And through the years those values I have found endorsed by Masatoshi Nagatomi, who introduced me to the Buddhist languages of India's past and to whom I once again express my gratitude. Those in the program then, and long since now, have found that rigorous studies and demanding assignments are readily, even happily, discharged when those studies have to do with one's friends and are undertaken among friends.

Those of us in the study of the religious life of humankind are fortunate to have traveled afar and to have found friends upon arrival, then to have returned home to work among friends. In this setting we are prepared to learn from each other, knowing fully that the difficulty of our study tends to make our conclusions tentative, to share our work, offered to be evaluated, and to trust that in so working we all move toward greater understanding.

Originally distributed in books and journals published in the United States, England, India, Sri Lanka, and Japan, most of the chapters that follow remained inaccessible to all but the most patient researcher in Buddhist Studies. Making these studies available in one volume will indicate clearly the significant contributions made by Wilfred Cantwell Smith, an Islamicist and a scholar of the religious history of humankind, to my thinking as I have turned my attention, rather, to important issues both in a study of the Theravāda Buddhist tradition and for Buddhists, who have perpetuated that remarkable tradition as fellow participants in our global religious history.

With gratitude for Wilfred Smith, who has demonstrated the inseparable interrelatedness of a thoroughgoing commitment to the pursuit of truth, intellectual cogency, and good will, this series of inquiries has been brought together and made available.

I wish to express my thanks to Marie A. Nardi for checking most of the typed copy of this text and indicating wherein corrections were necessary. The typing I did myself, but my son, Christopher John, came to my rescue on several occasions, helping me to understand the workings of a word processor. For the understanding my daughter, Mary Elizabeth, has extended to an occasionally preoccupied father, I am thankful. To Sandra, my wife, who has accompanied me through the journey that lies behind these inquiries and who has befriended those whom I am fortunate to call friends, I say thank you.

ACKNOWLEDGMENTS

I wish to acknowledge with gratitude the following publishing agencies for permission to reprint, with revisions, articles or chapters that appear in this book:

The first chapter, entitled "The Origin and Development of '*Buddhism*' and '*Religion*' in the Study of the Theravāda Buddhist Tradition," and the second, "The Coming of '*Early Buddhism*' to Sri Lanka," originally appeared as an essay entitled "A History of *Early Buddhism*," *Religious Studies* 13 (1977): 263–286. Chapter 3, "*Dhamma* at the Center," first appeared as "*Dhamma* as a Religious Concept: A Brief Investigation of Its History in the Western Academic Tradition and Its Centrality Within the Sinhalese Theravāda Tradition," *Journal of the American Academy of Religion* 44, Part 4 (1976): 661–674. "The Notion of Refuge," chapter 4, was published as part of a memorial volume in honor of Bhikkhu Jagdish Kashyap, *Studies in Pali and Buddhism*, edited by A. K. Narain (Delhi: B. R. Publishing Corporation, 1979), pp. 41–52. With some minor revisions, the piece became the first chapter of *The Threefold Refuge in the Theravāda Buddhist Tradition*, edited by John Ross Carter with George Doherty Bond, Edmund F. Perry, and Shanta Ratnayaka (Chambersburg, Penn.: Anima Books, 1982), pp. 1–15. With a few further revisions, it appears here. Chapter 6, "Beyond 'Beyond Good and Evil'," originally appeared in *Buddhist Studies in Honour of Hammalava Saddhātissa*, edited by Gatare

Dhammapala, Richard Gombrich, and K. R. Norman (Nugegoda, Sri Lanka: University of Sri Jayewardenepura, 1984), pp. 41–55. The eighth chapter, "There Are Buddhists Living in Sri Lanka Today," originally appeared as Chapter 10, "The Buddhist Tradition," in *Modern Sri Lanka: A Society in Transition*, edited by Tissa Fernando and Robert N. Kearney, (Foreign and Comparative Studies/South Asian Series 4, Maxwell School of Citizenship and Public Affairs, Syracuse, N.Y.: Syracuse University, 1979), pp. 181–200. "Music in the Theravāda Buddhist Heritage: In Chant, in Song, in Sri Lanka," Chapter 9, first appeared in *Sacred Sound: Music in Religious Thought and Practice*, edited by Joyce Irwin (Journal of the American Academy of Religion Thematic Studies, 50, no. 1; Chico, Calif.: Scholars Press, 1983), pp. 127–147. The final chapter, "The Role of the American Scholar in Buddhist Studies in Sri Lanka," is a revised form of a plenary address originally delivered to the All Ceylon Buddhist Congress, Colombo, Sri Lanka, as part of a seminar on the theme of Buddhist Studies by American Scholars, on November 19, 1977, to mark the twenty-fifth anniversary of the United States Educational Foundation in Sri Lanka, established by agreement between the governments of Sri Lanka and the United States of America. That address subsequently appeared in *Dialogue*, issued by the Ecumenical Institute for Study and Dialogue, Colombo, Sri Lanka, New Series, 5, no. 1 (January–April, 1978): 45–52.

INTRODUCTION

Over a decade ago Willard G. Oxtoby began his "Editor's Introduction" to *Religious Diversity: Essays by Wilfred Cantwell Smith* by sharing an observation:

> "Before I met Wilfred, I had studied Buddhism as a system. What I learned from him was to look for the faith of Buddhists as persons." These words, from one of Wilfred Cantwell Smith's Harvard students, sum up as succinctly as any the influence of this Canadian scholar, by general consent one of the foremost in the "history of religions," or comparative religion, field.[1]

What follows in this volume is an attempt, developing through the subsequent decade, to elaborate that oral observation faithfully recorded and shared by Oxtoby. It represents a continuation of one person's attempt "to look for the faith of Buddhists as persons."

The subject of this study is twofold: the Theravāda Buddhist tradition, particularly the shape or form that this cumulative tradition has taken in Sri Lanka, and the men and women who, by becoming engaged with this heritage and the message it conveys, have been enabled to live this human life as Buddhists. This study attempts to extrapolate from text and tradition, from doctrine and ritual, by thinking through new notions and reflecting on old issues, an understanding of the faith of men and women representing, through their participation in the Theravāda Buddhist tradition, a significant portion of humankind.

Within the past two decades, men and women living in Sri Lanka have experienced an eruption of conflicting ideologies representing the conceptual underpinnings of aspirations for an ideal social order. Sinhala men and women have seen this conflict defined along the extremely troubling lines of ethnic, linguistic, and religious differences: an abysmal vortex drawing into it apparently as much hatred, bitterness, misunderstanding, and lack of trust as persons are willing to project. These men and women have also witnessed an eruption among Sinhalas, bringing with it a saddening spectacle of slashing destruction of life and property, driven by a pent-up frustration of economic deprivation and political ineffectiveness, unventilated by insightful articulation. Indian troops have come, have left their mark singed into the memory both of Sinhalas and Tamils of Sri Lanka, and have gone.

Wherein is the calm and dispassionate voice of the Buddha? One receives in the United States a letter from a Sri Lankan Tamil Christian female professor of the Hindu tradition in which newspaper articles written by a Sri Lankan Sinhala Buddhist male professor of Sanskrit were applauded. The voice is there—it needs to be given sound by Buddhist men and women. We await this, alertly listening.

This book does not offer an account of these recent clashes and upheavals, nor does it provide a study of Buddhist responses, defensively mundane or compassionately creative. Information about these events is still being gathered and, although being chronologically near and personally close to these events—even still somewhat baffled by the intensity of the hatred and benumbed by the pain—we await further reporting. Interpretation, however, requires perspective; and the essays in this volume are designed to provide a perspective whereby one might discern assumptions, affirmations, and aspirations held and celebrated by persons seeking to enhance the quality of human living as this quality has been demonstrated in the Theravāda Buddhist heritage. Once these are seen, and it is important that they be seen, wherein some of us have failed in Sri Lanka will become more fully, more humanely, understood.

Further, we will not be concerned primarily with a study of "religion." We will be concerned with understanding what persons who are Theravāda Buddhists have said and are saying about living life religiously. This differentiation is neither pedantic nor flippant. The difference between studying the notion "religion" and studying what men and women in India and Sri Lanka, and Southeast Asia, China and Japan, too, have been saying about the good life, the life lived well, an authentically human life, is profound. We will be reflecting on their thoughts and interpreting their actions in terms of those thoughts and in light of that to which those thoughts point.

We do well, at the outset of this study, to put aside the term and concept *religion*. This term, originally from Latin *religio*, has been around in the West for over two thousand years and the development of its meanings through these centuries has not been entirely consistent. Rather early in the use of the Latin word *religio* two strands of meaning developed. One was more personalistic and communicated a sense of personal involvement, an engaged attitude towards deity. Another strand of interpretation, also appearing quite early, understood the term *religion* to pertain to something impersonal, "out there" as it were. Wilfred Cantwell Smith draws our attention to the uneven development of this peculiarly Western term and points to Lucretius (fl. 99–95 B.C.) as the one who might have first used the word in such a way that one could say "the concept of religion as a Great Something is born."[2]

The ambiguity of the personal and impersonal senses held within the noun *religion* has continued in the West. Consider, for example, the phrase *the Christian religion*. When one is met with the query "What is the Christian religion?" one might sally forth to reply by discussing the "founder," bits about the history of the Christian religion, and mention several doctrines. When *religion* is used in this sense it refers, most probably, to a "great something." It tends to mean some entity, something that can be analyzed, studied, something "out there," so to speak, about which we can talk, argue, disagree, or agree.

Consider, as another example, the following: "it would be better if I had religion" or "give me that old time religion." Here, one is met with that personal sense. The word here refers to an attitude, a quality of life, a personal orientation to life.

We are familiar with some of the old uses of the noun *religion* in some areas of intellectual inquiry: "what is religion?" "the essence of religion," "the origin and development of religion," and the like. We also are aware that the plural form of this word has been put to a peculiar use: the "religions" or "the great religions" or "religions of Asia," and the like. In this usage, the tendency has been to demarcate, differentiate, conceptualized entities that carried the labels of Judaism, Christianity, Islam, Hinduism, Buddhism, Jainism, Confucianism, Taoism, Shintoism, and so forth. One might note that what seven of the nine reified entities have in common is the *-ism* suffix thereby indicating, strikingly, the degree of reification that has occurred in this conceptualization.

If we were to agree that the term *religion* continues to be ambiguous and in its Western cultural specificity remains inadequate for understanding Buddhists, if we further were to agree that the notion of "religions" as clearly demarcated great systems is both historically untenable and divisive, then how would we set about to carry out this study? Wilfred Cantwell Smith has contributed mightily to our clearer discernment of the task. Two categories that he has proposed are "the cumulative tradition" and "faith."[3] The cumulative tradition is made up partly by the externals: the texts, doctrines, institutions, rites, rituals, practices, art, chants and songs—the things that have developed over time, the things one can study. The cumulative tradition is passed down from generation to generation, changes, and is part of the historical process. Faith represents that personal quality of life by means of which one responds to participate in some authentic way in the cumulative tradition because one has discerned the point of the tradition, the source of which the tradition is but a mundane manifestation.

Today the Theravāda Buddhist tradition is receiving the attention of an impressive group of extraordinarily talented scholars representing several of the major disciplines: anthropology, art, history, language and literature, philosophy, political science, religious studies, and sociology. And their studies run the gamut from village contexts to urban developments, from monastic institutions to political movements, from translations to ethics.[4]

We have carried out the study that follows by reconsidering

modes of conceptualizing that have been utilized customarily in seeking to understand doctrinal formulations, ritual and social expressions, facets of the "cumulative tradition" of Theravāda Buddhists, that which lies most readily before us for scrutiny. Consequently, our present study is not an attempt to present a history of the Theravāda Buddhist movement. Although, conceivably, an outsider might write the definitive history of this movement, it would be more difficult, indeed perhaps impossible, for an outsider to write the definitive work on the faith of Theravāda Buddhists. The cumulative tradition we can grasp through our careful gathering of information and thorough analyses. We need also to penetrate through this material to probe for the faith of persons who have engendered and sustained this material or have been transformed by it. And, of course, inference is the mode by means of which one seeks to understand the faith of others.

We will attempt to move but a small step nearer to an understanding of the faith of Theravāda Buddhists. Faith is not a static, generic, substitute term for *religion* in the sense that one might speak of the "faiths of the world" or of "different faiths." Faith is not a conglomerate of texts, doctrines, institutions, rites, rituals, practices, art, chants and songs. Rather, faith is that which sustains these more external elements of a religious tradition. Smith has established the point that there

> is no such thing...as religion or a religion; and when one divides what has been called that into two parts, an overt tangible tradition on the one hand and a vital personal faith on the other, neither of the resultant parts is a thing either, definite, stable, static, complete, definable, metaphysically given. To see faith truly is to see it actually, not ideally.[5]

There is a dynamic dimension to our study, then, both in the changes brought about in a religious tradition in the course of history and in the living dynamic quality of the personal faith of men and women who are Buddhists. Smith has argued that to "understand the faith of Buddhists, one must look not at something called 'Buddhism.' Rather, one must look at the world, so far as possible, through Buddhist eyes." Further, Smith has suggested, "The faith of a Buddhist does not lie in the data of the Buddhist tradition. The locus of faith is persons."[6] Another dimension is also present in our study: the process of becoming personally engaged in an academic subject, developing a disciplined self-consciousness[7] in an inclusive approach to understanding religious persons.

From time to time one reads a book dealing with something called *Buddhism* in which the author might write about "religion." Usually, in the course of such studies, the author demonstrates a restlessness with these two concepts. And also, in most cases, when one speaks of "Buddhism" or "the Buddhist religion" one slips into speaking about an impersonal, reified concept, an "It." Here we shall try to move beyond this, to attempt to move beyond description to provide also interpretation.[8]

This is no easy task, indeed occasionally it looms before one as ominous because of the antiquity of the tradition, the complexity of its development, the intricacies of several languages that carried the conceptual expressions of the insights, the enormity of the canonical and commentarial literature, the interrelatedness of the doctrinal formulations for ethics and the changing, historical, contextual moral ethos, the magnificent art and variegated architecture, the old rituals and ancient chants, the village and more recent urban configurations of the social patterns of those who have participated in the heritage, and the manifold creative contributions of countless men and women, all of which have provided a dynamic reciprocity of human life and religious heritage, of faith and cumulative tradition, ever changing, ever exceeding one's grasp. Attempting to provide an interpretation of all of this is, to say the least, formidable.

To see this, and to feel its force—indeed, to be made humble by it, insofar as one discovers the capacity to become impressed by a study of what persons cherish precisely because it has made manifest authentic human living for them—provides both motivation and modesty. Inspiring is the testimony of persons who recognize their indebtedness to others who, by being exemplars, simultaneously have gone on before and have handed down to subsequent generations patterns for progress along the way to living life well. To try to understand this activity of recognizing, this sense of indebtedness, this orientation to what is entailed in living life well, is refreshingly alluring. This way lies human self-understanding.

Moreover, it is hardly wise to think that one, unaided, can achieve a comprehensive understanding of a subject like ours. Immediately one notes the obvious: had our human history not witnessed the significant presence of men and women who became Buddhists, studies such as this would not have occurred. Further, without Buddhists who are scholars and scholars who study Buddhists, this particular quest for understanding certainly would not have been launched. And the conclusions presented here are offered tentatively. One is fully cognizant that all the data is not yet in; and what is in is not comprehensively available to any one person but remains distributed, or scattered, in the hands of numerous scholars diligently working in many areas on many issues with many differing approaches: historical, anthropological, philological, political, social, theological, textual, economic.

However, the academic tradition has not yet totally lost its sense of community; one spots it from time to time in some of our colleges and universities and among colleagues committed to a study of the same subject or to a shared approach to the study of that subject. Persons contribute and assist and are acknowledged. Opinions differ, of course, but argument yields to discussion and leads to knowledge that discloses understanding. Into this context of community, ideally, a study like this is to be placed as one more attempt to move us, however tentatively, even, perhaps from the perspective of some, tangentially, nevertheless quite seriously, toward a deeper understanding of those of us on this globe who are Theravāda Buddhists.

Time and again in our efforts to overcome detrimental circumstances that we find both embarrassing and demeaning to the dignity of the human personality we find that our creative responses into resolution have occurred precisely at those moments when we have found ourselves discerning community, speaking about ourselves, whether those moments be occasions for political negotiations to resolve conflicts among us, attempts to create housing for those of us who have no shelter, or to find employment for those of us without jobs. Speaking of nationalities or of political ideologies or of the homeless or "the jobless" has not brought us far enough. The poor we will probably continue to have with us, perhaps, because some persons will continue to be seen primarily as "the poor" and not fundamentally as *us.* This is an old issue, of course; it hinges on how one conceptualizes what constitutes one's neighbor.

Quite similar is the religious issue, also historical, also human. Insofar as one understands Buddhists as persons following a conceptualized and reified system called *Buddhism,* those persons will be seen as different as a consequence of their having made a different choice, to follow one system rather than another. Their being Buddhists is an indication primarily of difference. But it would seem that the religious issue, which fundamentally is a matter of faith, and the historical evidence, which is a matter of record, and the distinctively human enterprise, which is the integration of compassion and understanding, would lead to an acknowledgment that persons, by becoming Buddhists, have participated in a global community, a community not at all restricted to Buddhists, whose foundations have long been in place but are only recently coming to be uncovered. Further, persons, by becoming Buddhists, have demonstrated unquestionably magnificent qualities of faith, have contributed to, have influenced, have absorbed and appropriated rites and rituals, concepts and orientations, patterns and processes of human living on various occasions through many years in different cultures during our one human history, and have done so as men and women who have set about to attempt to live their human lives as human life ought to be lived. Their being Buddhist is an indication not primarily of difference but of impressive human living and a testimony of what human life can become.

We turn then to a study of the Theravāda Buddhist tradition in an attempt to understand the faith of some of us, of men and women who are Theravāda Buddhists.

1

THE ORIGIN AND DEVELOPMENT OF "BUDDHISM" AND "RELIGION" IN THE STUDY OF THE THERAVĀDA BUDDHIST TRADITION

We launch our discussion in this chapter by turning again to the ground-breaking theoretical contributions made by Wilfred Cantwell Smith. In his classic study, *The Meaning and End of Religion*,[1] Smith made the point that the concepts "religion," "religions," "Hinduism," and "Buddhism" are rather recent, of Western origin and, in an attempt to understand humankind's religiousness, are inadequate.[2] In developing his argument, Smith considered the Buddhist case with penetrating insight but, because his thesis was of such comprehensive scope, chose not to go into a detailed consideration of relevant matters in the Theravāda Buddhist tradition.

In the historical considerations that led Smith to his conclusions, he considered the Buddhist case in India and noted an absence of the reified concepts "religion" and "Buddhism."[3] He wrote,

> Perhaps the most eloquent testimony to the inappropriateness of the new concept ["an entity-concept 'religion'"] to that situation and those processes lies in the persistent problem of whether or not primitive Buddhism was a religion. The modern West has proven incapable of answering this question.
>
> The early Buddhists and their neighbours, we may note, were incapable of asking it.[4]

Smith was quite right, as we will come to see by focusing on the Buddhist case in general, the Theravāda in particular, and the Sinhala Theravāda Buddhist tradition specifically.

Western scholars of the Buddhist tradition have not been totally unaware that the languages of that tradition had no words representing the concepts "religion"[5] and "Buddhism."[6] And now more than a quarter century has passed since Smith reminded us—and this in a compelling way that should lead us not soon to forget—that Buddhist men and women had lived religiously, had gone about the process of living life well, without conceptualizing that what they were doing was practicing Buddhism.

In studying the classical Sanskrit, Pāli, and Sinhala languages, one confronts an unalterable difficulty in trying to propose words in these languages that would carry the weight of the concepts "religion" and "Buddhism." Sinhala Theravāda Buddhists, within the last two hundred years, I would suggest, have become acquainted, however vaguely, with the concepts "religion" and "Buddhism" and have either attempted to coin Sinhala terms to match the concepts or have decided to adopt new terms or new meanings first proposed by Westerners, perhaps by Christian missionaries.

A brief survey of some of the terms most frequently used by Sinhala Buddhists to represent the notions "religion" and "Buddhism" should, on the one hand, demonstrate the degree to which those indigenous terms have tended to lose precision and, on the other hand, indicate the novelty of the rather recently acquired notions of "religion" and "Buddhism." Further, this survey might suggest that persons who study the Buddhist tradition and attempt to discern the faith of Buddhist men and women should refrain from imposing upon the data the concepts "religion" and "Buddhism" without an awareness that these concepts have had a history and that they were not originally proposed by Buddhists to represent their understanding of the religious life.

I

The first term we might consider is *bauddha-samaya*, or *budu-samaya*, a term occasionally found in literary Sinhala as a counterpart to the concept "Buddhism." This term, formed by the words *bauddha/budu* and *samaya*, carries, through extension, wide connotations. *Samaya* is the pivotal word in this compound; whatever its meaning, it is modified by the adjective *Buddhist*. *Samaya* literally means "a coming together," and through extension the word means "convention," both in the sense of what is customary among Buddhists—tenets (*maṭa*), opinions (*diṭṭhi/dṛṣti*), teachings (*dhamma/dharma*)—and, perhaps, also in the sense of multitude, collectivity, or, better still, community (*samūha*).[7]

If one were to take *bauddha-samaya* or *budu-samaya* to mean "the Buddhist community," although this meaning has not been clearly supported by frequent and wide-ranging evidence, one would be dealing with those men and women who see themselves as forming a community and who have found community by becoming Buddhists. The difference between *bauddha-samaya* and *Buddhism* would be significant; without the former the latter would not have had a history. Had there not been a community of men and women who, through their common orientation to each other, to the world, to life, enabled outsiders to discern a uniform pattern in their views and behavior and consequently call them *Buddhists*, or had there not been a community of men and women who discovered through the teachings of the Buddha a capacity to participate meaningfully in a common heritage, there would not have been present before the Western observer that which first caught his or her eye and for which, later, was conceived a generalized classification, a reified concept "Buddhism."

If one were to take *bauddha-samaya* to mean "Buddhist tenets, doctrines, opinions, views, teachings," as reflected in the terms *maṭa*, *diṭṭhi/dṛṣti*, and *dhamma/dharma*, one might have a meaning rather close to a frequent use of *Buddhism*, namely, "Buddhist thought." And one might move further, through extension in meaning, to understand *samaya* as connoting also rites, institutions, and practices that have been customary among Buddhists. The antiquity of this latter extension in a compound *bauddha-samaya* or *budu-samaya* is not clear. We have yet to see written the history of this compound; and Sorata Thera makes no reference to a Sinhala text when he glosses *budu-samaya* with *buddhāgama* (a compound to which we will turn later) in his impressive Sinhala-Sinhala dictionary, *Śrī Sumaṅgala Śabdakoṣaya*.

It appears that *bauddha-samaya* or *budu-samaya* probably meant something like "Buddhist views" or "Buddhist thought" and subsequently had added to it the extended meanings of Buddhist rites, institutions, and practices. In any case, when this compound is met, one moves closer to grasping its import when one takes it to mean "Buddhist thought" in a straightforward sense or "Buddhist tradition" in an extended sense.

One might interject that my point thus far is obvious. Of course, one might contend, there is a significant difference between the concepts "Buddhist community," "Buddhist thought," and "Buddhist tradition," on the one hand, and "Buddhism" on the other; the latter is much broader in scope, more comprehensive, and this comprehensiveness is the rationale for its continued use by those who study also texts, rituals, monastic and lay institutions, practices, doctrines, and customs. I would reply that Buddhists have had terms for these latter areas of inquiry, and they have had them for many centuries. Moreover, Buddhists have considered aspects in these areas, discussed those aspects, debated them, understood them, might have discarded a few of them and incorporated others, without trying to maintain that a particular combination was important because it represented "Buddhism;" rather, they did so because they found a particular combination consistent with mutually endorsed tenets, consistent within their community, and consistent with a tradition, on the one hand, and the process of living life well, on the other. Apparently Buddhists, for centuries, never sensed a need for a concept like "Buddhism" because such a concept, in its lack of clarity and precision, would have been of assistance only for those who were not very familiar with what is involved in living one's life within the Buddhist community and, as an expression of one's faith, participating actively in that community as that community is given form by and informs the Buddhist heritage.

Another old and significant term is *sāsana.* It occurs both by itself and in compounds such as *buddhasāsana* (*buddhaśāsana, buduśasna*). In the compound *buddhasāsana*, the term *sāsana* provides a straightforward meaning: "instruction, admonition of the Buddha." Standing by itself, the term *sāsana* appears not always unequivocal in its meaning. This term, too, has had a history and it appears that throughout its long history a degree of reification might have occurred.

Basically the term *sāsana* means "instruction, admonition, message, order"; and this seems to have been a customary meaning in the canonical literature. A very well-known verse among Buddhists reads,

> Refraining from all that is detrimental,
> The attainment of what is wholesome,
> The purification of one's mind:
> This is the instruction [*sāsana*] of Awakened Ones.[8]

This usage of *sāsana* is frequently met in conjunction with the terms *awakened one* (*buddha*)[9] and *teacher* (*satthar*).[10] Of passing interest is the use of *sāsana* with the name Gotama.[11] Thus far, it should be apparent that *sāsana* represents an equivalent for neither *religion* nor *Buddhism*. Certainly the verse quoted would be misrepresented if one were to translate it so as to read "This is the religion of Awakened Ones" (for *etaṃ buddhāna sāsanam*) or elsewhere to offer in English "religion of the Teacher" (for *satthu sāsanam*) or "in the Buddhism of Gotama" (for *Gotamasāsane*).

The term *sāsana* has had a history, yet a careful study of its history would require more space than available here. It seems that in the course of time the term *sāsana* came to designate a patterned or established set of teachings, systematic injunctions, connoting a system of training.[12] This can be noted in those passages that relate one's "going forth into the *sāsana*,"[13] that is to say, entering the monastic order. *Sāsana* seems also to have reflected in its usage a self-conscious institutional awareness on the part of Theravāda Buddhists. There are occasions in which the canonical texts speak of a person accomplishing this or that "right here" (*idh'eva*) and the commentarial tradition frequently understood the emphasis as "in just this *sāsana*."[14]

An interesting process of interpretation can be noted in the commentary on the *Suttanipāta* with regard to the term *brahmacariya* as it occurs in verses 693 and 696. *Brahmacariya* is a rather complex term but basically it means "mode of chaste living," "chaste behavior," and in a broad sense, "the higher life."[15] In verse 693 the phrase under consideration reads "His mode of chaste living [*brahmacariyam*] will be widespread." The commentary takes *brahmacariya* as meaning *sāsana*.[16] The commentary interprets *brahmacariya* in verse 696 as *samaṇadhamma*, that is, the *dhamma* for those striving for inner calm or, following traditional interpretations, duties for monks (*bhikkhus*). The spatial references, "widespread" (*vitthārika*) together with the notion "right here," seem to suggest an awareness of a recognized set of distinctive principles and practices that readily differentiate the Theravāda Buddhist movement from others and, within that movement, demarcate prescribed behavior for monks. Consider, moreover, a commentarial gloss: "thus announcing, expounding, roaring the lion's roar he both announces and expounds 'just here in this *sāsana* is this *dhamma*; it is not so elsewhere'."[17]

Sāsana, although closely identified with established principles and a system of training prescribed for *bhikkhus*, was also broad enough to include laymen (*upāsakas*) and laywomen (*upāsikās*). Consider, for example, a passage in the *Mahāvaṃsa* in which one who has gone to the Buddha, Dhamma, and Sangha as refuge is considered a layman (*upāsaka*) in the *sāsana* of Sakyaputta (i.e., the Buddha, the Sakyan son, the son of Suddhodana).[18] And Visākā, preeminent among the laywomen (*upāsikās*) is said to have been endowed with faith in the *Buddhasāsana*,[19] no doubt seeing herself as actively engaged in this *sāsana*.

At times *sāsana* is used interchangeably with *dhamma* when the latter means portions of the received teaching[20] or prescribed practice.[21] And *sāsana* occurs as a gloss for "teaching and training" (*dhammavinaya*).[22] Moreover, it is recorded that a question was raised at the first council, shortly after the demise of the Buddha, whether the "teaching" (*dhamma*) or "training" (*vinaya*) should be recited first. The *vinaya*, it was decided, was to be recited first because "when the *vinaya* is established, the *sāsana* is established."[23]

The *Mahāvaṃsa*,[24] the old chronicle of Sri Lanka, provides passages that suggest a reification of the earlier notion of *sāsana* and a tendency to use the term in close connection with the way of life prescribed for those in the monastic order, the Sangha.[25]

The use of the term *sāsana* to reflect an awareness of an institutional understanding of the Sinhala Buddhist community, monks and laity, is noted in the *Mahāvaṃsa* when Duṭṭhagāmaṇi interprets his conquering the Tamils (*Damiḷa*) as a means of bringing glory to the *sāsana*.[26]

Having gone to Tissamahārāma, having
reverenced the Sangha [he] said,
"I, myself, shall go to the further side of the river
to brighten the *sāsana*.
Give us, that we might honor them, *bhikkhus* to
accompany us,
For the sight of *bhikkhus* is both auspicious and
a protection for us."

One can infer from this passage that an attempt to drive away a Tamil army, and in the process slaying a few hundred Tamils and creating a situation in which many Sinhala warriors would be slain, was interpreted and remembered as an act that would bring glory to, make illustrious, brighten, the *sāsana*. In this context *sāsana* clearly does not mean "order, message, instruction;" nor, for that matter, "doctrine." It would be difficult, moreover, to maintain that *sāsana* in this context meant the *buddhasāsana* upon recalling the verse quoted previously in which the *sāsana* of the Awakened Ones referred to, "Refraining from all that is detrimental, The attainment of what is wholesome, The purification of one's mind." This sense of *sāsana* appears diametrically opposed to the activities of Duṭṭhugāmaṇi. No, *sāsana* had, by this time, acquired a broader, reified, indeed, institutional meaning. Consider another passage:[27]

Having thoroughly cleared the country [Of Tamils (*Damiḷas*)] and
having put the populace at ease,
He established the *sāsana*, which was destroyed by the foreigners,
In its former place.

Geiger, when he came across *sāsana* in this passage made the comment, "P[āli]. *sāsanam* 'the doctrine' is used in exactly the same sense as we speak of 'church'. He restored the Buddhist church."[28] Our concern is not to take issue with Geiger's comparison by arguing that the notion of "church" is considerably different from *sāsana*. What is important is Geiger's discernment that *sāsana* was used in a particular way—and one worth noting—to suggest an institutional meaning. He elsewhere translates *sāsana* (in a compound *sugatasāsanam*) with "he reformed the Order [*sāsana*] of the Perfected One."[29]

Sāsana has undergone a development in meaning, one not entirely uniform, not always unequivocal. In the course of its history and varied usage, *sāsana* has developed from a meaning much like *institute*, in the sense of authoritative precept or rule, to *institute*, that is, an *institution*, in the sense of an organization promoting the precepts; a shift akin to one from *order* as command, say, to *order* as organization.

For some time Sinhala Buddhists have been aware of a notion of the decline and disappearance of the *sāsana*.[30] They have addressed this notion by noting that, first, there will be a decline and disappearance of persons who follow the precepts and rules and that, subsequently, when all of the texts containing the precepts and rules are lost and forgotten, the *sāsana* will have disappeared. In other words, the institutes, precepts laid down by the Buddha, are the basis of the institute, the institution promoting those precepts; and when the latter becomes dissolved and the former are forgotten one can speak of a disappearance of the institute—*sāsana* in both meanings.

Now then, can *sāsana* be translated "Buddhism?" Hardly. Consider the awkwardness of the phrase, "The purification of one's mind, This is the Buddhism of Awakened Ones." And one must allow room for a translation to represent accurately the use of the term *sāsana* when it refers to Nigaṇṭha Nātaputta, the leader of the Jain movement.[31] Nor would the matter be made clearer were one to speak of a person "going forth into the *sāsana*," undergoing the ceremony that symbolizes one's entering the monastic community, as "going forth into Buddhism."

Perhaps one might speak of a king going into battle in order to bring glory to "Buddhism" (*sāsana*) and, in other contexts, as one protecting "Buddhism," or cleansing "Buddhism," or establishing "Buddhism" in its former place. Such understanding is closer to the extended, institutional meaning of *sāsana* but is lacking in precision not because of the scope of meaning of the term *sāsana* but, rather, because of the inherent vagueness of the notion "Buddhism." Expressed more accurately, to bring glory to the *sāsana* is to create a situation in which the monastic organization can flourish, the laity can express its loyalty and thereby make manifest, make illustrious the teachings of the Buddha. By establishing, cleansing, and protecting the *sāsana*, one creates the conditions in which there are neither internal nor external threats of destruction for the monastic organization and no radical barriers or pressures inhibiting the support of the laity; one seeks to maintain consistency between the inculcations of the Buddha and the mode of conduct of the *bhikkhus*, who are exemplars for the laity. These dimensions are held in the one term, *sāsana*; they are relatively obscured by the vague term *Buddhism*.

In the involved and demanding process of translating from one language into another, one might adopt as a working principle the practicability of retranslating into the former language what has been translated into the latter. This principle would lead one not to translate *sāsana* as "religion" because, for example, a Sinhala Buddhist upon reading the phrase "the origin and development of *sāsana*," if he or she were reading it in the Sinhala language, would wonder what might have happened to the marker equivalent to the definite article in English, that is, *the sāsana* or, if he or she were reading it in Pāli, would anticipate a discussion of the doctrines and organizations in the Buddhist tradition. *Sāsana* is both too specific for the generalized and reified notion of "religion" and too definite in its frame of reference to represent that personal, engaged, attitudinal sense of "religion."

II

Rather recently, Sinhala Buddhists have introduced terms to represent the concepts "religion" and "Buddhism"—*āgama* and *buddhāgama*.

Āgama is an old Sanskrit and Pāli word. Its basic meaning is "coming, approach, arrival," and it is used also to mean "that which has come down to the present" in the sense of tradition preserved in writing. Through this extension the term means also "religious text," "authoritative text," and further, "established procedure, discipline."

The manner in which *āgama* came to be chosen to represent the notion "religion" is by no means clear. I have not found the word *āgama* so used in canonical, commentarial, or medieval Pāli texts nor in classical and medieval Sinhala texts. It is difficult to note the precise date for its first usage to represent "religion"; my guess would be in the later part of the eighteenth century or the early part of the nineteenth.

A cursory glance at the contexts in which *āgama* is used suggests its being closely affiliated with a consideration of the authoritative texts. One finds in the canonical collection known as the *Dīghanikāya* a passage in which *āgama* means "traditional or authoritative texts."[32] Further, The Pāli commentary on the *Dhammapada* (v. 208) glosses "one who has heard (and remembered) much," that is, a learned one, (*bahussuta*), with "one endowed with textual learning," that is, endowed with knowledge of the authoritative texts (*āgama*).[33] In the commentary on the *Vimānavatthu* one finds the term *āgamaṭṭhakathāsu*, meaning "in the commentaries on the authoritative texts" or "in the textual or traditional commentaries."[34] In 1886, E. R. Goonaratne, a provincial administrative assistant[35] in Galle, Ceylon (now, Sri Lanka), under the British reign, chose to translate this compound "in the Commentaries of the religion."[36] However, four years earlier, in 1882, Piyaratana Tissa Thera, in a letter written in Sinhala to Professor T. W. Rhys Davids, uses the term *āgama* to mean "authoritative text, canonical text."[37] In the same year, Ven. Paññānanda, also writing in the Sinhala language, mentions an *āgamadharma* that is worthy of respect.[38] This writer seems to use this compound to mean a system of teaching (*dharma*) that is based on canonical or authoritative texts (*āgama*). It is suggestive that approximately forty years after publishing these letters the editors of the *Pali Text Society's Pali-English Dictionary* did *not* introduce the English term "religion" into their discussion of *āgama*[39] and that at about the same time, in 1924, it is noted in Charles Carter's dictionary, *A Sinhalese-English Dictionary*, under the entry *āgama*, "*general usage* [*N. B.*]: religious system, religion."[40]

I say *suggestive* first because the scholars working on the Pali Text Society's dictionary did not "read into" the term *āgama* a meaning *not found* in the Pāli sources consulted and second because Carter noticed a disjunction of sorts between the traditional meanings of *āgama* and the "*general usage*" of the term, at the beginning of the twentieth century.

Thus far, it is possible to say that by 1924 *āgama* was used by quite a few people in Sri Lanka to represent the concept "religion." Goonaratne gives the reader some idea of how a bilingual Sinhala man or woman could interpret *āgama* in a Pāli text as meaning "religion"—and this in 1886. Where might one look for this change in meaning that the term *āgama* underwent? I would suggest, as mentioned previously, that Sinhala Theravāda Buddhists have become acquainted with the concepts "religion" and "Buddhism" and have either attempted to coin Sinhala terms to match the concepts or have decided to adopt new terms or new meanings first proposed by Westerners, perhaps by Christian missionaries.

In 1865, about two decades before Goonaratne presented his readers with an interpretation of *āgama* in a Pāli text as "religion," a series of debates began between representatives of the Buddhist and Christian communities in Sri Lanka.[41] Although it is an admirable quality in one's religious life to take religious affirmations seriously, the debates between those endorsing the Buddhist side or position (*buddhāgamē pakṣaya, bauddha pakṣaya*) and those holding the Christian position (*kristiyāni pakṣaya*) represent a period in which there was not only inadequate understanding of the other religious tradition, but also a deeply entrenched conviction that the one was in opposition (*viruddha*) to the other. Manifestly, there was demonstrated no concern to understand Buddhists or Christians; two monolithic giants had clashed, the one something called Christianity (*kristiyāni āgama*) and the other something called Buddhism (*buddhāgama*).

In some of the texts recording these debates[42] one notes the occurrence of *āgama* meaning "religion"[43] and occasionally the term appears in the plural, as "religions."[44] Throughout some of these sources the terms *buddhāgama* and *kristiyāni āgama* occur frequently.[45] So thoroughly reified had become the concepts "religion," "Buddhism," and "Christianity" that the debaters found it intelligible to speak of the "untrueness of Buddhism"[46] or the "untrueness of the Christian religion or Christianity,"[47] the "trueness of Buddhism,"[48] and meaningful to say that Christianity is "a deceitful religion,"[49] and to attempt to argue that "Christianity is not an authentic religion,"[50] and maintain that "Buddhism is a true religion."[51]

It is probable that the use of the terms *āgama* and *buddhāgama* to represent "religion" and "Buddhism" respectively antedates these debates. By how many years? I would suggest by about 100 at most.

Sinhala Buddhists scholars have been aware of the development of these terms and the meanings that they have acquired. In a splendid Sinhala-Sinhala dictionary, Venerable W. Sorata lists seven meanings for the term *āgama,* all of which, except the last, are very old; for *āgama* he notes *kristiyānidharmaya*[52] and provides a symbol that elsewhere he explains "that is in common parlance."[53]

The reader who turns to Sorata's entry for *buddhāgama* finds only one explanation, *buddhadharma,* which elsewhere Sorata explains as the *dharma* of the Buddha; that is, the eighteenfold *dharma* possessed by the Buddha and the *dharma* taught by the Buddha.[54] There is an enormous difference between *buddhāgama,* on the one hand, and *buddhadharma,* on the other, a difference not only in history, the latter being very old indeed, but also in attitude, which the concepts reflected by the two terms represent: the former is mundane, sectarian, provincial; and the latter is personal, of tremendous consequence for one's life. Let me provide some examples.

First, turning to booklets written rather recently for children at the upper kindergarten level one finds the use of both *buddhāgama* and *buddhadharmaya* in the titles.[55] The opening three sentences in a beginner's book written by J. Abēruvan, which utilizes *buddhāgama* in its title, read "Buddhism is our religion. It is according to Buddhism that we should act. For us, there is nothing more important than Buddhism."[56] Abēruvan, in his slightly more advanced book for children, also utilizing *buddhāgama* in its title, begins a section dealing with reverence for the triple gems—the Buddha, Dharma, and the Sangha—with the following remark: "Buddha, Dharma, Sangha are the highest treasure of Buddhists. Indeed, those are our three gems or triple-gem."[57] Now, consider how de Silva, Eratna and Vanigatunga, who utilized *buddhadharmaya* in the title of their book, begin their presentation of the three gems: "It is (i) our Lord Buddha, (ii) His Dharma, and (iii) the venerable Sangha that we call the triple gem. This, indeed, is the triple gem of Buddhism."[58]

The difference one detects in these approaches is more suggestive than conclusive. In both cases a young child is introduced to the notion of "Buddhism," and this quite early and in a formal setting. Yet there is a difference: in the former a child is made to be self-conscious of an institution and the way in which certain practices are important for that institution, that is, "Buddhism." In the latter case, a child reenacts a practice and is made to understand that what he or she has done is an important part of "Buddhism." The latter case seems to represent more accurately the way self-consciousness has developed in the history of the Sinhala Theravāda Buddhist tradition. There was a time in which one would recite the three gems without being aware that this practice was a part of "Buddhism." The former case represents the way in which many Sinhala Buddhists tend to speak about their religious heritage; there is a radical self-consciousness of a reified "something," a system that separates some of us from others of us.[59] When a booklet entitled *Buddhāgama* is placed before children a statement is needed to clarify the meaning of the term. When one entitled *Buddhadharmaya* is so placed, there is no apparent need to explain the term at the outset.

Sinhala Buddhists have been aware of *buddhadharma*, the Buddha's teachings about a way of life that could lead one to penetrate that which he rediscovered, have tried to live their lives according to it, have been buttressed by it in times of personal anxiety, and have found that it holds when all else seems to topple. *Buddhadharma* is for all humankind; the possessive pronoun in a sentence, "*buddhadharma* is our *dharma*" would be awry.

Let me provide another example that might inform the point. Consider the following passage written by a well-known Sinhala *bhikkhu* Walpola Rahula:

> The question has often been asked: Is Buddhism a religion or a philosophy? It does not matter what you call it. Buddhism remains what it is whatever label you may put on it. The label is immaterial. Even the label "Buddhism" which we give to the teaching of the Buddha is of little importance. The name one gives it is inessential.[60]

At first blush this passage appears straightforward, intelligible, if a whit Platonic. It is a passage that Sīripāla Līlāratna, who translated it and the book in which it occurs into Sinhala, most probably found rather subtle. There are terms, he might have thought, that communicate the concepts "religion" and "philosophy."[61] Yet, both "Buddhism" and "'Buddhism'" occur in the English passage.

Līlāratna, probably with the concurrence of the author, chose to take *buddhadharmaya* as the key term to represent "Buddhism" throughout the book not because they are equivalent, but, rather, because *buddhadharmaya* comes closer to the awareness on the part of Sinhala readers of that which is most noble in their religious heritage. The thrust of Rahula's book would have been severely limited, restricted, had his translator taken *buddhāgama* for the English term and concept *Buddhism*. The Buddha did not teach "Buddhism," he taught *dharma*, and the title of the Sinhala translation, *Budun vadala dharmaya*, "the *dharma* expounded (divulged?) by the Buddha," is more engagingly relevant than the English title, *What the Buddha Taught.*

To return to our passage, then, the force of the English term *Buddhism* together with the word *label* suggest that somehow the descriptive term under consideration is inadequate, a mere convenience. The translator chose the term *buddhāgama* for this use of *Buddhism*. The key points of the passage are, therefore,

> The question has often been asked: Is Buddhism [*buddhadharmaya*] a religion [*āgamak*, of course the use of *buddhāgama* previously would have required that one say *buddhāgama* is a religion, *āgamak*] or a philosophy [*darśanayak*]? It does not matter what you call it. Buddhism [*buddhadharmaya*] remains what it [*buddhadharmaya*] is. The label is immaterial. Even the label "Buddhism" ["*buddhāgama*"] which we [*apa*] give to the teaching of the Buddha [*budunvahansēgē dharmayata*] is of little importance. The name one gives it is inessential.[62]

The *we* in this passage referred originally to Westerners and, perhaps, Sinhala men and women capable of reading and speaking English. Non-English-reading Sinhala men and women are now able to see themselves in this pronoun and consequently in this conceptual activity. The passage is instructive for our purposes because it demonstrates the way in which the notion *Buddhism* is inadequate to catch and communicate the series of intricate, subtle thought patterns of Sinhala Buddhists. Obviously the passage as designed for Sinhala readers makes an important point not quite clear in its English original:

whether *buddhadharma* is called a *religion* or a *philosophy* or *Buddhism,* it is still *buddhadharma.*

To discuss what is entailed in the concept *buddhadharma* certainly would require more space than available here. Western students can move nearer its meaning by dropping the use of the term *Buddhism* when that concept does not represent the thinking of Buddhists. Should one want to continue to use the term *Buddhism*—admittedly an attractive convenience—in discussing the contemporary scene in Sri Lanka, one should be aware that this concept came into the thinking of Sinhala Buddhists rather recently. Further, even today, *Buddhism* is handled by Sinhala Buddhists religiously, conceptually, on a level more mundane than other concepts and is certainly secondary to *buddhadharma.*

Let me put it another way. The notion that *Buddhism* is "otherworldly" has been said before. My point is straightforward; *Buddhism* is "this-worldly" whereas *buddhadharma* is *both* "this-worldly" *and* "otherworldly." The *-ism* indicates a conceptual category into which several things in this world are placed and consequently are given some identifiable label for handling data; *-dharma,* the second member of the compound *buddhadharma,* provides the context in which everything in this world and beyond this world, conceived and beyond conception, is placed and thereby provides an intelligible structure for living life well.

III

In 1971, after months of public discussion led by the All Ceylon Buddhist Congress, a significant resolve made its way into the basic resolutions adopted by the Steering and Subjects Committee of the Sri Lanka Constituent Assembly. I quote the English, which was probably the language in which the draft was originally written.

RESOLUTIONS

The Republic of Sri Lanka

1. Sri Lanka shall be a Free, Sovereign and Independent Republic.
2. The Republic of Sri Lanka shall be a unitary state.

> *Buddhism*
>
> 3. In the Republic of Sri Lanka, Buddhism, the religion of the majority of the people, shall be given its rightful place, and accordingly, it shall be the duty of the State to protect and foster Buddhism, while assuring to all religions the rights granted by Basic Resolution 5 (iv).[63]

Sinhala men and women have worked with the concepts "religion" and "Buddhism" for at least a century—the major debates began in 1865 and 1866—possibly two. Since the late nineteenth century, we have noted representatives of religious organizations using the concepts, educators introducing them to children, and more recently politicians grappling with them. The passage drawn from the *Government Gazette* clearly shows the extent to which these Western concepts have been adopted. There are the terms *Buddhism, religion,* and *religions,* and they are matched in the Sinhala language today with *buddhāgama* and *āgama.*

This is not the place to enter a discussion of the merits of this basic resolution proposal, however ambiguous the notions "Buddhism/*buddhāgama,*" "rightful place/*nisitäna,*" and "religion/*āgama*" might be.[64] Obviously complex historical factors have given rise to the situation in which this basic resolution was submitted, and obviously, the issue remains delicate. The important thing to grasp is that our contemporaries in Sri Lanka seem to be aware of the concepts *religion* and *Buddhism,* and are using them in their discourse. All this is instructive for students of the Buddhist tradition.

First, one can discern the manner in which Sinhala Buddhists have chosen to utilize the concept "Buddhism": they have tended to use it in a restricted sense to refer to the external, the peripheral characteristics that have been manifested by a more personal, deeply significant awareness. Western students of the Buddhist tradition will do well to be alert to this.

In sensing a need to assure a continuing, flourishing presence of the Sangha, the All Ceylon Buddhist Congress and others, not fully aware of the precise program that would productively relate "Buddhism" (*buddhāgama*) with "its rightful place" (*nisitäna*), nevertheless led in the formulation of this resolution. They did not choose another term in place of *buddhāgama*. They could have tried to make a break with a trend, somewhat more than a century old at the time, and propose *buddhadharma* or, more engagingly, *dhamma/dharma*, instead of the concept *buddhāgama*. But they did not.

I think they made the move they did because they were well aware that *dhamma/dharma*, rediscovered by the Buddha, provides a foundation for living religiously, provides an underpinning for an integrative interpretation of that which underlies the notion of law, on the social level, personal level, indeed, for the reflective person, also the cosmic level. Sinhala Buddhists are saying that the rightful place (*nisitäna*) for *buddhadharma* is in the minds and hearts of men and women—and no proposed basic resolution can alter that or assure it.

We, therefore, put aside "religion" and "Buddhism" and continue our attempt to understand Buddhists.

2

THE COMING OF "EARLY BUDDHISM" TO SRI LANKA

Buddhism has been in Sri Lanka for at least a century, perhaps two. *Early Buddhism* arrived even later. I have not uncovered data in Sinhala sources treating something called *early Buddhism* (*pūrvakālīna-buddhāgama*, or for that matter in Pāli sources concerning *purima-buddhāgama*). Until rather recently Sinhala Buddhists have tended not to be significantly concerned about "getting back to" the early developments in the Buddhist tradition. Western academics took the lead in this, reflecting in the process a mind-set woven from three strands in the Western intellectual heritage: a "backward" look derived, perhaps, from the Renaissance; an "origin and development" fixation, issuing from the notion of evolution, epitomized by Darwin; and an interpretation foisted on the Reformation period by scholars of later generations. These strands became closely meshed and led historians to label a multiplicity of phenomena *Buddhism,* subsequently to attempt to "get back to" its origin, and even to cut away tradition in a quest for the historical Gotama.

Approximately 400 years stood between the birth of Martin Luther and the founding of the prestigious Pali Text Society in London, a society devoted to the publication of texts recording events believed to have occurred approximately 400 years before Julius Caesar. In this light a fascination with the early period of the Buddhist tradition was understandable. The label *Buddhism* was probably first given by people in the field, so to speak, who saw a variety of externals, rites, beliefs, institutions, and practices and sought to impose unity. Academics, men and women of outstanding ability, turned to the task of understanding this "something," that is, *Buddhism,* and to do this they thought they had first to "leapfrog" 2,000 years of tradition, to begin at a beginning, which they chose to be the life of Gotama in the sixth to fifth centuries B.C., and to start tracing subsequent developments. Sinhala Buddhists had been starting by hearing the *Jātaka* tales, stories of the former lives of the Buddha, and the *Dhammapada,* although discerning the support provided by refuge in the Buddha, *Dhamma,* and the Sangha. They had begun a process of probing *dhamma/dharma,* whereas academics and other authors, much more recently, have been interested in handling "Buddhism."

Buddhism has had a history in the West. It appears that the earliest label applied by Westerners to the activities of Buddhist men and women in Sri Lanka took the form of *Religion of Budu* or the like, and it is possible that this type of label might be found in records dating from the period of Dutch occupation (seventeenth to eighteenth centuries), possibly even from the time of the Portuguese presence (sixteenth to seventeenth centuries).

By 1797, one year after the Dutch were expelled from Sri Lanka by the British, *Budun,* understood as "the name of one of the Ceylonese Gods...."[1] was known to Westerners as recorded in the *Encyclopaedia Britannica.* In this same encyclopaedia, typically suited as are all encyclopaedias for the presentation of knowledge through categories, one does not note a separate entry, "BUDDHISM," until the ninth edition (1876, vol. 4, pp. 424–438).[2] However, the term *Buddhism* does occur in a discussion under the entry "BUDDHA OR BUDDHU" in the seventh edition (1842, vol. 5, p. 637a) and again in the eighth edition (1854, vol. 5, p. 724a).

Fifteen years after Napoleon I was defeated at Leipzig, in 1828, one of the earliest books dealing with "Buddhism" was published in this German city.[3] In the same year, in London, a small book on "Buddhism" appeared, focusing on Nepal[4] and, one year later, another dealing with the case in Ceylon,[5] and within sixteen years French readers could consult an introduction to "Buddhism" in India.[6] Then came a work drawing attention to the studies of "Buddhism"[7] followed by a manual of "Buddhism"[8] and a study of "Buddhism" including its founder and literature.[9]

About the time Abraham Lincoln was developing the Emancipation Proclamation, a Sinhala gentleman, James de Alwis, was putting the finishing touches to his book, *Buddhism: Its Origin, History and Doctrines, Its Scriptures, and Their Language, the Pali* (Colombo, 1862–1863). This work represents one of the first attempts by a Sinhala author to publish a book on "Buddhism" in English. A Russian author joined the ranks of those who wrote on "Buddhism"[10] and in 1877, Professor T. W. Rhys Davids, who was to play an important role in developing the study of the Theravāda Buddhist tradition, saw his book on "Buddhism" published.[11] By the close of the nineteenth century, work on "Buddhism" was underway in Sri Lanka[12] and elsewhere: in Germany,[13] in England,[14] in the United States,[15] in France,[16] and in Italy.[17] And between 1900 and 1907, works on "Buddhism" were being published in Edinburgh,[18] Calcutta,[19] and Madras,[20] and a Japanese Buddhist used *Buddhism* in the title of a study published in English.[21] *Buddhism* had gone around the world.

A living, dynamic, comprehensive religious tradition of bewildering variety and stunning complexity, capable of providing sustaining support for an insider, a Buddhist, presented an intellectual challenge of enormous proportions to outsiders. The response by outsiders was a process of conceptualization that led to the introduction of a term representing a generalized classification or characterization, *Buddhism,* and this process tended toward reification.

Now that a reified concept, *Buddhism,* was on the scene authors began to do things with it. It could be put into translations,[22] its essence could be discussed,[23] its quintessence sought,[24] its heart disclosed,[25] and its spirit made known.[26] And the quest for a core continued, not always in accord; what one scholar considered the central conception of "Buddhism"[27] another considered a view contrary to its central philosophy.[28]

How have scholars tended to handle "Buddhism"? Three general procedures have emerged: (1) a study of Buddhist schools, that is, Mahāyāna, "Hīnayāna," or Theravāda Buddhism;[29] (2) a study demarcated by geographical setting, that is, Northern or Southern Buddhism or Buddhism in India, Tibet, China, Japan, and so on; and (3) general or particular historical, topical studies.

The historical approach to the study of the Buddhist tradition has tended to be the one most frequently adopted by Westerners. Of particular interest is the patent penchant for discerning the origin of the Buddhist tradition. As early as 1847, this quest for origins had begun[30] and by no means did it cease.[31] Yet, in spite of a drive for origins and a broadly based interest in "origin and development,"[32] Western scholarship tended to move in a direction focusing on the early period of the Buddhist tradition. This focus seems to have been most prominent among those scholars who worked in Pāli and Sanskrit sources. Or, conversely, because of this focus or interest, scholars turned to Pāli and Sanskrit sources.

Although scholars of the Mahāyāna movement have reported studies dealing with almost every century through which that movement entered and every country in which it flourished, within the last century in the West the main focus of investigations dealing with the Theravāda has been directed toward the early period of this movement. The study of the Theravāda tradition tended to be a study of something called *early Buddhism*. Not a great deal has been done in the history of the Theravāda and less is being done about the situation of the Theravāda Buddhist tradition today.

In the case of Sri Lanka, and perhaps that of Burma and Thailand, whereas Christian missionaries and British civil servants introduced the Buddhist tradition to the West as they understood it at the time and setting in which they wrote a century or so ago, it has been the task and accomplishment of cultural and social anthropologists to reintroduce the contemporary religious scene in these countries in which the Theravāda is prevalent. Scholars in the study of religion, historians of religion, comparative religion specialists and buddhologists have tended to confine their studies to the distant past, to something called *early Buddhism*.

By 1876, at the latest, "early Buddhism,"[33] in contrast to "later Buddhism," was in books in the West and by 1881 readers in the West met a title depicting a direction in which a great deal of scholarly energy was to move: "Buddha and early Buddhism."[34] Some chose to speak of what they discerned in this period as "primitive Buddhism"[35] or "ancient Buddhism,"[36] but probably T. W. Rhys Davids was most influential in bringing into full view the notion of and scholarly interest in "early Buddhism."[37]

Since the second decade of this century the West has been treated to a scintillating variety of investigations and enormous productivity in scholarship dealing with aspects of the early Buddhist tradition: monasticism,[38] the spread of "Buddhism,"[39] the role of women,[40] geography,[41] caste,[42] scriptures,[43] a concept of becoming,[44] and the notion of "man perfected,"[45] jurisprudence,[46] psychoethical philosophy,[47] aspects of movement,[48] *dhamma*,[49] causality,[50] psychological attitude,[51] poetry,[52] epistemology,[53] the general background[54] and relationships between systems,[55] the notion that knowledge has to do with salvation,[56] kingship,[57] the view of the state,[58] and the doctrine of *karma*.[59]

In a sense, *early* has come to designate a particular form of "Buddhism," a form that theoretically can be differentiated, analyzed, "approached," a form about which persons can debate.[60] When one speaks of "early Buddhism" as, in some sense, a "Buddhism" distinct from "Mahāyāna Buddhism," "Theravāda Buddhism," "Indian Buddhism," "Burmese Buddhism," "Sinhalese/Sinhala Buddhism" and so forth, one usually has in mind a system of doctrines, practices, institutions, and the like. In this view, one aspect of study has been taken for granted and another overlooked or not adequately stressed. One thing that was not present at that time to which "early Buddhism" refers is the notion *early Buddhism*, yet the presence of this notion has been assumed. One thing that has been overlooked or not adequately stressed in this early period is *persons*. One certainly misrepresents the fact when it is suggested "Buddhism said" or "early Buddhism says, believes, represents, provides, demonstrates, disagrees, endorses, maintains." Only quite recently has "Buddhism" done anything, more recently still has "early Buddhism." *Persons* have been doing these things, have done them in the past in India, are doing them today.

If we will turn the flank, if we will recognize that history is also, and primarily, the activity of persons, we can clarify anew the task of the historian, to represent accurately the thoughts, motives, and aspirations of the persons who caused the events, responded to them, or forgot them in that period or place under investigation. It has been said, "Mahinda brought Buddhism to Ceylon/Sri Lanka." Westerners did this. Mahinda probably thought he was sharing a way of life that provided support in a process leading to transcendence, a process of transcending; he called it *Dhamma*. Further, even a cursory glance at some of the texts (*suttas*) from which he is said to have preached would demonstrate a "Buddhism" quite foreign to "Buddhism" as generally understood in the West. "Buddhism" did not come to Sri Lanka until the eighteenth or nineteenth century, and within a century of its coming it had become known around the globe.

It is not difficult to discern the contributions to the Buddhist tradition by Westerners,[61] those who saw themselves as Buddhists and those who did not. Of significance is the fact that Westerners, to the degree that they study the Buddhist tradition, regardless of whether they see themselves as Buddhists, have been and are participating in that tradition, and more dramatically so to the extent to which the results of their investigations are made known to Buddhists.

Theravāda Buddhists in Sri Lanka have had a self-consciousness of their religious community for a longer time and to a more pervasive degree than has the Christian tradition in the West. The Academic tradition, developed in the West, is only recently developing a comparable self-consciousness. Academics who study the Theravāda tradition are, by the nature of their work, participating in the Theravāda tradition; and the method of their approach to their study, the results of their investigations, and the manner in which they report their findings and provide interpretations have had and might continue to have significant ramifications in this religious tradition in Sri Lanka.

Where, for example, might one turn to find a serious, sustained scholarly study in book length written by either a Western or a Sinhala Buddhist scholar dealing with the significance of the Sangha for the laity today in Sri Lanka;[62] or, for that matter, the role of women; the place of caste in a total world-view, if any; the relevance of the authoritative text or the notion of scripture; the freeing qualitative dimension of the notion of becoming; the importance of the concept of release as a fulfillment of human potential; clinical and pastoral psychology; contemporary philosophical discussions among Sinhala philosophers on causality or epistemology; sensitive, probing interpretations of Buddhist and Hindu understanding of religious living, by a Buddhist about the Hindu case or by a Hindu concerning the Buddhist;[63] what Buddhists are thinking about the notions of the "State" or jurisprudence; what poetry is being written, novels lauded, or plays being applauded by Sinhala Buddhists? We know a great deal about the notion of *karma* in "early Buddhism," but where can one find a scholarly study of *karma* that would tell one the way Sinhala Buddhists today view the world in which we live, a world in which that portion of humankind living in Sri Lanka has been receiving staggering blows by insurgency, armed skirmishes, and more recently civil war over the past fifteen years?

History is in process—past tense, past perfect, and present tense. In the past, a person in Sri Lanka could find meaning in life, a sense of belonging, support in the face of challenge, propriety in behavior, and through this, an awareness of coherence in living life by becoming Buddhist. Recently, this comprehensive orientation is much more difficult to attain. "Buddhism" is becoming the standard jargon; all the manifold fluidity of a dynamic, comprehensive way of life is becoming a vague "it," which has been separated, isolated, looked at, put out there in space and time, so to speak, almost as an extended thing on a post-Cartesian scale, has become a "one over against others," and hence one reads of "Buddhism and Society" or "Buddhism, State and Society."[64] Where does a Sinhala Buddhist look for a coherent view now either lost or in decline? The point is that he or she now needs to *look* whereas formerly he or she was *confronted.* Men and women are now expected to look here or there in society to find something that might help them in their cultural identity somewhere else, to look in what is seen now as one aspect of their lives for answers to questions raised in another dimension of living. This is all very Western; it represents a view of the world probably less than one-fifth as old as the Buddhist tradition and yet a view that seems to have carried the day.

Until rather recently, Theravāda Buddhists in Sri Lanka had not been much concerned with "Buddhism"; they had made their concern the teachings of the Buddha and the well-being of the community of those who followed his teaching in the hope of penetrating through it to that which he rediscovered. Westerners have contributed a reified concept and have sought to explain not the history of that concept but the history of the divergent entity that was believed to have existed. As a consequence, Theravāda Buddhists in Sri Lanka have tended to endorse both the concepts and the reverse chronological orientation, both "Buddhism" and "early Buddhism."

A Western scholar of the Theravāda tradition in India and Sri Lanka who was to choose to continue using the terms *religion, Buddhism,* and *early Buddhism,* at least should be aware that doing so imposes a burden on a translator were he or she to make his or her research known to non-English-reading Sinhala Buddhists. *Religion* as a system of rites, institutions, and practices could be translated, and this only within the last 200 years, as we have seen, by *āgama.* The scholar should be prepared to have the term *religion* in a phrase like *deeper religion,* or *a person filled with religion* translated by either *śraddhāva* ("faith") or *bhaktiya,* ("loving devotion"). *Āgama* cannot carry the weight; it just will not do.

A scholar who was to continue to use *Buddhism,* were he or she to write about the early period of the tradition in India, would be working with a conceptual anachronism. Further, should one decide to hold the concept *Buddhism* primary in one's consideration, one should be aware, at least, that in the minds of Sinhala Buddhists there are other, more precise terms, concepts: "tradition" (*āgama/sampradāya*), "instruction, institution" (*sāsana*), "Buddhist thought" or "Buddhist tradition" or "Buddhist community" (*bauddhasamaya*), *buddhadharma* and "way" or "path" (*magga/mārgaya*), and so on. One should also be aware that a Sinhala Buddhist would readily detect a significant difference in meaning between *buddhāgama, Buddhism,* and *buddhadharmaya,* a difference almost as profound as that between *Christmas* and *Xmas* for one not really knowing the significance of the Greek letter *chi* (*X*) in the latter term.

Those of us who study the Theravāda tradition, which, of course, assumes the study of Theravāda Buddhists, should attempt to see the world as Theravāda Buddhists view it. This means becoming aware that Theravāda Buddhists have only rather recently seen *Buddhism,* or looked for *early Buddhism*. They have continued to see more than this, have seen themselves as part of more than this, within more than this, and such seeing enables them to see themselves as insiders. For an outsider who attempts to catch their views, how they have continued in history, to understand them, a study of "Buddhism" is not good enough. Further, a study of "early Buddhism" aids little in understanding how Buddhists saw themselves during the lifetime of the Buddha and fifty years thereafter, and obviously, it is of little assistance in understanding what Sinhala Buddhists think today about how to live life well.

3

DHAMMA *AT THE CENTER*

Whether or not those of us who study the Buddhist tradition see ourselves as Hindus, Jews, Christians, Buddhists, Muslims or secular humanists, most of us participate in at least two traditions: the Western Academic tradition, insofar as we undertake our studies in a university setting with a commitment to reason and the pursuit of truth, and the Buddhist tradition, insofar as we study Buddhists, write about Buddhists, and make our work known to those among us on this globe who are Buddhists. In continuing this study of the Theravāda Buddhist tradition we are aware of the legitimacy of the study of the religious traditions of humankind and more particularly the study of the Buddhist tradition in the Academic tradition. We also recognize that our subject touches on the loyalty of Buddhist men and women, through centuries, to the meaning of, and purpose in, life discerned within and through their cumulative religious heritage. An academic is concerned, or ought to be concerned, with the pursuit of truth; a Theravāda Buddhist is concerned with living in accordance with, living in pursuit of, *dhamma*.

I have presented elsewhere a study of a century and a half of scholarly discussion, indeed even debate, by Western scholars about the meaning of *dhamma* and have attempted there to relate what Theravāda Buddhists have apperceived in *dhamma* in the course of two millennia.[1] In this chapter, I shall sketch briefly the high points in that short history of Western investigations of *dhamma*. Next, and this will represent my major concern, I shall try to indicate what *dhamma* has meant to Theravāda Buddhists generally and Sinhala Theravāda Buddhists particularly. Finally, I will offer for further reflection a few of the grand and lofty notions that have inspired men and women who have lived in the intellectual heritage of the West, which might enable some of us in the West to begin to measure the profundity of the concept *dhamma*.

I

For nearly a century and a half, Western scholars have been aware of the term *dhamma*; they have pondered philological difficulties involved in the wide spectrum of meaning given to this term by Buddhists; and they have grappled with some implications suggested by the concept.

Eugene Burnouf, in 1844, translated *dharma* as "la Loi" and in so doing placed that Western concept as an interpretation of *dharma* on the scene in Western academic circles where it has been one of the most frequent renderings of the term.[2] Six years later, R. Spence Hardy, noting that *dhamma* had various meanings, wrote, "It is not unfrequently [*sic*] translated 'the law,' but this interpretation gives an idea contrary to the entire genius of Budhism [*sic*]. The Dharmma [Hardy here is following a form of Sinhala orthography] is therefore emphatically, the truth."[3]

Two decades later, Robert C. Childers provided a dictionary entry in which he defined *dhamma* as "Nature, condition, quality, property, characteristic; function, practice, duty; object, thing, idea, phenomenon; doctrine; law; virtue, piety; justice; the law or Truth of Buddha; the Buddhist scriptures; religion."[4] In his dictionary, generally superseded now but nevertheless still valuable regarding certain entries, Childers established over a century ago the meanings of *dhamma* generally accepted thereafter in the West.

Then there followed T. W. Rhys Davids (1877) who, like Hardy, suggested a move behind or beyond the notion of "law" to "truth or righteousness";[5] and Hermann Oldenberg (1881), who noted *dhamma* as "teaching or truth."[6]

In 1897, Professor Müller's edition of a Pāli commentary appeared (the *Atthasālinī*, a commentary on the *Dhammasaṅgaṇī*, which itself was published in 1885), and Western scholars were able to note a brief fourfold definition of *dhamma* current in Sri Lanka 1,500 years ago. In 1900, Mrs. Rhys Davids translated the *Dhammasaṅgaṇī* and in her introduction noted a fourfold definition of *dhamma* provided in the *Atthasālinī: pariyatti*, she understood as "doctrine"; *hetu*, she took as "condition or cause"; *guṇa*, she translated "virtue or good quality"; and for *nissattanijjīvatā*, she gave "absence of essence or living soul."[7]

The next quarter of a century, from 1900 to 1925, witnessed a flurry of scholarly activity regarding *dhamma*. Mrs. Rhys Davids began the move by placing *dhamma* in the center of her interpretive considerations of the Theravāda. She did this in 1912 with her perceptive little volume *Buddhism: A Study of the Buddhist Norm*,[8] wherein she proposed the concept "Norm" for *dhamma*. She and her husband continued to speak also of "cosmic law" as a meaning for *dhamma*.

In Germany, in 1916, H. Beckh made a provocative probe into the meaning of *dhamma*. *Dhamma*, Beckh suggested, is "the highest spiritual essence" that the Buddha discerned. Beckh noted that within the Buddhist world-view this spiritual essence, or as he also suggested, "spiritual reality," cannot be described as something substantial.[9]

In 1920, from Munich came an impressive work by Wilhelm and Magdalene Geiger, *Pāli Dhamma: vornehmlich in der kanonischen Literatur*.[10] The Geigers concentrated on the canonical literature, making a passing reference, now known to have been incomplete, to commentarial sources and, in the process, missing the remarkable contributions of the later Theravāda tradition. However, the importance of *dhamma* in the canonical literature the Geigers discerned. Early in their work they noted that *dhamma* is an expression "for the greatest and most comprehensive that there is, for the highest transcendental concept, for the absolute." They continued, "*Dhamma* is the essential central concept of the Buddhist system."[11] So resolutely did the Geigers endorse this comprehensiveness and centrality of *dhamma* that they stressed their observation, "For Buddhists *dhamma* is the same as *brahman* is for Brahmanic philosophy. *With deliberate intention the Buddha has placed the concept dhamma in the place of brahman.*"[12] One year later, in 1921, Wilhelm Geiger wrote a significant article, entitled "Dhamma und Brahman," in which he said, "*The concept dhamma had been placed, by the founder of the Buddhist system, in the place of the older concept brahman and was destined to dislodge and to replace it.*"[13] Certainly, Geiger was not suggesting an identity, nor was he saying the two concepts were analogous. We would catch his point were we to say that *dhamma* and *brahman* are homologous; that is, *dhamma* has within the general Buddhist frame of reference the same relative position as *brahman* in brahmanic philosophy, that each within its relative context suggests a similarity of structure.

Since the important work of the Geigers several strands can be discerned in Western scholarly investigations into the meaning of *dhamma*. First, some have considered it sufficient to speak of "cosmic law" or "order," as did Masson-Oursel;[14] of "truth" or "righteousness," as did T. W. Rhys Davids, to refer to a twin dimension of "that which is" and "that which should be," as did Paul Oltramare.[15] Second, a strand reflected a concern about a so-called *dharma*-theory, a technical compound first introduced by Otto Rosenberg[16] and popularized by Th. Stcherbatsky,[17] and continued by others. Quite lively have been some debates related to that so-called *dharma*-theory; whether the Buddha preached such theory and how early schools variously considered it. There is a suggestion of subtle interpretive insights by scholars who have refrained from introducing the notion of "a theory" when discussing *dhamma* as a central religious concept; that is, abiding salvific Truth, the presence of which enabled Gotama to become awakened, to become the Buddha. Third, there was the persistent activity of Mrs. Rhys Davids, a remarkable woman, who continued probing for the meaning of *dhamma*.

Finding it difficult to sense any religious force in the Buddhist affirmation of three characteristics (*tilakkhaṇā*) of life (*saṃsāra*) as it is found, as characterized by impermanence, inadequacy, and insubstantiality, Mrs. Rhys Davids appears to have read into Wilhelm Geiger's comments about *dhamma* and *brahman* more than the illustrious German professor intended. Starting where she did, Mrs. Rhys Davids drew conclusions not readily acceptable by either Western scholars or Theravāda Buddhists. She discarded her notion "Norm," tried "conscience," then "will," and even "inner controller" (*antaryāmin*). She wrote about the insight of the Buddha, "A Something it is he is placing where his country, before his day and during his day, placed That Who is Highest: *Brahman, Atman.*"[18] Further, she said,

> To this dual concept of the One (Atman, Brahman) the first Sakyans brought their own new concept of a term it is hard for us to render exactly: their own concept of Deity as *dharma* (Pali *dhamma*). In this they sought to conceive Deity, as not only immanent, but as moving, urgent, ideal, as "conscience," as "duty," as "the ought and ought not."[19]

Mrs. Rhys Davids's work was significant not because of her conclusions but because of her quest for the meaning of *dhamma*; she appears to have been probing for the force of *dhamma* as a religious concept. Somehow, she seems to have thought, the depth of meaning of *dhamma* was more engaging than the notion of "absolute" suggests; somehow this most comprehensive concept, "absolute," seemed too sterile, too aloof and impersonal.

Other Western scholars have written on *dhamma*: Helena Willman-Grabowska, I. B. Horner, Edward Conze, Helmuth von Glasenapp, to name a few. I might add, parenthetically, that attempts to probe the meaning of *nirvāna* (*nibbāna*) have been more frequent.

For some time now Western scholars have been able to suggest a reasonably adequate translation for the term *dhamma* in the *canonical literature*, thanks largely to the efforts of the Geigers. Also, it seems, Western scholars have not been entirely convinced that they have understood what Buddhists have meant by the concept, thanks, possibly, to the tenacious conviction of Mrs. Rhys Davids that *dhamma* is a forceful, lively concept, a religious concept somehow integrally related to persons.

Three more recent Western scholars, who have been associated with American universities, have discussed the significance of *dhamma* for Theravāda Buddhists. Robert Lawson Slater, in his perceptive study *Paradox and Nirvana*, argued for the centrality of *nirvāna* (Pāli, *nibbāna*) in Theravāda thought from several perspectives, one of which was through contrast with the Buddha and *dhamma*.[20]

> Nibbāna is the *gospel* of Buddhism, the term which signifies emancipation, salvation. The greatest assurance which can encourage the devout disciple is the assurance that he is indeed in the Path-of-the-Stream and will now, without doubt, attain Nibbāna. It is the term which turns pessimism into optimism and makes it absurd to describe Buddhism as a pessimistic religion. At the same time, it is the term which makes it true to say that Buddhism *IS* a religion—not merely an ethic or a philosophy.[21]

However, Theravāda Buddhists have discussed this assurance, this path, and this optimism in terms of *dhamma*. One of the standard definitions of *dhamma* given by Theravāda Buddhists is "*dhamma* in the sense that it supports," or "*dhamma* because it holds, supports" (*dhāretī ti dhammo*). Slater appeared to have been a bit restless about his notion of *nibbāna* as the "*gospel* of Buddhism" because he notes, at the close of his observation just quoted, "For this reason, *Nibbāna* rather than *Dhamma* is the consummating, central term of Buddhism—though much depends on the connotation assigned to *Dhamma*."[22]

Winston King took the notions of the Buddha, *kamma, dhamma,* and *nibbāna* and suggested that when taken together they provide what he called a "*reality-complex* or *reality-structure*."[23] King mentioned that of the four notions, *nibbāna* "in every way, is the most important of them all."[24] *Nibbāna*, he wrote, "is a 'gift of grace,' for there *might* have been a world without Nirvana, hence a world without the hope of salvation."[25] In another work, King mitigated the force of his earlier observation when, speaking of the Buddha as "revealer of truth [*dhamma*?]," he wrote, "*Without the teaching of a Buddha, sentient beings can never come to the knowledge, let alone the attainment, of Nibbana*."[26]

Wilfred Cantwell Smith placed the consideration of *dhamma* as a religious concept in its proper perspective. He wrote,

> though Nirvana was a distant reality, indescribable, not profitable of discussion, yet the Buddha saw and preached another absolute reality immediately available to every man. This is the moral law. To speak linguistically: while other scholars have argued that Nirvana is in some ways an equivalent or overlapping term to "God," I would like to argue that Dharma is so also, and in fact first.[27]

In considering the relationship of *dhamma* with the Buddha, Smith said,

> The Dharma that he taught does not owe its validity or authority to the fact that he was a wise and great man; on the contrary, he became a wise and great man because he awoke to its pre-existent truth. He became a Buddha by discovering what if we were to speak in Greek terms we could only call the pre-existent logos.[28]

Alert to the religious dimension of *dhamma*, salvific Truth, Smith mentioned succinctly, "Because there is Dharma, he [humankind] can be saved."[29]

II

As brief and restrictively selective as our comments about interpretations of *dhamma* among Western scholars during a century and a half have been, it is far more challenging to indicate comprehensively what Theravāda Buddhists, particularly Theravāda Buddhists in Sri Lanka, have said about *dhamma* in the course of well over a thousand years.

At the outset of our considerations of traditional interpretations of *dhamma*, let me note that I have ruled out an attempt to research the canonical material that was covered by the Geigers from a philological perspective. They were aware that in many cases when readers press for the meaning of *dhamma* in this or that passage in the canon, the definitions those readers discern are more or less a matter left to their personal inclinations. Philological considerations aside, such a situation suggests to a historian of religion that the personally engaging, multivalent quality of the term *dhamma* indicates a religious factor of utmost significance—one is made alert to the presence of a weighty religious concept when probing the meaning of *dhamma* in the canonical literature and elsewhere. To attempt to determine the meaning of *dhamma* in every occurrence in the canonical texts not only would be an exhausting enterprise but universal agreement on the conclusions proffered would be impossible, certainly. Much less ambitious, and perhaps more instructive in the long run, would be a study of what leading exponents within the Theravāda tradition have said about the concept.

In addition to the fact that *dhamma* has a variety of meanings, one must also come to realize that *dhamma* has several levels of meaning. Consequently one is concerned not so much with an attempt to discern a philological basis for extrapolating an inherent relationship between different meanings of the concept in different contexts as with probing the depth of meaning of the central religious concept, which for Buddhists would necessarily involve a concerted effort to become personally engaged with that which *dhamma* designates, that for which *dhamma* stands, by living one's life according to the concept and in so living coming to understand the concept and that to which the concept points.

The Theravāda Pāli commentarial tradition has given us fifteen or, in another reckoning, seventeen definitions of *dhamma*.[30] If one were to include Sinhala literature up to the nineteenth century, one would find twenty-four definitions.[31] Were one to include more recent Sinhala sources, one would have at hand thirty-four traditional definitions of the one term *dhamma*.[32]

Lexicographical entries can occasionally play tricks, so to speak, on an outsider—one for whom an obvious meaning of a term or concept is not immediately apparent. For example, only one Pāli commentarial source explicitly and unequivocally lists the four noble truths (realities?) as a definition of *dhamma*.[33] Yet, a cursory reading of the Pāli commentaries will lead one to no less than twenty-two occasions where *dhamma* is glossed by "*dhamma* that pertains to the four [noble] truths" (*catusaccadhamma*). Only one source, a twelfth century Sinhala text, provides "the [four] paths, [four] fruits, and *nibbāna*" (*maggaphalanibbāna*) as a definition of *dhamma*.[34] However, a cursory reading of Pāli commentaries will yield no less than forty-three occasions where the notion of four paths and four fruits together with *nibbāna*, to which we will shortly return, represent a meaning of *dhamma*.

The thesis that I wish to maintain is one that Theravāda Buddhists have maintained for centuries and one hitherto not fully elaborated by Western scholars whose opinions have been published. Succinctly stated, the central religious concept in the Theravāda tradition is *dhamma*, the presence of which provides doctrinal coherence in the entire Theravāda system of thought, and soteriological continuity from this life to that which transcends. Let me attempt to explain this as Theravāda Buddhists have tended to do.

There is a dimension of *dhamma* that is immediately at hand, and frequently one finds this dimension generally defined as "teaching" (*desanā*); that is, *dhamma* taught by the Buddha about *dhamma* that he "rediscovered." To designate this sense of *dhamma* as taught by the Buddha, Theravāda Buddhists have used a forceful term, *pariyatti*, a term designating that which is to be taken up and held in the mind, in the heart, mastered, pondered, repeated, and made a part of one's waking consciousness, a part of one's life, discerned as a norm and perceived as authoritative. This is a fundamental dimension of *dhamma*: *dhamma* as the authoritative teaching.

Another dimension is stressed in the commentarial tradition; namely, the dimension of *dhamma* that transcends the ordinary, the commonplace, this world as one customarily perceives it, and its customs, its mores. When one moves to this level of *dhamma*, one is nudged into the presence of a soteriological process, a process of transcending as Buddhists have tended to describe it. To understand *dhamma* fully on this higher or deeper level requires a *metanoetic* process, a simultaneous activity of "turning away from" fetters that bind us, from that which is detrimental, and a direct penetration of salvific Truth, an activity that is holistic; consequently one becomes what one was not before—one enters into a process of transcending.

Dhamma, we are told, is ninefold;[35] and it is composed of four paths, four fruits, and *nibbāna*. These four paths represent four stages in this soteriological process, a process of transcending. The first path or stage is "stream-attainment" (*sotāpatti*). When a person enters this first stage, enters into what has come to be referred to as a stream, a stream that leads onward, there comes to him or her, in a fructifying instance, a realization that indeed he or she has attained this stream. This realization is spoken of as "fruit of stream-attainment" (*sotāpatti-phala*). The second path or stage is that of a "once returner" (*sakadāgāmin*), which has its own fruit. A person who has entered into this path is said to enter, in the next life, into a realm of the *devas* for one life span and subsequently to enter this world of human life once more, therein to attain *nibbāna*.[36] The third path, that of a "nonreturner" (*anāgāmin*), has also its fruit. A person who is a "nonreturner" is said to enter, in the next life, into pure abodes (*suddhāvāsa*) and there will attain *nibbāna*. The fourth path is that of the *arahant*, the person who has achieved salvific insight, and with the fruit of this path or stage, not elaborated in detail in the sources, one has the eighth item that completes the list of four paths and four fruits. When we add to this *nibbāna* we have the ninth factor in the ninefold *dhamma* that transcends the world, or the ninefold world-transcending *dhamma* (*navavidhalokuttaradhamma*). When we note *nibbāna* here, we see it placed in its proper context, in the context of *dhamma*.

Now, *nibbāna* is considered to be uncompounded, that is, not made up of constituent dependent parts (*asankhata*), and to this extent, *nibbāna* is to be differentiated from the four paths and four fruits. Although the four paths and four fruits are considered as not included in, not comprehended by, not encapsulated within (*apariyapānna*), the mundane (*loka*) realms, they are nevertheless not themselves uncompounded like *nibbāna*. This means that the four paths and four fruits are at one and the same time world transcending (*lokuttara*) and compounded (*sankhata*).[37] Quite clearly, and quite profoundly, the ninefold world-transcending *dhamma* is *in* the world, is involved with the world, but is not *of* the world.

Another way of communicating this centrality of *dhamma* in living life religiously was formulated in the Pāli commentaries. There was a concerted attempt to assure that the Theravāda tradition not forget that *dhamma* meant more than authoritative teaching (*pariyatti*).

In some of the commentaries there are passages that mention

dhamma as twofold, "authoritative teaching" and "penetration" (*pariyatti* and *paṭivedha*),[38] or "religious texts" and "attainment" (*āgama* and *adhigama*).[39] One also notes a threefold classification of "authoritative teaching," "practice," and "penetration" or "attainment" (*pariyatti, paṭipatti, paṭivedha,* or *adhigama*).[40] In later Sinhala Buddhist literature this threefold classification of "authoritative teaching" (*pariyatti*), "practice" (*paṭipatti*), and "penetration" (*paṭivedha*) became standard and is used frequently.[41] The commentarial tradition, in the course of many centuries, has consistently and impressively maintained that the ninefold world-transcending *dhamma* (that is, the four paths, four fruits, and *nibbāna*) is represented or classified as "penetration" (*paṭivedha*) or "attainment" (*adhigama*).[42]

Along with this standard threefold classification, and parallel to it, we note next a discussion offered by Buddhaghosa, a great Buddhist commentator who flourished in the fifth century A.D.,[43] in which he elaborates *dhamma* as "authoritative teaching" (*pariyatti*), on the one hand, and also as the ninefold world-transcending *dhamma*, on the other.[44] The author of the *Upāsakajanālaṅkāra*, of uncertain date but prior to the eighteenth century, refers to Buddhaghosa's discussion and speaks of *dhamma* as tenfold.[45]

Dhamma, as the ninefold world-transcending *dhamma*, continued to be the central concept of the Theravāda tradition among Sinhala Buddhists;[46] and often, when *dhamma* is considered as one of the gems of the threefold refuge, it is interpreted as the ninefold *dhamma* and the authoritative teaching (*pariyatti*).[47] This way of understanding the meaning of *dhamma* as refuge has continued among Sinhala Buddhists into the more recent setting.[48]

Whether *dhamma* is considered as twofold (authoritative teaching and attainment); threefold (authoritative teaching, practice, and penetration); ninefold, or tenfold, it can be heard, held in one's hands, put into one's life, practiced, and penetrated, realized. This is a calming notion representing a profound religious awareness. Throughout the various classifications of *dhamma*, from twofold to tenfold, what strikes one as remarkable is a fundamental assumption behind all of these classifications: the relation of *dhamma* with persons. If one were to erase the assumption that persons can—that is, have the capacity to, are enabled to—become engaged with *dhamma* and are to—that is, should, ought to—become involved with *dhamma*, the classifications would lose their coherence.

Dhamma is the central religious concept in the Theravāda Buddhist tradition, providing coherence in the entire system of Theravāda thought, providing soteriological continuity from this life to that which transcends.

III

Dhamma, salvific truth, abides and it is not remote from persons.

Western scholars have discerned that *dhamma* can mean truth and they have written about the way leading to the state of an *arahant*, a perfected person; but, unlike Buddhists over the centuries, they have not written about *dhamma* as encompassing both. Salvific truth, *dhamma*, Buddhists have said, is available, and one lives truly when one lives according to truth. In so living, one can realize salvific truth. What have Buddhists said about the relevance of the particular term *dhamma* in this context? One of the oldest and most frequent glosses given by Buddhists for the term *dhamma* has been "*dhamma* is so called because it holds, supports" (*dhāretī ti dhammo*). "In effect," the commentarial tradition maintains, "It [*dhamma*] is both the noble way (*ariyamagga*) and *nibbāna*."[49]

Perhaps a Western student of the Buddhist tradition might begin to grasp some of the profundity of *dhamma* for Sinhala Theravāda Buddhists by drawing on strands from the heritage of Greece and considering the Platonic notion of "the Good" (*agathon*/ἀγαθόν),[50] or the comprehensive Greek notion of *logos* (λόγος).[51] The Western student who is a Christian might ponder anew notions drawn from the Christian tradition to assist in catching dimensions of meaning held by Sinhala Theravāda Buddhists in the concept *dhamma*: "preaching," "proclamation" (*kerugma*/κήρυγμα), "teaching," "instruction" (*didache*/διδαχή), "righteousness," "uprightness" (*dikaiosune*/δικαιοσύνη), "truth," "reality" (*aletheia*/ἀλήθεια). Further, as an academic participating in both the Academic tradition and the Christian tradition, one might propose that *dhamma* means something like "holy wisdom" (*hagia sophia*/ἅγια σοφια: *sancta sapientia*), or "salvific truth" (*salvifica veritas*) with a full conviction that truth, when known, is liberating, freeing, salvific.

One might object that "holy" (*hagia*/*sancta*), by definition, would be foreign to Theravāda Buddhist perspectives. If by "holy" one means that which is pure, untainted, held in deepest religious reverence, the application of the notion to *dhamma* is on the mark.

For example, one important way to discern a part of the delicately religious attitudinal orientation of Sinhala Buddhists toward *dhamma* is to reflect on the way they have viewed the life of the Buddha of this era as being the culmination of the many lives of the Bodhisattva ("the being for enlightenment, aiming for enlightenment"; "the being whose purpose is enlightenment" [Sanskrit: *bodhisattva*, Pāli: *bodhisatta*]). These lives have long served as a model of virtuous living for men and women who aspire to emulate more fully, reflect more adequately, characteristics of the life lived by the Buddha when he preached *dhamma* nearly 2,500 years ago. When did that series of lives begin? What was the objective of the Bodhisattva's quest? In what way is one to become involved religiously?

> "Of what sort is *dhamma* as refuge?: One should go to *dhamma* as refuge [thinking], "I go to *dhamma* as refuge, [to *dhamma*] that was realized by our Guru of the three worlds, Fully Enlightened One, noble Lord, who had toiled in search, throughout four innumerable one hundred thousands (*laks*) of aeons, until the moment, while seated on the diamond seat at the base of the *bodhi* tree, everything to be known was understood."[52]

For the author of the *Dhamma-Refuge* (*Daham Saraṇa*), a Sinhala text written in the twelfth or thirteenth century, there was a beginning to those lives but one so long ago that pausing to consider it begins to fascinate the mind and tends to nudge one toward mystery. The Bodhisattva's quest was for *dhamma* and to *dhamma*, NOW, one can go for refuge.

The Bodhisattva's attitude toward *dhamma*, as mentioned throughout Sinhala Buddhist texts, obviously provides structure for the attitudes of the authors of those texts and, it is likely, represents the way a considerable number of Sinhala men and women have viewed *dhamma.* The Bodhisattva aspired to the realization of *dhamma,*[53] to *dhamma* that was realized by former Buddhas,[54] and his aspiration is to be instrumental in shaping the attitude of one who goes to *dhamma* as refuge.

A sense of gratitude was present in the mind of the author of the *Daham Saraṇa* when he wrote, "I received without effort this *dhamma* true (*saddharma*) that was accomplished by many efforts by this my noble Lord."[55] Elsewhere in the same work the author referred to this true *dharma* as, "*dharma* true that was aspired for with such great effort by the Great One and has been met by us without effort."[56]

And the author of a Pāli text of the fourteenth century, the *Rasavāhinī,* wrote: "I will hear only *dhamma.* In *dhamma* my mind delights. There is nothing higher than *dhamma.* The three prosperities have *dhamma* as [their] foundation."[57]

Dhamma, holy wisdom, salvific truth, has been placed in the center of Buddhist soteriological considerations because of a recognition that when a person becomes engaged with *dhamma* it preserves, provides security, protects, is a guarantee of safety, provides deliverance, supports, keeps from falling. Through metaphors and similes Sinhala authors of old sought to adorn a message singularly straightforward—*dhamma* enables one to move beyond the miseries and fears of *saṃsāra*[58] and effects the attainment of heaven and *nibbāna.*[59]

Truth or reality, *sacca* (Skt. *satya*) are one, the texts tell us.[60] Although Buddhists speak of "path" (*magga*) and *nibbāna* in this context,[61] and consequently one might think somehow two different things are presented here, Buddhaghosa[62] and another great commentator, Dhammapāla,[63] remind us that there is no contradiction.

Let me quote from the commentarial tradition a passage that further demonstrates this unifying force of the concept *dhamma.*

> *Dhamma* that transcends the world (*lokuttaradhamma*) is well proclaimed because of the proclamation of the practice (*paṭipatti*) that conforms with *nibbana* and of *nibbāna* that conforms with the practice. As it is said, "Indeed, the mode of progress going to *nibbāna* is well demonstrated by the *Bhagavant* to the disciples; both *nibbāna*

> and the mode of progress merge. Just as the water of the Ganges [river] merges with, comes together with, the water of the Yamunā [river], just so the mode of progress going to *nibbāna* is well demonstrated by the *Bhagavant* to the disciples; both *nibbāna* and the mode of progress merge."[64]

This passage, as it is presented here, is quoted by Buddhaghosa and originally appears in a canonical text, the *Dīghanikāya*. The commentary on that passage as it appears in the *Dīghanikāya* provides the following elaboration:

> "The water of the Ganges with the water of the Yamunā" means the water at the confluence of the Ganges and Yamunā [rivers] "merges, comes together" in color, smell, and also in taste. It becomes just like one, like gold that is split in the middle; it is not dissimilar, as on the occasion when it [fresh water] is mixed with the water of the great ocean [at an estuary].[65]

Salvific truth is one, and because of its preexisting availability Gotama was enabled to become the Buddha. *Dhamma*, salvific truth, Theravāda Buddhists have affirmed, does not change; we do, and we do so dramatically when we enter the stream that leads upward. The Buddha attained salvific truth, *dhamma*, and the teaching about the way that leads to this attainment is called, also, *dhamma*. Buddhists are to follow the teachings (*dhamma*) because by so living one can fully penetrate salvific truth (*dhamma*), which is the same as saying one can attain *nibbāna*. The one cohering notion is *dhamma*: one weighty religious concept that holds together authoritative teaching, practice, and penetration, that affirms that salvific truth is available to humankind, that manifests an efficaciousness contingent only on one's solemn decision to become engaged with it, that assures no discontinuity in the process of transcending.

We have seen that *dhamma* has several levels of meaning for Buddhists in Sri Lanka. Readers who are Buddhists probably are at ease with these overlapping levels and, perhaps, have found in this conceptual fluidity a subtlety of nuance that yields additional significance. Outsiders, because they have not discerned what Sinhala Buddhists have apprehended, might find these levels—from text to practice to penetration—perplexing.

English-reading Christians, since the early seventeenth century with the appearance of the King James version of the Bible, have been exposed to a notion that outsiders might find a bit baffling on first blush. One might call to mind the notion "Word of God," which has arisen from interpretations of the Prologue to John's Gospel. Although the notion "Word of God" has been given a content expressed differently from the way Sinhala Buddhists have spoken about *dhamma*, the notion has a homologous relationship with *dhamma*; it has the same relative position within a general Christian perspective as *dhamma* holds within the Sinhala Buddhist view.

Within the Christian tradition, *Word of God,* like *dhamma* in the Theravāda tradition, can mean religious text, authoritative teaching, and more recently, perhaps, scripture (Bible: cf. *āgama/tipiṭaka*). Further, one in the Christian tradition can be said to preach and to hear the "Word of God," as would be the case among Theravāda Buddhists with *dhamma*. Moreover, the "Word of God" can be taken up and held in mind, as it were, pondered, mastered, made a part of one's waking consciousness (cf. *dhamma* as *pariyatti*). Persons are enjoined to follow the "Word of God," to put the "Word of God" into practice, to make it a part of one's daily life (cf. *dhamma* as *paṭipatti*). The "Word of God" is to be discerned, understood, penetrated and when this occurs it is said that the old person is put aside and things become new, become seen in a new way (cf. *dhamma* as *paṭivedha*). Christians have said that the "Word of God" is a support, will keep one from falling, leads on. And Theravāda Buddhists are not strangers to a similar sense of confidence. Lastly, religious persons have affirmed that there was a time in our common history on this planet when the preexistent "Word of God" became known and dwelled among us. There was also a time in our common history when *dhamma* was "rediscovered" and launched in the hearts of men and women.

I have spoken of the concepts *dhamma* and "Word of God" as homologous and have done so keeping in mind that we are working with two notions differently elaborated in two religious traditions.

Were we to put aside, for a moment, doctrinal extrapolations and institutional consciousness and put our focus on persons who have attempted and are attempting to live life religiously, that is, *homo religiosus*, one might propose that *dhamma* and "Word of God" are *analogous*, not insofar as one might want to argue that there is a close resemblance between the content of the two concepts themselves, but, rather, because of the resemblance of attributes given to the concepts, resemblance of effects engendered by becoming engaged with the concepts, and because of the similarity in the associated circumstances in the lives of religious persons, Buddhists and Christians.

Persons living in different parts of the globe have made it clear that without these impressive religious concepts their lives would have remained awry, that because these impressive concepts are discerned a way, a path to follow (Pāli: *magga*, Greek *hodos*/ὁδός), and salvific truth (Pāli: *dhamma*, Greek: *soterios logos*/σῶτήριος λόγος—even, perhaps, "the *logos* [that] became 'enfleshed'" καί ὁ λόγος σὰρξ ἐγένετο [John 1:14]) is at hand, and life as it should be lived is known.

4

THE NOTION OF REFUGE

I go the the Buddha as refuge;
I go to Dhamma as refuge;
I go to the Sangha as refuge.[1]

For many centuries Buddhist men and women—monks, nuns, and laypersons—have taken refuge (*saraṇa*), found refuge in the Buddha, in Dhamma, and in the Sangha. At first glance a notion of refuge might suggest a passive, retrogressive move, a retreat, a withdrawal on the part of such persons; and one might interpret this as corroborating an interpretation that "Buddhism is world denying or world negating."

Buddhists have demonstrated otherwise; they have entered into commerce, have written poetry, have dug canals and tanks for irrigation, have tried to minimize overhead and increase profits, have frequented royal courts, have given to the poor, have coped with famine, have celebrated colorful festivals. Very little withdrawal is manifested here—and yet Buddhists have participated in these activities while taking refuge.

The notion of refuge is both delicate and complicated. Perhaps many who have seen themselves as part of the Buddhist community have given little thought to what is meant when one chooses to take refuge in the "triple gem": the Buddha, Dhamma, the Sangha. Yet, others, in one way or another, have thought about it, and it is largely due to their efforts that one can note the presence of Buddhists living in the world today.

Buddhists have said that refuge (*saraṇa*) is like a caveshelter (*leṇa*), like a protective enclosure (*tāṇa*). At the same time they have stressed that refuge is not a passive matter, a recoiling in the face of the world(s). Rather, it seems the point has been that this refuge provides a recourse, a source of aid. When one finds this refuge one is not fleeing from the world; rather, one is entering a process of transcending. Simultaneously with a discernment that one has found refuge, it would seem, there is a recognition that the world is defined (Latin, *definire*), limited. So the movement into refuge, this protective enclosure, represents an understanding that one is moving onwards in a liberating process because the world has been placed into a meaningful context, that is, defined.

Very early in the Buddhist movement the notion of going for refuge, taking refuge, was made the standard, formalized expression representing a new relationship that was the consequence of a profoundly personal reorientation of one's life. It appears that at an early stage of the Buddhist movement, refuge was taken in the Buddha as the glorious exemplar (*Bhagavant*), and Dhamma as the supportive process of living well and the supportive ideal; that is, salvific truth. Those who made this move and professed this commitment, confessed this protection, were called, in the canonical text known as the *Vinaya*, "two-word-ones" (*dvevācikā*).[2] Theravāda Buddhists, over the course of centuries, have tended not to forget this early historical setting.[3]

Rather soon in the history of the Buddhist movement, a threefold formula became established and, for centuries, has remained the standard expression representing one's reorientation. Also in the *Vinaya*, one meets the term "three-word-one" (*tevācika*), used to designate a person who had found refuge in the *Bhagavant*, Dhamma, and the Sangha, or the order of monks (*bhikkhusangha*).[4] The commentarial tradition has been consistent in insisting on the regularity of the triple refuge; that refuge is found in the Buddha, Dhamma, and the Sangha. On occasion when the canonical texts mention praise only of the Buddha and Dhamma, the commentaries remind the reader of the standard expression for praising also the Sangha.[5]

Over the course of time, the term *Buddha* became standard in this formula, and it appears that *sāvakasangha,* in a comprehensive sense designating all those persons, the eight noble persons, engaged in a process that leads to liberation, was also used along with *bhikkhu-sangha,* which designated the order of monks. In time, Theravāda Buddhists preferred an interpretation of the Sangha in the threefold refuge to mean the community of disciples (*sāvakasangha*) who had made the breakthrough into Dhamma, who had entered the stream—in short, those realizing the effectiveness of the way characterized as having four paths and four fruits with *nibbāna* as the culmination. Apparently, Theravāda Buddhists have been aware for quite some time that institutions, the status of being a monk, a *bhikkhu,* that rites and rituals—what some Western scholars tend to mean when they write about something called *Buddhism*—in themselves are not an adequate basis for refuge.[6]

Frequently the English terms *gems* or *jewels* (*ratana*) are used to designate the Buddha, Dhamma, and the Sangha; hence, one speaks of the *triple gem,* or three gems or jewels (*tiratana*). The commentary on the *Khuddakapāṭha* provides a more comprehensive meaning of *ratana,* our word here for *gem* or *jewel,* as follows: "*Ratana* is a synonym for that which induces, brings, produces, increases delight (*rati*), for whatever is valued, very costly, inestimable, rarely seen, an enjoyment for incomparable beings."[7] Obviously the point is not that this refuge is like a stone. This refuge is delightful, highly valued, inestimable, and a source of enjoyment even for extraordinary human beings. In considering the relationship Buddhists have continually discerned in the Buddha, Dhamma, and the Sangha, one becomes aware that for Buddhists this relationship is one of delightful refuge, joyful protection.

What, then, is meant by going for refuge? The commentarial tradition provides a sevenfold classification. "For the sake of proficiency in the acts of going for refuge, this classification should be understood: namely [1] refuge, [2] the going for refuge, [3] the one who goes for refuge, [4] the mode of going for refuge, [5] the effect of going for refuge, [6] defilement, and [7] breach [of the going for refuge]."[8] And why is this called refuge? Note the dynamic thrust of what follows:

> "Refuge" (*saraṇa*) is so called because it slays (*hiṃsati*); such is the force of the term. Of those who have gone for refuge, by just this act of going for refuge, it [i.e., *saraṇa*] slays, it destroys, the fear, trembling, *dukkha*, the hindrance of a poor destination [on rebirth].[9] This [i.e., *saraṇa*] is a synonym for the three gems themselves.
>
> In other words, the Buddha, by causing the performance of what is beneficial and by causing one to turn from what is not beneficial, destroys fear on the part of beings. And Dhamma, by causing one to cross over the wilderness of becoming, by giving consolation [destroys fear], and the Sangha, by causing even those who have done little [by way of giving alms] to derive great benefits [by the ennobling effect of meritorious behavior, destroys fear]. Therefore in this manner are the three gems a refuge.[10]

Going for refuge, taking refuge, discovering refuge represents a lively religious awareness demonstrated by Theravāda Buddhists. When this credal statement is pondered, a reflective person might recall the moment when first he or she found the statement true, and because the threefold refuge is frequently uttered a person has repeated occasions to determine whether he or she is being consistent. The triple refuge can be said either in a private setting or in public, as a part of a corporate religious service. In any setting, the process involved is deeply personal. The recitation of the triple refuge is ritually structured in a threefold repetition to develop reflective alertness. This repetitive pattern sets the expression apart from routine patterns in normal discourse, serves to check a participant from running roughshod through a communal affirmation that has echoed through history, and tends to engender a sense of thoroughness in personal involvement.

Part of what it means to live religiously is to discover that in so living one is engaged in a process of transcending, in the widest sense; transcending what one has known, how one has thought, what one has been, how one has lived. Theravāda Buddhists have attested that in this process of transcending there is an exemplar (the Buddha); there is his testimony (*dhamma*) that truth (*dhamma*) is salvific; and there is a crowd of witnesses, those disciples (*sāvakasangha*) who have entered and gone far in the paths that fructify (a mixed metaphor that falls sharply into focus in the lives of persons); also there is the monastic order (*bhikkhusangha*) that has contributed magnificently to continuity within the tradition.

One has not begun to understand what going for refuge (*saraṇagamana*) has meant to Theravāda Buddhists without taking seriously their affirmation that anxieties and pressures can be extinguished thereby and that a fragmented life can be made whole. The commentarial tradition has long known the human predicament, subtly held in the notion of *dukkha*; and it is noteworthy that going for refuge is said to slay, to put an end to *dukkha*, to misery, anxiety, anguish, with regard to one's future existence(s) and thereby to destroy the sting, to remove the victory, of *dukkha* now and at the time of one's own death. We are on to something weighty here. *Dukkha* "reflects a meaning of disarrangement, disorientation, disorder, being disjointed, and through extension, discontent, discord, and 'dis-ease,' concerning the physical (*kāyikadukkha*) and mental (*mānasadukkha*) dimensions of life, individually and socially considered."[11] To say that *dukkha* suggests "the world is out of joint"[12] or "all life is awry"[13] would be on the mark. And all of this is sensed as causing oppression (*paṭipīlana*).[14]

So the movement involved in going for refuge represents a process of putting an end to *dukkha*. For such a person the world becomes defined, placed in perspective; fear of the future and bitterness for the past are put at rest; a purpose for living is discerned, and a mode of conduct remarkably consistent with that purpose is endorsed. On the deepest level, going for refuge represents an orientation to transcendence as a goal and as a process in which one's personality is holistically integrated in the commonality of living beings, in community among men and women.

A delicate transformation occurs when one goes for refuge, a transformation within that enables one no longer to rail with disoriented frustration against a world that is out of joint, no longer to whimper because all life is awry, no longer to engage in a grand revolt against meaninglessness, which, it is said, enables some to live meaningfully, but, rather, now to live with an admirable composure that reflects an awareness of the efficacy of a gospel message, now to instill order where there is disorder, to heal the wounds of life, to put an end to *dukkha*. *Dukkha* can be terminated. This is part of the gospel; *dukkha* is antepenultimate.

A reader of the Pāli commentaries learns that going for refuge is not merely a ritual that a Buddhist does or a bit of liturgy that some people perform. The commentaries tell the reader to turn his or her attention to what one might call the seat of emotions, even the heart (*citta*), to look there to discern the depth of the thoughts involved in this going for refuge: "The going for refuge is the arousing of thoughts (*cittuppāda*), which are free of defilement by virtue of being gladdened in it [going for refuge] and showing respect for it, which are activated by reason of being inclined to it. It is a being endowed with this [going for refuge] that does [in fact] go for refuge."[15] Nor are we dealing here with what one might consider merely an inchoate religious awareness, an incipient emotional sensitivity. The commentarial tradition has interpreted this going, this movement, as an activity of knowing, of understanding. "Whatever [philological] roots convey the meaning of 'going' convey also the meaning of 'knowing' (*buddhi*). Hence, for this [expression] 'I go' the meaning 'I know, I understand' is expressed."[16]

A person who is inclined to go for refuge, who considers going for refuge a weighty matter, who makes the commitment with a pure and joyous heart and mind enters a process of knowing, of deepening understanding of himself or herself, his or her neighbor, his or her world, and that which transcends the world.

So refuge, the going for refuge, and the person who goes for refuge are three elements inseparably fused in a momentous religious experience.

The commentarial discussion also provides an explanation of the modes of going for refuge, and it does this by introducing two fundamental categories: a *lokiya* going for refuge and a *lokuttara* going for refuge. These two terms, *lokiya* and *lokuttara*, are well known to students of Pāli and have been frequently translated as "mundane" (*lokiya*) and "transcendental" (*lokuttara*). It might come as as surprise to some for one to suggest that in reflecting on the meaning of refuge the former term, *lokiya*, seemed to be the more problematic to translate adequately. As contrasting terms, one might say whatever *lokiya* means, *lokuttara* somehow transcends, goes beyond (*uttara*) the world(s) (*loka, lokiya*) and hence one occasionally finds *lokuttara* translated as "supramundane."

Loka, the noun, has a broad spectrum of meaning, but basically it means "world" or "realm" and also "people" or "humankind." In most cases *lokiya*, the derivative adjective, means "like the world," that is, common, ordinary, usual, customary, and hence has been translated as "mundane." To describe something as mundane suggests that it somehow has to do with human activity that in most cases has a practical orientation concerned with the immediate situation, which is, like the world, transient and which is, like the world, common, ordinary. Some might interpret *mundane* as having to do with things of the world with little or no concern for the ideal or for what is heavenly.

To use the term *mundane* in attempting to communicate what is involved in the activity that Theravāda Buddhists have called *lokiya going for refuge* (*lokiyasaraṇagamana*) might be misleading. Western students of the Theravāda tradition are well aware of the attitudes expressed by Theravāda men and women about the ultimate objective in living. Ordinarily, Buddhologists tend to speak of this objective as *nibbāna*, though I prefer to represent it as *dhamma/nibbāna*. It is difficult to overstress the significance of this objective for Theravāda Buddhist men and women or the impact of this vision on the religious history of humankind generally. Yet in stressing the ultimacy of this objective and the centrality of this pursuit within the Theravāda tradition, one might tend to underrate the legitimate religious expression involved in the *lokiya* going for refuge. Making it peripheral or merely secondary, one might then interpret this *lokiya* going for refuge as *merely mundane.*

Buddhists have seen this world in which we are living as part of a larger whole, as one world among many. Some worlds, or planes of existence, are more enjoyable than this one, some are much worse; and one is where one is because of past deeds. Where one will be depends on how one lives now—this is sobering. Buddhists have spoken of the justice perceived in one's coursing through the worlds as integrally related to how one lives and thinks; that is, one's *kamma.*

Buddhists have come to discern that *kamma*, volitional activity expressed in body, mind, and speech, is set in a context in which justice reigns; a context in which a concomitant subtle presence of righteousness and mercy seems to be acknowledged (i.e., it is a context not discerned to be arbitrary, whimsical, despotic, chaotic, nor is there fate). In this setting *kamma* represents an affirmation that a moral order (*dhamma*) abides, that we reap what we sow; wholesomeness insofar as our intentions and actions are in accordance with *dhamma* or detrimental consequences insofar as our intentions and actions are divergent from *dhamma*. Lest one consider the notion of *kamma* to be a "theory" of impressive intellectual cogency only, Buddhists have tried to make the point that faith (*saddhā*) is involved. One puts one's heart (*saddahati*)[17] in the moral significance of volitional activity, and one sets about to arrange one's life in accordance with the norm that volitional activities yield consequences.[18] And, of course, the *lokiya* going for refuge yields significant consequences in this world and in the future in the other existences or worlds.

Fortunately, we are not without instructive testimony about what is involved in this *lokiya* going for refuge. The commentarial discussion says,

> The *lokiya* going for refuge is this: by arresting whatever defiles the going for refuge on the part of the average person it [*lokiya* going for refuge] takes on the virtues of the Buddha *etc.* [Dhamma, Sangha] to be its objective and flourishes in this way. In effect, it means the attainment of faith (*saddhā*) in the Buddha and the other subjects [Dhamma, Sangha]. Proper vision conditioned by faith is called straight conduct following from proper views and this pertains to the ten fields of meritorious action. That [proper action with regard to the subjects, Buddha, Dhamma, and Sangha] functions in four modes: [1] by the dedication of oneself, [2] by being inclined to them, [3] by undertaking the state of a pupil, [4] by prostration.[19]

A reader is struck by two phrases that occur in a brief transitional passage, introduced by the commentary, used to catch the force of the four modes of going for refuge being considered here.[20] First, one meets "from today onwards," and one is placed face to face with the seriousness of the dedication, the orientation, the discipleship, and prostration. Persons are putting their lives on the line. Second, this is not exclusively a private matter, though it is deeply personal. One reads the phrase "you all consider (*dhāretha*) me as one who has done thusly," and this public dimension adds to the totality of the commitment in the person, and the person senses the buttressing influence of others by his or her movement into a religious community.

With impressive conciseness the commentary, following a long established procedure in Theravāda hermeneutics, quotes passages from the older literature. In this way one who goes for refuge is enabled to interpret one's own activity as a participation in a communal continuity of faith.

1. Dedication: "And also I dedicate myself to the *Bhagavant*, I dedicate myself to Dhamma and to the Sangha, and my life I dedicate; dedicated indeed is myself, dedicated also is my life even until the end of my life. I go for refuge to the Buddha. The Buddha is my refuge, shelter (*leṇa*), protection (*tāṇa*)."[21]

2. The state of a resident pupil: "And indeed I would see the teacher (*satthar*), I would see only the *Bhagavant*, and I would see the One Well-gone (*sugata*), I would see only the *Bhagavant*. And indeed I would see the Perfectly Awakened One (*sammāsambuddha*), I would see only the *Bhagavant*."[22] This passage is quoted from a canonical text, the *Samyutta-nikāya*, and there the original continues, "And then I, having fallen prostrate at the feet of the *Bhagavant* thusly, said to the *Bhagavant*, 'Sir, my teacher (*satthar*) is the *Bhagavant*, I am his disciple.'"[23]

3. On inclination:

> Thus I will wander from village to village,
> From town to town,
> Revering the *Sambuddha*
> And the excellent reliability of *dhamma*
> (*dhammassa ca sudhammatam*).[24]

4. On prostration:

> Now Brahmāyu, a brahman, stood up from his seat, placed the outer robe on his shoulder, bowed his head to the feet of the *Bhagavant* and [now] covers the feet of the *Bhagavant* with kisses with his mouth and strokes [them] with his hands and announces his name, saying, "I am, O Gotama, Brahmāyu, a brahman, I am, O Gotama, Brahmāyu, a brahman."[25]

The commentarial discussion does not intend to suggest different ways of *lokiya* going for refuge, or different levels or steps, with an assumption that a Buddhist is to see himself or herself at any one time as participating in only one way or mode and not the others. Rather, it appears that the discussion works along the line of a "this too" principle, a principle of inclusion: this, too, is a way of going for refuge, as is noted in this or that passage; and further, this, too, is a dimension of one's personal interpretation of what is involved in one's activity of going for refuge on, perhaps, the first occasion some years ago and even now, today.

The commentarial tradition has made a significant contribution to the continuity of the tradition in which the commentator participated. With regard to the notion of going for refuge the commentators drew together strands of religious awareness embedded in passages scattered throughout the canonical literature not only because the strands were there to be collected but also, and profoundly I think, because these strands had been interwoven in the lives of Buddhists for quite some time. It would seem that for centuries men and women have sat at the feet of *bhikkhus*, who utilized the commentarial discussion in preaching *dhamma*, and have been inspired by an exhortation to dedicate their lives, to study and to learn, to trust the reliability of *dhamma* in the context of loving devotion springing not from a state of frenzy but from a calm heart delicately quickened with a delightful sense of being taken up.

The attitude suggested by the act of prostration in going for refuge has been further interpreted by considering what constitutes proper motivation for obeisance. The commentarial tradition makes the point quite clearly that family loyalty is no basis for going for refuge, neither is fear of retribution, nor an appreciation for practical benefits imparted by one's instructor (*ācariya*). Rather, the discernment of the inherent incomparable worthiness of that before which prostration is made (i.e., the Buddha, Dhamma, the Sangha) provides the proper motivation.[26] And further, prostration before others as a socially sanctioned gesture of respect does not, in this case, constitute a breach in commitment involved in going for refuge. Consequently the commentarial tradition notes that paying homage to one's elder relatives, even should it be the case that an elder relative has become committed to the way of another religious teacher and tradition, does not rupture the commitment of going for refuge. Similarly, when homage motivated by fear is paid to a great king and when homage motivated by sincere appreciation is paid to an instructor (*ācariya*) who has imparted the skills of a craft, even though this instructor be committed to the way of another religious teacher and tradition, no rupture occurs in the commitment of going for refuge.[27]

The *lokiya* going for refuge is certainly a religious act: we have noticed the seriousness of the activity, the presence of faith, an awareness thereby of the eradication of fear and dread about one's future existences and a concomitant commitment to the eradication of *dukkha*, the discernment of the inherent worthiness of that which constitutes this refuge, among other things. There is, further, an affirmation that living one's life in accordance with the commitment to and confidence in this refuge leads to a better life in this world and in worlds to come in the future. The commentarial tradition reminds one that being faithful to this refuge has as its effect the enjoyment of future existence among the gods and the enjoyment of plenty.[28]

Ignorance, doubt, and misapprehension with regard to the Buddha, Dhamma, and the Sangha taint this *lokiya* going for refuge and, consequently, inhibit the effulgence of the religious awareness and the efflorescence of the experience in one's life now and in the future. And the continuity of the commitment can be ruptured by devoting oneself, as depicted in this *lokiya* going for refuge, to another religious teacher and on death. In the former case, the breach in the continuity of commitment is censurable and carries with it unfavorable consequences. In the latter case, the act of death itself, being without volition or desire, yields no consequence, and consequently this act causing a breach in such commitment is blameless.

Such is the *lokiya* going for refuge. Is this going for refuge mundane? Yes and no. It is mundane in the Buddhist sense insofar as taking refuge in this way will enable one to live in a process of transcending but a process, nevertheless, not finally transcending the worlds (i.e., *saṃsāra*, the whirl [*vaṭṭa*] of existence as Buddhists customarily speak of it). However, the *lokiya* going for refuge is not mundane, as some Westerners might tend to understand what is usually considered mundane. The *lokiya* going for refuge (*lokiyasaraṇagamana*) is not in opposition to what might be considered spiritual or lofty as the term *mundane* might suggest. Nor is the *lokiya* going for refuge to be viewed as a practical activity—again as the term *mundane* might suggest—an activity that is primarily considered useful. This activity of going for refuge is praised for being beneficial; yet, for one to pose as having taken refuge for this reason, because it is useful for making better one's station in life, would be to overlook, indeed not to see, the swift pungent reminder that craving (*taṇhā*) and greed (*lobha*), in whatever conceptual garb they might be disguised, drag one downward, cause one to stumble, and check a process of transcending.

Perhaps one might suggest "customary"[29] as an English concept bordering on adequacy for the Pāli word *lokiya* in *lokiyasaraṇagamana*, recognizing that what are customary forms of religious expression for one community might strike an observer as remarkably engaging and profoundly significant. A Westerner might catch the force of *lokiya* in *lokiyasaraṇagamana* by interpreting *lokiya* to mean something akin to "heavenly," keeping in mind that Buddhists have apperceived the heavens to be a part of *saṃsāra* and remembering that Buddhists have discerned a higher stage in the process of transcending, one called *lokuttara.* consequently, one might understand the relationship between the adjectives *lokiya* and *lokuttara* as roughly homologous to "heavenly" and, say, "godly" in Western religious terminology. To speak of *lokiya* in the context of going for refuge as representing an activity that is mundane or worldly might tend to lead a Westerner, a non-Buddhist, not to be aware of the lively religious emotion and active commitment to a way of life that is with purpose, that is integrative, that seeks to alleviate *dukkha* in one's present life, in one's future, and in the world.

Perhaps a further step in interpretation might be made: one might say that the *lokiya* going for refuge enables one to see oneself as *a* Buddhist, a member of an impressive religious community. The *lokuttara* going for refuge however enables those qualities to arise that lead others to speak of one as being *Buddhist*. The religious force and significance of these two terms is entirely comparable, it seems to me, to the two dimensions represented in theological discourse when one speaks of a person as being *a* Christian (i.e., one who is authentically engaged with the customary [*lokiya*] forms of expressing religious commitment) and being *Christian*[30] (i.e., Christlike, one who has been enabled to manifest those extraordinary, world-present but world-transcending [*lokuttara*], qualities characteristic of the life and passion of Jesus Christ).

The second dimension of going for refuge, one that is transcendental, refers to a going for refuge that transcends the world(s), this world and the heavens (*lokuttarasaraṇagamana*). One is told that this transcendental going for refuge has as its consequence not the attainment of the heavens, but the realization of the four fruitions of one striving for inward calm (*samaṇa*): stream entrance, once-returner, nonreturner, and *arahant*. This going for refuge has as its reward not the acquisition of plenty, not just the removal of a possibility of *dukkha* in one's future existence, but, rather, the destruction of all *dukkha*.[31]

Such *lokuttara* going for refuge occurs when one has had a vision of the four noble truths, which is concomitant to the moment of entering the path (*maggakkhaṇa*), together with a complete cutting off[32] of what harms this going for refuge. The objective is the realization of *nibbāna*[33] (*dhamma/nibbāna*), which is synonymous with a penetration of *dhamma*, salvific truth. This realization, this penetration, provided the basis for the virtuous qualities of the Buddha, continues to provide a corroboration of the virtuous qualities of *dhamma*, and yields in the lives of the community of noble disciples (*sāvakasangha*) an increasing pervasiveness of virtuous qualities as these noble persons penetrate *dhamma* more deeply, realize *nibbāna* more fully.

Proper insight into the four noble truths is of utmost importance in this transcendental going for refuge. The commentarial tradition quotes from the *Dhammapada*,

> But who to the Buddha, Dhamma,
> And Sangha as refuge has gone,
> Sees with full insight
> The four noble truths;
>
> Misery [*dukkha*], the arising of misery,
> And the transcending of misery,
> The noble Eightfold Path
> Leading to the allaying of misery.
>
> This, indeed, is a refuge secure.
> This is the highest refuge.
> Having come to this refuge,
> One is released from all misery.[34]

The reward of this transcendental going for refuge is the termination of one's proclivity to regard conditions as permanent. The commentarial tradition again provides a quotation.

> This, O *bhikkhus*, is impossible...that a person possessed of [proper] view [i.e., stream attainer] would regard any psycho-physical synergy (*sankhāra*) as permanent (*nicca*), would regard them as blissful (*sukha*), would regard any *dhamma* as self (*atta*),[35] would deprive his mother of life, would deprive his father of life, would deprive an *arahant* of life...would with a corrupt heart draw the blood of the *Tathāgata*, would cause disunity in the Sangha, would turn towards another teacher; this cannot take place.[36]

On reading this quotation one might wonder why it was chosen to elaborate what is involved in the *lokuttara* going for refuge—indeed, murder is a stunning transgression of the commitment involved even in the customary (*lokiya*) going for refuge by one who takes seriously the first precept of virtue (*sīla*), that is, to refrain from taking life. The passage was probably chosen first to elaborate the integral relationship of the three characteristics of sentient existence (*tilakkhaṇā*)—

that all *sankhāras* are fleeting (*anicca*), awry (*dukkha*) and that all things that are capable of being known, that is, all knowables (*dhammas*),[37] are without self (*anattā*)—with the four noble truths. Second, the commentary is working in the realm of *certainty* and doing so by quoting a passage from a canonical text, the *Aṅguttara-nikāya* (I.26–27), enumerating patterns of behavior resolutely dissociated from the behavior of one possessed of proper vision. The point is straightforward and is made with full confidence—the transcendental going for refuge is never soiled by misapprehension nor is it ever ruptured. "There is not at all a rupture of the transcendental [going for refuge]. Even in the transition from one life to another the noble disciple does not propose another teacher."[38]

Were there a possibility of a rupture in the transcendental going for refuge, there would remain a gap of sorts within the Theravāda soteriological vision, a zone of uncertainty engendered by a recognition of one's capacity to delude oneself, crowning oneself ruler of one's future by the exercise of one's will. It appears that Buddhists are affirming that one does not take refuge in one's will because one knows oneself well enough to realize oneself as other than the source of liberation. There is no need of a savior, as Buddhists continually remind one, not because humankind is its own savior but because of the efficacy of *dhamma* when made the integral basis of one's life.

Nor would there be a need to quest for another teacher. In the customary mode of going for refuge (*lokiyasaraṇagamana*) one is to maintain a loyalty to the Buddha as one's teacher. In the transcendental mode of going for refuge (*lokuttarasaraṇagamana*) one has already penetrated that about which the teacher taught, that which will lead onward, will not fail, and is sufficient to meet every situation. When one recognizes that this breakthrough has occurred, it is not necessary to look for another teacher. One does not consider abandoning this process of living, nor think of standing in the way of others who are engaged with similar pursuits. Such would be inconceivable.

Refuge, although elaborated within the tradition as threefold, is one. And for Buddhists it is not locked within the vicissitudes of history—we are. But because there is refuge, persons who discern that refuge are thereby enabled to transcend the vicissitudes of history, or *saṃsāra* as some of us view the situation, not because history or *saṃsāra* has changed but because persons have changed.

The study of the life of the Buddha, the four noble truths, dependent origination, *kamma*, the monastic institution, and on and on, indeed is important. However, such study would remain incomplete in an attempt to understand what has been momentous for the history of a religious community, which has participated in and has perpetuated an impressive religious tradition, without an understanding of what Buddhists have discerned in the notion of refuge (*saraṇa*).

5

A RESPONSE TO THE FOUR NOBLE TRUTHS

I

Increasingly men and women who study the cumulative religious traditions of humankind are becoming more pervasively aware that the results of their studies will be read by persons participating in those religious traditions that are being studied. Increasingly, also, students of these traditions are considering afresh the matter of attitude in their research. When a Western academic studies with Buddhist scholars in Asia, raises questions about textual interpretations and contextual religious orientations to life, it is difficult for that Westerner not to appreciate deeply the consistency of scholarly competence and personal faithfulness of his or her host colleagues. This appreciation cannot fail to be carried over into that Westerner's reflection on and writing about the Buddhist tradition. On the one hand, such Westerner is fully aware that superb scholarship will be applied meticulously to what he or she has written whereas, on the other hand, evaluations and constructive criticism will be shared in the context of friendship and mutual interest. This scholarly environment is hardly hostile.

The context of friendship, which has been brought about to no small degree by an increase in international travel and continuity of indigenous hospitality, has begun to shift the ground from under the self-imposed intellectual barriers of the different disciplines. The barriers, or disciplinary distinctions, have not fallen, of course, but have become askew, having been devised initially to be analytically precise and practically executed by drawing "data" from one's friends in order to evaluate theories of interest primarily for one's academic colleagues. Friendship, increasingly, is having a direct bearing on scholarly method.

The academic disciplines that hitherto have been helpful, not altogether uniformly, in the study of religious traditions have been defined customarily in terms of method, the way of conducting the study, the "how" of the matter.[1] The subject remains, of course, to be studied, the "how to approach" the study becomes the basis for differentiation. When methods of study become modes for research there is a tendency for them also to become fashions of discourse; one ends up doing what one's colleagues are doing, and philosophy becomes defined merely as "what philosophers are doing." But the context of friendship in the study of religious traditions presses this "how" beyond the scope of method, beyond the initial phase of "approach," to include as well the manner of giving expression to the results of the study; friendship requires continuity in the entirety of the study and consistency in the mind of the author. If friendship be merely a social matter that does not also constructively impinge on one's thinking as an intellectual, if one argues that one must stay within one's discipline, one could find it possible to comment about one's study of the religious life of other persons, as it was once put to me: "I cannot respond to those concerns as a theologian. I am not a theologian. Nor can I consider those issues as a philosopher. I am not a philosopher. I have my own thoughts on the matter, but I will keep myself to a sociological analysis; I am now wearing my sociologist's hat." One wonders where the thinking of such a person is really moving, where the weight of real intellectual power is being placed; in short, one wonders where the person is centered as an intellectual, where the person really is.

The context of friendship provides a setting for intellectual inquiry that raises the question of how to manage the "how" of the study: the approach to the study, the method of conducting the study, the mode of communicating the results of the study. Friendship, then, is not one method to be placed over against others. Friendship has bearing on methodology, the systematic reflection on methods. It has to do with attitude.

For several decades if the matter of "attitude" were to have arisen in scholarly studies of religious traditions it would have been held in check, as it were, considered liable to mislead. A development occurred, one highly instructive for us today, that established what was considered the only legitimate attitude toward attitude; namely, that any attitude that indicated emotion or mood, any feeling, any human empathy on the part of a scholar was to be replaced by an "objective" disposition, an impersonal manner of thinking—in short, to be replaced with, what passed unobserved, a new attitude about attitude.

In the study of history, scholars uncover facts and provide disciplined interpretations, substantiated by the facts. Generally the only emotion or mood allowed for the historian has been the emotion with which he or she would argue about an interpretation of the facts that had been uncovered; hardly would such be allowed in the search for the facts. It appears, however, that an objective, impersonal approach to history has yielded to what historians know as "historical sensitivity," an attempt to place oneself in the context of a historical event in order to be particularly alert to the possible relevant factors among numerous alternatives, operating at the time, in light of which persons reached decisions. Usually the most incisive interpretations of historical events have been provided by those historians who have had the ability to exercise this "historical sensitivity" disciplined by methodical research. In the classroom, such historians are usually praised as being those teachers who make "history come alive."

The hold that secularity, even secularism, this peculiarly recent and Western development, has had on the intellectual pursuits of the academic community might be indicated, in passing, by noting applause one receives for making "history come alive," for making "philosophy come alive." What might be the response of one's colleagues in learning that a teacher has made "religion come alive" or that one has made the "Buddhist tradition come alive"? Would such educational activity become suspect? In most institutions in the United

States, such response would probably be forthcoming. But such response overlooks the force of the undergraduate vernacular, "come alive." Students tend to speak this way when they have discerned that a subject under study addresses the human condition. And in the study of religious traditions, which have been maintained through human history precisely because those traditions have addressed the human condition and have enabled persons creatively to respond in light of this condition, one ventures into scholarly inadequacy when one steps into a method that rules out an attitude of friendship with persons whose religious heritage is being studied.

In the study of the religious traditions of humankind, there is, of course, the historical, cumulative tradition that is part of the subject of study, a part that yields its secrets to a methodical, careful, and patient inquirer willing to read the records and marshal evidence. In the study of these religious traditions, the past does not, strictly speaking, appear. One, to understand, must infer one's conclusions from facts that can be established, from events that can be assumed to have occurred on the basis of what is known or on the basis of what can be considered reasonable in light of the evidence.

In the study of the religious traditions of humankind another dimension of the total complex has been awaiting one's attempt to understand. That dimension is the faith of persons, without which the religious traditions would not have continued, because of which there has been a dynamic relationship between receiving one's heritage and giving it to one's posterity, a relationship of creative change, of supportive continuity. When a historian demonstrates that a change occurred in a religious tradition, that change had come about because of the acitivity of persons, obviously, most would agree. Similarly, when there has been continuity for centuries, that, too, is the result of what persons have chosen to do, to remember, preserve, cherish, maintain. Scholars, of course, are interested in change—one wonders whether scholars have forgotten about, or have failed to marvel at, continuity. Perhaps some have found change to be exciting, like the daily news, and continuity to be boring (possibly being superficially put aside as "to be expected" or "natural" or "inevitable," while actually being the more difficult actually to explain).

In the study of religious traditions with the dynamic interrelationship between human faith and cumulative tradition—a conceptual reformulation that we have already met and for which we are indebted to Wilfred Cantwell Smith—the matter of attitude arises anew and cannot be put aside, simply, as "dangerous to real [read "impersonal"] scholarship." It might be possible to write about facets of the historical development of a religious tradition in an impersonal way, but persons who have lived through those facets of that same historical development of a religious tradition have neither responded to that tradition nor to life in an impersonal way. The issue is even more complicated: persons participating in a religious tradition today have deeply personal orientations toward, opinions about, even commitments shaped in light of, the cumulative tradition that has become their heritage, the historical tradition that one seeks to study. A scholar might *approach* a religious tradition; a person who has been enabled to express his or her faith through that tradition *receives* and *responds to* that tradition, and not only that, but receives and responds to that which the tradition has enabled him or her to discern beyond the historical vicissitudes to which that tradition itself has been and is subject.

A historian should be on guard not to read too much into the subject being studied, of course; but a historian would do well to drop his or her guard in the study of religious traditions in order not to "read out" too much. Attitude is important, a particular attitude that subsumes the best in the old disposition stressing objectivity by holding to methodical research, careful inferences, clarity in expression, while subsuming also the old anathema of scholarship, sensitivity and empathy, because one is dealing with what persons have done.

Empathy, which has much to do with feeling, I use in the straightforward sense of intellectual identification with others, a sincere projection of one's own self-understanding as a human being into the total human experience of others, as far as possible. Some might say that empathy in scholarship inevitably leads to misunderstanding if not to distortion. One could reply that scholarship disciplines empathy and empathy contributes to what Wilfred Cantwell Smith has demonstrated to be humane scholarship, that disciplined empathy and humane scholarship prevent intellectual solipsism of a given inquirer conducting an independent study and that they serve as a gadfly to keep one from settling into a kind of solipsism of a discipline. Scholarship, too, is cumulative, open to change and development. Empathy in scholarship in the context of friendship will lead one to try one's best "to get it straight and to say it well" while being assured that one's friends participating in the religious tradition being studied will gently set one straight were one to fail to understand or propose a distorted conclusion. Part of the celebratory genius of being human is that we communicate.

II

And so we return one more time, yet again, to the four noble truths, so often discussed in books on the Theravāda Buddhist tradition, about which we know so much, and yet we return. In the texts one frequently meets an abbreviated, staccato, phrase: "He illustrated to him the very eminent preaching of *dhamma* of the Buddhas—*dukkha*, origin, cessation, and path."[2]

This is an insider's communication, obviously opaque to one not informed of the point. A reader or hearer who comes across this kind of mnemonic formulation recognizes that a cluster of key concepts has been held together in a particular way in the development of the cumulative tradition. A formula like this, which has been designed, apparently self-consciously, to help persons remember also draws one's attention, simultaneously, to a recognition that the item to be remembered has been evaluated as worthy of not being forgotten by those who have gone on before, who have established the mnemonic pattern. The brief passage just quoted is probably not early in the formulation of the oral-textual tradition. By formally interrelating these four ideas and presenting them as a standard form of *dhamma* preaching common to Buddhas (in the plural), one can infer, but only infer, that this passage is probably relatively late. Yet the form of this passage indicates its importance.

It appears that the standard formulation of the four noble truths, long entrenched in the texts, is the result of some oral reconstruction or redaction.[3] There is some evidence that participants in the early formative period of the Buddhist tradition were uncertain about the syntax, about the grammar and gender, that was carrying linguistically the weight of the profound insights of the Buddha. K. R. Norman has suggested that perhaps the earliest formulation of what became known as the four noble truths did not have the Pāli equivalents of either "four" or "noble truth(s)." In translating Norman's suggestion of what might have been the original form, one would have "This is *dukkha*, this is the origin of *dukkha*, this is the cessation of *dukkha*, this is the path leading to the cessation of *dukkha*." Norman writes, "When these items became known as 'truths', they were so designated...."[4]

Norman's patient and insightful textual, grammatical study demonstrates brilliantly a parallel corroboration of my inquiry on a more existential level: in the lives of human beings (Norman's study refers to human beings of long ago) the teachings about *dukkha* have become known, have been affirmed, as *truths*.

It is striking that these four truths are on the lips of men and women living today, four truths that have been passed on from generation to generation for roughly 2,000 years. That the four noble truths are heard today, that today they are in the hearts and minds of men and women who aspire to understand them more fully, is remarkable. That these truths are there, in this sense, before the person who initiates his or her study of the Theravāda Buddhist tradition, is exhilaratingly fascinating. Why has this come to be?

What are the four noble truths? On first blush this is a rather straightforward question, one for which there is a quick response, a repetition of a doctrinal formulation capable of elaboration to monograph length or phrased succinctly. But this response does not measure the depth of the question. Coming to know what the four noble truths are requires a massive effort to probe with sensitive and disciplined insight into the view of life that Buddhists have been enabled to bring into focus by means of them, to interpret a vision of life to which Buddhists have been enabled to aspire through them, an effort far exceeding the restrictions of a brief chapter.

One might ask why there are four truths, no less, no more, or in what sense they are considered "noble." Buddhaghosa, whom we have mentioned previously, provided in the *The Path of Purity* (*Visud-*

dhimagga) a summary of interpretations on the scene approximately fifteen centuries ago. One might ask, In what sense are the four noble truths true?—and one immediately moves to the cutting-edge of the question, What are the four noble truths? because, it seems, one does not know what these truths are until one considers in what sense they are true. When Buddhists began to discern wherein the four noble truths were true is, of course, important. That Buddhists have found the truths to be true, in what sense this discovery has been made, and the ramifications in human life and human history that this discovery has brought about are the fundamental issues of global and personal and cosmic significance.[5]

In a valuable bibliographical reference work, one reads the following about Walpola Rahula's book *What the Buddha Taught*, listed under an entry on the four noble truths: "Perhaps still the best simple introduction for the beginning student who wants only to know what the Four Noble Truths are, and who is totally uninterested in whether the Buddha actually taught them, or in how the doctrine developed and changed and was used over the centuries."[6] Of course the annotations to bibliographic entries of a reference work of this magnitude cannot be said to represent the sterling conclusions of elaborate arguments; deadlines are met, space limitations are required, entries are restrictingly categorized. At first glance, the entry quoted might appear innocent. Yet, a bias is present with such overwhelming pervasiveness that it makes one wonder whether it would be worth one's time to read the book noted. I am not arguing the merits of Walpola Rahula's book here, rather I wish to make it clear that much more is assumed in the brief entry than might first strike one's awareness. For our purposes in this chapter, let me note the following implications in this annotated bibliographical entry: (1) that a beginner can discern, by means of a simple introduction, what the four noble truths are; (2) that one somehow remains a beginner or one somehow remains on a simple level of understanding until one at least grapples with the issue whether the Buddha actually taught this, and (3) one is not considered to be advanced until one has at least become informed of the possible changes the doctrine underwent.

My point, and Buddhist readers will spot this immediately, is as follows: it is assumed, in the quoted passage, that one can understand what the four noble truths are and understand this quickly, rather simply, at least straightforwardly. This is so, it is assumed, while Buddhist men and women have moved through the years of their lives in quest of such understanding and have been doing so for centuries. It appears that two different "four noble truths" are being talked about: one, a doctrine, a formulation in statements (the implication of the annotation quoted); the other, the truth about living life well, the point I am here suggesting.

Another point needs making: neither in the quoted passage nor in the book noted is there a discussion of how a person might come to explore the depth of meaning in the four noble truths; how, for example, one first learned them, perhaps as a child, and how one might continue to consider them with growing maturity in a life of faith. Whether the Buddha actually taught the four noble truths is an important question, although probably beyond one's grasp through historical research, and properly a question the resolution of which it is perhaps more fitting for Buddhist researchers to provide. What changes in interpretation were offered in the past, what changes in formulation the doctrine might have undergone, are also important questions, especially for those interested primarily in the history of the doctrine. Answers to these questions would certainly add to our knowledge. Learning of the responses that Buddhists have made to life by means of the four noble truths would add to our understanding.

> This, monks, is the noble truth of *dukkha*: birth is *dukkha*, old age is *dukkha*, disease is *dukkha*, dying is *dukkha*, association with what is not dear is *dukkha*, separation from what is dear is *dukkha*; in brief, the five groups of grasping [that are the aggregates constituting an individual] are *dukkha*.
>
> And this, monks, is the noble truth of the uprising of *dukkha*: this craving, which is characterized by repeated existence, accompanied by passion for joys, delighting in this and that; that is to say, craving for sensual desires, craving for existence, craving for cessation of existence.
>
> And this, monks, is the noble truth of the cessation of *dukkha*: complete dispassion and cessation of craving, abandonment, rejection, release of it, without attachment to it.

> And this, monks, is the noble truth of the path leading to the cessation of *dukkha*: just this noble eightfold way; that is to say, proper view, proper intention, proper speech, proper action, proper livelihood, proper effort, proper mindfulness, proper concentration.[7]

This passage, quoted from the Pāli canonical texts, from a discourse that came to be known in the Theravāda Buddhist tradition as the "Discourse on the Launching of the Wheel of *Dhamma*," (*Dhammacakkappavattana-sutta*), is considered one of the earliest formulations in words of the salvific insight realized by the Buddha on the occasion of his enlightenment.

The tradition has continued to maintain that these truths are applicable to the human situation. They are true because they are capable of becoming true in human experience and in the human realization that this life situation does not ultimately constitute the limit of human understanding.

The fundamental appraisal of the life situation communicated in these truths is that life remains awry for one who interprets the quest for ultimate meaning to depend on a perspective that is ego centered. The ego-centered life is in search of value structures defined by that ego centeredness. Such value structures, to maintain assumed supportiveness, must be maintained in some conceivable stability, a stability that tends to require a variable yet centrifugal orientation. To this life situation and to this ego-centered interpretation of meaning, the four noble truths have spoken for Buddhists, and these truths have been long held as being at the basis of the religious life.

The four noble truths affirm that life is unsatisfactory, awry, sorrowful, a misery (*dukkha*), because of craving, a thirsting for what is desired. As long as one maintains this craving, disappointment and sorrow will be the resultant experience.

The four noble truths (*sacca/saccāni*) are not propositionally formulated as assertions whose truth or falsity is to be determined by appealing to verificative criteria developed within intellectual systems that do not (1) recognize as legitimate a frank and candid appraisal of the life situation, and (2) do not acknowledge as meaningful statements about the transformational potential of an engagement with salvific truth in the religious life. From the Buddhist frame of reference, these truths are not merely teachings, or doctrines, or propositional statements; they have been affirmed as realities (*saccāni*).

The first noble truth indicates that a reality of human life is *dukkha.* There is a second truth, namely, that a reality of life is the causal sequence of craving, that it leads to this *dukkha.* The third noble truth describes another reality, that the situation can be altered, that a life awry is not the final judgment, that the human predicament of *dukkha* is not unalterable, that things can change, and change radically, through cutting off entirely this craving. And the fourth noble truth discloses another reality: there is a way, a path, a means by which persons can bring about a delicate and subtle moment in which the mind is receptively poised for the occurrence of the complete cutting off of craving, and hence the burning sense of *dukkha* becomes extinguished. There is, then, in the presentation of the four noble truths a formulation of a gospel message, a message of good news—not a series of "truth claims" proffered by one seeking to stake out an argumentative position.

Regularly a reader of literature about the Buddhist tradition is introduced to the four noble truths as a doctrine. As a doctrine, the concepts tend to hold together multiple strands of Buddhist thought; the succinctness of the formulation and the comprehensiveness of the frame of reference is truly remarkable. Some Western scholars have found the four noble truths to be a "borrowing" from something called *medical science* or *medical practice* in India at the time of the Buddha, representing a standard approach to illness: (1) symptom or illness, (2) cause of the disease, (3) cure, and (4) medication or remedy. Such might well be so—but to what extent this can be seen as "borrowing" is problematic. The healing ministry, whether one attempts dubiously to maintain that a clear separation between "medicine" and "religion" existed in India at the time, is nevertheless the healing ministry. Whether the Buddha chose this formula from "another area" of the healing ministry, the formulation is brilliant, not only in its obviously remarkable mnemonic utility but also in its obviously remarkable versatility in containing converging strands of interpretation that focus through these four truths, beyond these truths, to the realization by the

Buddha of salvific truth and to the intention of the Buddha as a wise and great teacher.

The Buddha rediscovered *dhamma*, which is salvific, and taught *dhamma*, which really having been heard (that is, penetrated), is also salvific. The Theravāda Buddhist tradition has held for millennia that in the formulation into words of that rediscovery and the means leading to it, the Buddha uttered the four noble truths. Of crucial significance is the understanding that the Buddha did not rediscover a doctrine. Soteriology does not hinge on a doctrine, a conceptual construct. Of no less significance is the understanding that the Buddha did not propose the four noble truths as statements that were the result of his reflection and speculation, thought out in quiet deliberation. These are not statements held out before all comers to be defended by argumentation and debate. These are not to be held out as "truth claims" unless one is prepared to suggest that the Buddha might have been wrong and Buddhists who have lived and died since the Buddha's ministry also might have been wrong. To what court of appeals might one turn to determine the truth or falsity of the alleged "truth claims"? Those who most often speak of such "truth claims" hold forth from a position within the Western philosophical heritage, making the case that the Buddhist tradition must come out of its internally coherent system, as it were, to appeal for arbitration to some form or pattern of human thinking that is other than that particular system. In a religiously plural world, one has witnessed in the West, at least, a diehard tendency to demand both of Christians and of Buddhists that they appeal to this court of impartial reason, which is undergirded by a massive bias that a particular way of determining the proper function of a particular notion of human reason is the sole method by which one ascertains truth.

The four noble truths are religious symbols, hardly "truth claims." Twin processes are operative through the four noble truths when one becomes engaged with them: an ordered clustering of cognitive activity combined with a total orientation of a person in the life context. These processes coalesce in the four noble truths, reach focal awareness in a coherent way; and when the four noble truths are penetrated, these twin processes become enlarged, ever expanding, continually becoming more comprehensive so that a person understands through and through reality as it really has become, reality as it really is.

III

In what sense then are the four noble truths true? In his extended discussion of the four noble truths, Buddhaghosa long ago asked, "What is the meaning of truth (*sacca*)?" He wrote in response,

> For those who examine closely with the eye of salvific insight-wisdom (*paññā*), it [*sacca*] is not distorted, like an illusion, equivocated, like a mirage, and of an undiscoverable inherent nature, like the self among sectarians, but, rather, it is the pasture of noble gnosis (*ñāṇa*) by means of its actual, undistorted, authentic condition. Just as with regard to the characteristic of fire, like the nature of the world, the actual, undistorted, authentic condition is to be understood as the meaning of [the word] truth.[8]

The suggestion that one should understand these truths as also realities is fully consonant with Buddhaghosa's interpretation. Buddhaghosa does not slip into a mode of interpretation not recommended in the Buddhist heritage—he does not say, in the context of his discussion of the four noble truths, "this alone is true, all else is falsehood." His thrust is to underscore the discoverability of these truths, that they represent, unequivocally, reality, and of course, that one becomes transformed when this discovery occurs.

In the context of the four noble truths, one will have noted that I chose to translate the adjectives modifying the terms of the eightfold path with the English word *proper* rather than the more customary *right*. The Pāli term under consideration is *sammā* (Skt., *samyag-*), customarily translated "right" as in "right view." *Right* is an accurate translation for *sammā*, but it appears not to be adequate. Let me attempt to advance the point.

In contrast to *sammā* is *micchā*, usually translated as "wrong"; that is, "wrong view." However, *right* and *wrong* have tended, in interreligious discussions, to carry with them connotations of truth and falsehood; right view is true, wrong view is contrary to truth, is false.

Moreover, what makes "right view" *proper* view is that it is appropriate, fitting, is in full accord with the means leading to the eradication of craving and ignorance. Proper view does not digress from, is not at variance with, tends not to turn one aside from the soteriological mode of progress, tends not to distort the reality of the salvific moment. Proper view is full view, comprehensive, is internally consistent, is conducive to the objective in view, and involves coherence, requiring personal engagement. Proper view is true in the life context of the person who becomes true through this view to that to which this view points.[9]

What makes "wrong view" wrong is the way it is placed in juxtaposition with "proper view"; wrong view is the opposite of proper view. It is a view that is not focused on, not consistent with, not conducive to, is separate from the mode leading to the salvific insight realized by the Buddha. "Wrong view" is "wrong" in so far as it fails to provide the perspective for living life consistent with the mode faithfully indicated by the Buddha as the Tathāgata, "the one who has gone (fully attained) thus (in the manner in which he has taught)."

It appears that "proper" communicates the central sense of *sammā* without introducing "right" over against "wrong" with the implication that "right" alone is true, all else is falsehood. "Proper" means that that which is so considered is especially suitable to a specific purpose which, in this context, is the eradication of craving and ignorance that provide the cause of the specific condition of *dukkha*. A life lived with the "proper view" is one that fully conforms with an established and accepted standard, the example of the Buddha and the admirable disciples. Similarly, the use of *proper* as an adjective to modify the other elements of the eightfold path would also indicate the sense of being in full accord with the mode of living that is conducive to *nibbāna* and reflects the example of the Buddha.

In the case of *sammā* in the grand epithet of the Buddha, the *Sammāsambuddha*, "Properly Awakened One" or "Fully Enlightened One," one finds the term being used in a way that is in accord with the suggestion here, of translating *sammā* in the factors of the eightfold path by "proper." The force of *sammā* occurring in the epithet would suggest that the one who is awakened is properly awakened, fully awakened, authentically and genuinely awakened, really completely enlightened. The implied negative or contrasting implication would not be that other teachings are wrong, false, in error; they are inadequate for the objectives in light of which the Buddha shared his realized teaching.

Consequently, orientations to life that have been nurtured by other religious traditions might well be considered inadequate or improper—that is, as not being fully in accord with a person's, a Buddhist's, fundamental orientation to the mode of living conducive to *nibbāna* and reflecting the example of the Buddha—if one would be sufficiently bold even to make this assertion. But it would not necessarily follow that such orientations to life that have been nurtured by other religious traditions would be wrong with the connotation that they would be false, in error, contrary to truth. They might not be in accord with what one's heritage has provided as a directive for living life, but one would naturally tend to suspend judgment. Nor would it follow that such orientations would be false. To refer to such orientations as "false" would require either complete and total familiarization with those orientations, or realization of the goal to which proper view is designed to lead one, or an appeal to authority. The first criterion is rarely met. The second is subtly held to oneself in patient silence. And the third, an appeal to authority, tends to go contrary to the old and wise Buddhist suggestion that one not cling to views.

This interpretation of the meaning of *sammā* in the eightfold path could provide a constructive and creative posture in interreligious colloquia. One would tend not to speak of one's position as "right" and positions held by others as "wrong." One would be in position to speak of one's apperception as fitting, as proper, appropriate within one's heritage, within the frame of reference through which one lives one's life, even as appropriate for human living at its noblest. The problem with *right* is not that it is wrong as a workable English translation of *sammā*. The problem with *right* is that it often connotes a contrastive implication, *wrong,* which in English can carry the meaning "contrary to truth," "false."

Proper, however, indicates the presence of value structures in light of which what is under consideration can be determined to be fitting or appropriate. The discernment and placement of those structures in our day depends largely on one's openness to others, relies heavily on one's attitude toward other persons of faith. The topic of consideration in interreligious colloquia could become a consideration of the extent to which one might understand the manner Christians aspire to eradicate craving, desire, and ignorance. To what extent might that process of living be considered proper? Wherein might one have appropriated a mode of life fully consonant in human living with what Christians have appropriated? The context of the discussions shifts; one does not begin with a point of view holding the other to be in error, and then to seek to determine to what degree the other is not in error, not endorsing a false doctrine, is not wrong. One does not begin by holding one's position as right, either. One approaches the discussions with a calm confidence that the way one is molding one's life is fitting, is proper for life that is genuinely human, is appropriate for the quest to which one has made the fundamental commitment. One then listens to the other, to learn how that person interprets a fitting human life, one suitable for human living at its noblest.

The four noble truths are also four realities that, when realized, become true in one's life. When this realization, this act of making real, occurs, one has understood the four noble truths on the world-transcending level—not that one miraculously escapes the world, as it were, but that one now is enabled to live through the world, unlimited by the world, a life unlimited by an inexorable process of *saṃsāra*, a life unhindered, a life that is genuinely, humanly free.

When one seeks to understand the four noble truths as a doctrinal formulation that might or might not have been taught by the Buddha in the earliest phase of a historical tradition, to learn whether the formulation might have undergone change and development over the centuries, one is working on an important level, but a mundane level, on a level of information gathering, on a level of gaining knowledge. There is nothing inherently wrong in working on this level—most of us do. Yet, not to recognizes that this is only one level, and a mundane level at that, is to fail to understand what Buddhsts have seen in and have been enabled to discern through the four noble truths, is to fail to understand what the four noble truths are.

Students of the religious traditions of humankind are beginning to take account of both levels of understanding, of developments within the cumulative religious traditions and within the hearts and minds of persons of faith. These are the two wings without which the bird of adequate understanding in religious studies cannot fly. One needs both methodical research and empathy, a willingness to inquire thoroughly but to reflect sensitively. We who are studying the religious traditions of humankind today are indeed fortunate to have with us colleagues participating in those religious traditions, colleagues with whom we study and for whom we write. Scholars enter colloquia also, and when one writes the conclusions of one's interpretive study one is aware that one is writing for friends for whom the topic being considered is deeply meaningful. Attitude is very important. And empathy, combined with humane sensitivity in the context of ongoing colloquia, produces a foundation for enlarging human understanding in the area of human experience that is most fundamental, in religious living.

6

BEYOND "BEYOND GOOD AND EVIL"

I

One of the problems in comparative studies or cross-cultural studies, but also one of the most exhilarating dimensions of the ongoing enterprise, we are coming to see, is the difficulty of matching concepts. The student of a tradition that developed within and also shaped another cultural and intellectual complex is continually challenged by a reciprocal dynamic of gathering the facts and determining the reliability of that information within the tradition under study, while at the same time checking the concepts with which the student is working in his or her own thinking. On occasion a scholar will discern at the outset an inappropriateness of previously matched categories of thought and set about to provide a sustained argument putting the matter straight, demonstrating that terms, concepts, ideas present in one cultural complex do not coincide with customarily established, allegedly corresponding concepts in the tradition or traditions being studied. On occasion scholars have been able to advance our understanding of another tradition being studied by reinterpreting terms and concepts derived from their own cultural and intellectual context, or by placing terms in a comparative study into a new juxtaposition, or by developing new phrases or categories incorporating those concepts. On both occasions the subject is being advanced by contributions to clarity that lead to a deeper understanding.

In this chapter, I would like first to draw attention to the way five representative scholars, four Westerners and one Theravāda *bhikkhu*, have made contributions to a general understanding of what some might call Theravāda Buddhist ethics. Two scholars consider the Theravāda case in a context of comparative religious ethics, one touches on our subject in the context of South Asian ethical theories, another writes from a perspective within the Theravāda frame of reference, and the fifth, a *bhikkhu*, seeks to present the teachings of his heritage to a Western audience. On a first reading, what these writers are sharing might appear confusing; their definitions appear poles apart. Their probes, however, are moving Western considerations of ethics and/or morality closer to an indigenous Theravāda orientation. There is among these authors an awareness that ethics and/or morality represent a universal human category of behavior and an inchoate sense that ethics and/or morality might have been definitionally culturally specific. This dynamic issue is seen readily in their considerations of the notions of "that which is without soul" or "absence of substantiality" (*anattā*) and *nibbāna*.

On occasion a problem arises when a phrase gets picked up in comparative studies, becomes used here and there initially, then almost on its own becomes a frequent way of discussing a matter. One such phrase, *beyond good and evil*, has entered into discussions about ethics in the Theravāda Buddhist tradition and has tended to remain in place like a grain of dust in a highly sophisticated, intricate, interlocking piece of machinery, being itself of foreign origin, making its presence known but in no way contributing to the functioning of the unit.

In this chapter, I would like second to attempt to go beyond the current usage of *beyond good and evil* in order to deal more adequately with a complex of positive evaluative concepts in the Theravāda Buddhist tradition that indicates clearly an appraisal of what is considered good in human conduct, in the quality of character that represents humanity at its best.

In developing this chapter, I do not wish to be argumentative, to parade a sequence of ideas held by a host of competent scholars before the reader and to set about chipping here and there—one usually can write a lot in doing this, but also one usually ends up proposing little that is of general interest and perhaps less, too, that will serve us well in our study of Buddhists past and present.

II

It is becoming apparent that the West has worked with a complex of ideas, for example ethics, morals (morality), religion, and law, that has had a history peculiar to the West, that has led generations of scholars to seek for clarification by definitional differentiation between these concepts,[1] and that has led generations of scholars to interpret non-Western human behavior in light of them.[2]

In recent times, *ethics* has come to be the preferred English term to designate systematic reflection on morality, apparently, on the American scene, having supplanted the study known more prominently in England as moral philosophy. *Morality* has come to refer to a composite of volitions, actions, and character of responsible persons in the process of differentiating between right and wrong, good and bad, and so on. *Ethics* has tended to represent the activity of justifying or validating this process of differentiation.

The Theravāda tradition has developed within a broad cultural matrix different from the West, of course. This tradition also presents to Western students a pattern of concepts within a complex, interlocking, and specialized formulation that is novel and forms a constellation not readily matched or replicated by customary English usage of terms like *ethics, morals* (morality), *religion*, and *law*.

Two notions within the Theravāda heritage that have given pause to Western students of comparative ethics are *anattā*, referring to "that which is without soul" or "absence of substantiality," and *nibbāna*. The former, *anattā*, seems at first blush to stand in direct opposition to much that has provided the cornerstone of Western ethical theory, the moral accountability of a discrete, autonomous self. And *nibbāna*, discerned by Western students as the ultimate goal in human life as Theravāda Buddhists have maintained, remains ineffable.

David Little and Sumner B. Twiss have attempted to deal with this *anattā* dimension and, noting both the outward orientation of Buddhist religious living as well as the inward, reflective and developmental dimension in Buddhist religious discipline, have suggested that the prominent posture of Theravāda Buddhist ethics represents a "transpersonal teleology," either in a "qualified intrapersonal teleology" or in a "qualified extrapersonal teleology"[3] with regard to final justification. For these scholars, the teleology involved concerns the attainment of *nibbāna*. The qualification noted deals with the affirmation of *anattā*, that ultimately there is no real, substantial, differentiated, discrete self. Hence, there is the stress on "transpersonal."

Little and Twiss find in their consideration of the early Buddhist records a set of guidelines for behavior that is practical, cognitive, and teleologically oriented. These authors want to qualify this because of a transpersonal dimension suggested by an interpretation of *nibbāna* in light of the *anattā* doctrine. They write,

> Fundamentally, morality, while present and important in Theravadin thought, is there provisionally at best. "In the ultimate sense," which is to say when looked at in respect to "the supreme dharma" [*nirvāna*, "the supreme dharma"], discussion of morality is inappropriate because the notion of morality presupposes persons, or at least intentions normally associated with persons, and these are not found in nirvana.[4]

Gerald Larson has made a probe into related ethical considerations in South Asia and has suggested two categories that represent distinct positions within the range of moral theorizing relevant to the Buddhist case: (1) a position classified as "naturalistic, nonintuitionist cognitivism," with regard to what is good, which he attributes to "the early Buddhist positions"; and (2) a position classified as "nonnaturalistic, intuitionist a-moralism" from which perspective Larson mentions "there is nothing that is truly good." This perspective he notes is characteristic of "Sāmkhya, Yoga, Vedānta, and certain varieties of Mahāyāna Buddhist reflection (Mādhyamika and Yogācāra)."[5] About the second position, Larson observes,

> There may be some contributory or instrumental (or, in other words, extrinsic) "value" in the world in that it can point one in a certain

> direction or prepare one for ultimate insight, but, finally, the ultimate experience itself is *not* a moral experience—it is "beyond good and evil," or, putting the matter directly, it is the denial that moral and ethical theorizing has any value at all![6]

Further, Larson suggests that these two positions, when characterized as normative ethical formulations, would respectively yield theoretical classification as (1) "teleological cognitivism" and (2) "gnoseological intuitionism."[7] Larson's second position, a "nonnaturalistic, intuitionist a-moralism," which is also "gnoseological intuitionism," is nevertheless presented as a normative ethical position, "a serious normative ethical claim." To fail to discern this characteristic would be, for Larson, "a serious interpretive mistake on analogy, for example, with the kind of mistake an interpreter makes who fails to see a Sartrean atheism as an authentic theological position."[8]

The two concepts of cognitivism and intuitionism are not sufficiently subtle, are much too sharply drawn to relate the activity of the human mind at the transitional moments of personal transformation for those engaged in the process of transcending as Theravāda Buddhists have apprehended it. The Theravāda position appears to me, on careful inquiry into the arising of the supramundane or world-transcending path (*magga*) in the awareness of a person, to be very close to Larson's second category, where reference is made to the Mahāyāna.

Little, Twiss, and Larson are developing our thinking about the Theravāda Buddhist case *within* the concepts of ethics and morality. Larson thinks that in the second category of ethical theorizing the highest objective realized through intuitive wisdom "totally transcends the good."[9] Yet, he urges that this position be seen as a serious normative ethical claim that can be so interpreted only within its total framework. This emphasis on the need for placing ethical structures within the context of a total framework is entirely on the mark, it seems to me. Little and Twiss, having noted a transpersonal teleology in Theravāda Buddhist morality, also mention that this position is a "religious-moral system,"[10] by which they mean "Other-impinging acts, together with whatever sacred-impinging acts there are in the system, are validated by a religious norm."[11]

These writers, aware of the ineffability of *nibbāna*, the subtle openness of the notion of *nibbāna* and the *anattā* doctrine, see in the Buddhist complex a religious-moral system in which morality is provisionally present, or they see the presence of an ethical claim that there is nothing intrinsically good, more usually expressed by reference to an ultimate state beyond good and evil.

It seems that one is led to conclude that, on the one hand, if morality is "there provisionally at best" in the Theravāda Buddhist tradition it somehow no longer remains so were one to speak of the tradition as a religious-moral system justified by a transpersonal teleology; that is, *nibbāna.* Or, if nothing is held to be intrinsically good, that is, the ultimate state is beyond good and evil, the position nevertheless makes an ethical claim. This might strike one as a bit confusing, and well that it should. Yet at the same time these writers are making constructive contributions to our developing understanding of the Theravāda orientation by developing new methods and categories, by pressing the notion of ethics in the English medium.

Joanna Macy has found in contemporary systems theory a mode of interpreting the dynamic of *anattā* in the context of "dependent co-arising" or "dependent co-production," (*paṭiccasamuppāda*), a mode of interpreting that "presents the structure of a living system as interdeterminative with its function or behavior."[12] Quoting Karl Deutsch, "The cognitive system is changing and remaking itself with each decision in the present. Thanks to what it has learned in the past, it is not wholly subject to the present. Thanks to what it can still learn, it is not wholly subject to the past. . . ." Macy sets before the reader her observation that

> The Buddha's emphasis on will does not, then, run counter to the *anattā* doctrine and suggests there must be some hidden abiding self. Nor does the doctrine of *anattā* imply any weakening of moral responsibility. Indeed the very process of choice-making constitutes our changing, but continuous identity. We cannot escape the effect of our choices, because that is what we are. These consequences are inescapable, not because there is a God that watches and tallies, but because in dependent co-arising our acts co-determine what we become.[13]

Anattā, for Macy, provides a moral ground:

> Basic to the ethic is the radical view of the self, which the teachings present. It is an interdependent, self-organizing process shaped by the flow of experience and the choices that condition this flow. Possessed of no "I" apart from what it feels, sees, thinks, does, the self does not *have* experience, it *is* its experience. Hence in the Buddhist ethic the error is egoicity. The problem with "mine-ness" (*mamattā*) is not just the greed it engenders, but the fundamental error it expresses and reinforces—that of considering the self as an independent, autonomous entity.[14]

What some theorists might consider foundational for a viable system of ethics, namely, an independent, differentiated, autonomous agent bearing moral responsibility, Theravāda Buddhists have tended to consider a fundamental error, as Macy puts it. Further, the doctrine of *anattā*, which has played a major role in the development of the presentation by Little and Twiss, wherein is recognized consequently a *provisional* presence of morality in the Theravāda framework,[15] is considered by Macy to be a "moral ground."[16]

What is one to do with an investigation of ethics or morality, which notions have been nurtured in Western intellectual history in an arena of discursive dualities such as good and bad, right and wrong, and so on, on turning to a religious tradition that has rigorously and delicately maintained that the highest state, *nibbāna*, transcends the ability of human discursive conceptualizations to comprehend it? Ven. Dr. H. Saddhatissa has written,

> In the first place, according to Buddhist and other Indian thought the highest state is one which lies beyond good and evil. In the second place, according to Buddhism there is no break between the moral teaching and that which pertains directly to the ideal state.[17]

He continues by stating that

> the ultimate ideal aim which may serve as the ultimate standard of right conduct, relates, according to Buddhist thought, to the supra-

> mundane or *lokuttara* state, and the connection between the moralities of everyday life and this *lokuttara* state is one which is entirely covered by the Buddha's teaching. It is, in fact, that which is known to Buddhists as *mārga, magga,* the Path, the Road, along which each person must travel for himself beginning with the practice of the common moralities up to the supramundane state beyond good and evil. From this point of view Buddhism can be said to provide the complete ethical study.[18]

Although Saddhatissa speaks of the highest state being beyond good and evil, by locating the focus of consideration on the path (*magga*), this Buddhist scholar interprets the Buddhist teachings as providing, in his words just quoted, "the complete ethical study."

Our authors are in basic agreement, although this might not be readily apparent. Acknowledging that the *anattā* notion involves in some sense a transpersonal orientation (in some ways going beyond a sense of "personal" customarily used in the English medium), recognizing, too, that *nibbāna* transcends conceptualization, somehow we meet in the Theravāda case a position that these writers conclude is religious, moral, and ethical. But the journey to this conclusion has not been without some confusion.

Perhaps we might move further into clarity by taking up focal Pāli terms and by giving some consideration to the application of those terms within the framework of the Theravāda perspective, which is not primarily concerned with doctrinal formulations and subsequent conceptual ramifications but with the function of those views in providing orientation in the life setting, as Macy has done with the *anattā* notion, as Saddhatissa has done with *magga.*

III

One no doubt has read or heard in the English language something like, "the objective in Buddhism is to go beyond good and evil," or that "the *arahant* is beyond good and evil," or "has gone beyond good and evil," or that "the ultimate is beyond good and evil," as we have just noted. I think we can move beyond this observation, represented in the general pattern of "beyond good and evil," in an attempt to work more adequately, more subtly, with the complex and cumulative formulations within the Theravāda tradition about what constitutes the highest evaluative affirmation of the purpose of human life. In a consideration of human behavior at its best, when one stresses that an *arahant* has "gone beyond good and evil,"[19] one speaks too quickly, speaks not enough, and what is said is not adequate to catch the subtlety of Theravāda Buddhist statements about the transformational moment.

Let me state a few of the issues: whether or not a fully accomplished person, one who has realized *nibbāna*, has gone beyond good and evil depends (1) on what one means by good, (2) at what point such a person "goes beyond," which depends heavily on (3) which Pāli terms one chooses to represent the English word and concept(s) "good." Whether the Theravāda case provides a consistent ethic depends on (4) whether one understands good as primarily an ethical and/or moral category, and of course, (5) what one means by *ethics* and/or *morality*. The matter is not made less complex by reminding ourselves that there is no one Pāli term equivalent to the contemporary English use of *ethics* in "a study of ethics" or "a theory of ethics."

Space is much too limited for one to provide a discussion of all five points noted. I will address only matters related to issues 2 and 3 in the remainder of this chapter, leaving aside questions related to issues, 1, 4, and 5 for further reflection.

Why have a number of writers in the West, and more recently some Theravāda Buddhists, seized on the English expression of *beyond good and evil* in an analysis of a dimension of what is called Buddhist ethics? In a thorough study responding to this question, it would seem Nietzsche would loom large. But more intriguing would be the possibility that Nietzsche has been misunderstood in *this* use of *this* phrase, *beyond good and evil* (*jenseits von Gut und Boese*).[20] Conceivably, the relatively rapid adoption of *beyond good and evil* with its implication of going beyond a particular interpretation of what is ethical might have been due to some extent to a reading of the pseudonymous authors penned by Kierkegaard—one has read of the so-called three stages: the aesthetic, the ethical and the religious. But it is likely that these so-called stages do not represent the personal position of Kierkegaard,[21] and it is more likely that applying these stages to the religious perspective of Theravāda Buddhists will not go beyond the barriers of an "outsider" merely *imagining* the fundamental orientation of life of an "insider," a reflective, knowledgeable Theravāda Buddhist.

Theravāda Buddhists have an abundance of technical terms that communicate positive evaluative appraisals, terms that represent what is commendable both with regard to act and to quality of person. It is not an easy matter to choose which of these terms one wants to represent the English word *good* so that, if this be the intent, one can then say that an *arahant* has gone beyond it. The term that yields itself most easily as an equivalent of *good*, perhaps for those who want to press the point quickly that an *arahant* has gone beyond it, is *puñña*, roughly also translated as "merit." And besides its own negative, *apuñña*, one finds *pāpa*, a standard Pāli term very frequently met in opposition to *puñña*, which one could translate "evil," preferably "bad" or "wrong." There are references in the Pāli texts that indicate that a person in whom all defilements are destroyed, an *arahant*, an ideal person who has fully realized salvific truth, has gone beyond, has abandoned or has destroyed *puñña* and *pāpa*.[22]

But why choose *puñña* and *pāpa* to represent "good and evil" beyond which an *arahant* is said to have gone? Certainly an *arahant* must go beyond, that is, leave behind, become dissociated from "evil" or what is bad, *pāpa*. Likewise, within the framework of Buddhist thought it is equally clear that actions expressive of a desire for bettering one's present and future condition now and in the next life, when one enters another life sequence, are not the actions that are expressive of the mental state of an *arahant* for whom there is no again-becoming. Such *puñña* acts (*puñña-kamma*) are not those of an *arahant*. Saying that an *arahant* has left behind, has gone beyond "meritorious acts" (*puññakamma*) tells us little that is new. Saying, on the basis of an analysis of only these two terms, *puñña* and *pāpa*, that an *arahant* has entered into a nonethical or amoral or nonmoral (which should not imply "unethical" or "immoral") sphere hardly represents an attempt to grapple with and perhaps enlarge our Western notions of ethics.

There are other terms in Pāli with which we might work to lead us further into a consideration of the process that leads from the point of leaving behind meritorious acts (*puññakamma*), through a process "on the stages" of sanctification, that is, from the path of stream-attainer up through the path of arahantship. The evaluative term for the qualities of persons on these stages or paths is *kusala*, a term that readily yields much of what one means by *good.*

P. D. Premasiri of Peradeniya University has argued[23] that, in what he calls *early Buddhism,* the term *kusala* carried a spectrum of meaning much broader than the term *puñña* and that the later tradition tended to confuse these terms, tended to use them interchangeably, even synonymously. Premasiri is right, it seems to me, that even in the canonical strata, *kusala* and *puñña* are met in senses communicating an overlapping in meaning or semantic usage. In his conclusion to his study, Premasiri notes that *kusala*, unlike *puñña*, represents the qualities with which one who has attained *nibbāna*, who has become free from all that is designated by *akusala, puñña*, and *pāpa*, is endowed. He writes that an assertion "that the Buddhist saint [*arahant*] is beyond good and bad can therefore be seen to be the result of a terminological muddle."[24]

Perhaps two refinements of Premasiri's noteworthy contribution might be made. First, the overlapping in meaning of *kusala* and *puñña* in the earlier canonical texts (*nikāyas*) tends to be present in those passages where *kusala* suggests one's volition with regard to thought, speech, and action. Where there is a distinction between *kusala* and *puñña*, the semantic function of *kusala* has to do primarily with qualities (*dhamma*) with which a person is endowed. Second, although the Pāli commentarial and Sinhala Buddhist literary traditions have tended to fuse *kusala* and *puñña*,[25] of which Premasiri generally is aware, the commentarial tradition maintains the distinction that Premasiri argued was the case in the early period of the Buddhist tradition. Premasiri notes that the later tradition was aware of this distinction but does not go into the matter, save for two references.[26]

Fundamentally, the distinction between *kusala* and *puñña* is maintained in the commentarial tradition. First, the commentarial tradition maintains the interpretation of the roots of *kusala* (*kusala-*

mūla) to be threefold: the absence of greed (*alobha*), the absence of avarice (*adosa*), and the absence of delusion (*amoha*),[27] which three roots provide the foundation for *puñña* at its best, so to speak and for cultivating further training in the way.

Second, the commentarial tradition tends to restrict its explanations of *puñña* to categories pertaining to the three realms of sentient existence *within saṃsāra*,[28] while frequently interpreting *kusala* as extending beyond these three spheres to include also a fourth, the world-transcending soteriological process expressed directly as being conjoined with the four paths of stream-attainment, and so on (*catumaggasampayoga*),[29] or indirectly in the three spheres within *saṃsāra*, and a fourth, which leads to *nibbāna* (*catubhūmaka*).[30] With regard to this soteriological process, the commentarial tradition uses *kusala* to modify the four paths, including the path of arahantship (*arahattamagga*).[31] Although there is a basis for one to infer that *kusala* could also modify *nibbāna* in the commentarial tradition,[32] it seems that the mainstream of that tradition would have us pause before making this move, pause not because of a lack of certainty or lack of clarity, but pause so as not to rush headlong into a delicate matter.

The weight of the Theravāda tradition undoubtedly stresses the Buddha as the ideal person and holds that person and that life as the highest example worthy of emulation. In the standard formula recited on the occasion of remembering the Buddha, one finds a comment about the Buddha's conduct, which the commentarial tradition unhesitatingly interprets as being characterized by moral virtue (*sīla*),[33] as the fulfillment of great compassion (*mahākāruṇika*), as being directed toward what is beneficial for others (*attha*).[34] He is called the *well-gone one* (*sugata*) because of a mode of going that is beautiful (*sobhanagamatta*), because he has gone to a pure place (*sundaram thanam gatattā*), because he has gone properly (*sammāgatattā*), and so forth.[35] And one might also note another evaluative notion, "good" ("genuine?" "authentic?") (*sat*), in the following statement: "The sweet fragrance of the virtue of good persons (*sappurisānam*...sīlagandho)—of Buddhas, Paccekabuddhas, and disciples (*sāvakas*)—goes against the wind."[36] And, further, one might note the use of the highest gain, or attainment, or profit, or goal, or good, that which seems to be behind *summum bonum*, so frequently used in English writings by Theravāda Buddhists; namely, *uttamattham*.[37] And one will remember that *kusala* is used to modify numerous qualities, at one count over fifty;[38] several of which, particularly "proper view," "proper awareness," "absence of greed," "absence of envy," "absence of delusion," and "insight-wisdom" (*sammādiṭṭhi, sammāsati, alobha, adosa, amoha* and *paññā*) cannot be said to be foreign to an *arahant*.

Well then, an accomplished person, a Buddha, a solitary Buddha (*paccekabuddha*), an *arahant*, on the basis of all these positive evaluative terms surely, from the Theravāda perspective, must be pronounced *good*, both in act and in quality of person, albeit not as a substantial underlying continually existing entity. And it would seem that from the Theravāda perspective, even if not from a perspective that one might regard the realm of what constitutes ethics, the case is closed.

But to say this without further ado might be failing to perceive a subtle overtone delicately sounded and carefully sustained in the corporate memory of the Theravāda tradition.

The tradition has made a profound affirmation with two dimensions. First the arising of the moment of stream-attainment is not itself the immediate result of one's action. Although one might exert long and arduously to prepare for this moment, even to bring about the conditions for its occurrence, that this moment occurs, that it happens, that the path, *magga*, arises is not the immediate result of one's will or actions because there cannot simultaneously occur one's effort and defilements, toward the discarding of which that effort is exerted. Were this to be the case, "the development of *magga* would be tinged with the defiled conditions [of the mind]."[39] Mahinda Palihawadana, of the University of Sri Jayewardenepura, has drawn our attention to this point and traces its theme to a passage in the canonical literature, in a portion of that passage he quotes:

> Monks, for a person who is virtuous [*sīlavato*], well-endowed with virtue [*sīlasampannassa*], there is no need of the effort of will [*na cetanāya karanīyam*]: "Let freedom from remorse arise in me." It is a matter of nature [*dhammatā*] that freedom from remorse arises in such a person.[40]

Palihawadana concludes,

> the *magga* event, swiftly arising after a moment of the mind's creative passiveness, regenerates and makes a new person of the pilgrim and gives him his first vision of Nibbāna. It is the true blessed event of the religious life of the Theravada Buddhist.[41]

The second dimension of this profound affirmation is that *magga*, interpreted as four paths, does not yield a result or results that fall into the category of "actions and consequences" (*kamma-vipāka*). The results of these paths are the associated "fruit" (*phala*) or "fructifications" of the path attained. The activities of an *arahant* and the associated meditative states are said to be "good" (*kusala*) yet they are "karmically inoperative."[42]

The commentarial tradition records that there is a moment when even *kusala* that exists because of insight meditation (*vipassanā*) is dissolved.[43] It appears that the activity of mind referred to here is that known as "functioning consciousness" (*kiriyacitta*), or mental function in relation to action but ineffective as to "karmic results."[44] It seems to me that such mind would have "ejected wishes" (*vantāso*) and would be one that "knows the uncreated" (*akataññū*) as a verse in the *Dhammapada* and its commentarial gloss suggest. We are talking about a person supreme (*purisuttama*).[45]

One might attempt to move the position "beyond good and evil" one more step, from beyond *puñña* and *apuñña* or *pāpa* to beyond *kusala* and *akusala*. But such a move cannot be established because of the presence of *kusala* as well as what one might call a "good-complex" of associative positive evaluative terms used to characterize such person (*purisuttama*). But what of this subtle activity in the consciousness of an *arahant* that suggests the absence of karmic consequences? This functioning consciousness is present in one who has no desire to get something more because *nibbāna has arisen*. Were this functioning consciousness not present, how could one speak of *nibbāna* as arising or as having arisen? Were a consciousness capable of engendering consequences (*vipāka*) to be active at the arising of *nibbāna*, this consciousness, conceivably, could be said to taint such arising or to suggest that a person immediately caused the arising of *nibbāna*. And so the notion of functioning consciousness at this stage of an *arahant* has continued to be held by the Theravāda thinkers not because the point to be made is that the *arahant* has gone beyond "good and evil" or "good and bad," but, more than that, beyond that, to state with impressive insight and subtlety—while being simultaneously loyal to the tradition and faithful to the reality of *nibbāna* realization—that *nibbāna* arises when the conditions are present, but one does not cause this arising.

The tradition has spoken of this full realization of *nibbāna* and of those who have had this realization in the most positive evaluative terms the Pāli language carries. And also the tradition has made it clear that *nibbāna* can in no way be said to be immediately caused by one. For a person to say "I am good" and to say that such *nibbāna* realization has occurred would strike one as representing a situation gone awry.

So to speak of an *arahant* or a Buddha, or a solitary Buddha (*paccekabuddha*), as having "gone beyond good and evil" really tells us more about what interpretation of *good* is being used—it tells us little about the way the Theravāda tradition has valued such persons and little, too, about the person at the moment of *nibbāna* realization. Whether such persons function within the realm of what one might call ethics depends on whether one's notion of ethics is adequate.[46] And this is a problem of the English medium of the Western intellectual heritage, not of Theravāda Buddhists.

7

FAITH IN THE WAKE OF THE DHAMMAPADA

In turning to a chapter on this subject, one might expect to find at the outset a succinct definition of faith. But the subject and the notion of faith escape one's attempts to provide a succinct and adequate definition, especially here within the confines of a single chapter.[1] Moreover, let me acknowledge that I have narrowed the scope of this present inquiry by omitting some important Pāli notions, such as "a delicate sense of being 'taken up'," or "delightful, quiet equipoise," or "serene clarity [of heart and mind]" (*pasāda*), "going for, taking refuge" or "going beyond oneself, rising above oneself" (*saraṇagamana*), or "beholding the [arising of] the path" (*magga-dassana*), in order to focus on one key Pāli idea, *saddhā*, let us translate it "faith."

In spite of what might seem to be the case because of the great accomplishments of scholars who worked before us, there still remains a great deal in Theravāda studies awaiting our sustained investigation and interpretation. In a sense, we outsiders who are students of the Theravāda tradition have only just begun. On the matter of texts and translations, one needs to note that the great wealth of commentarial literature remains relatively untapped by Western scholarship. The deeper and more subtle issues of the classical Buddhist Abhidhamma reflections are generally untouched. Regarding thorough historical or theoretical studies, we are continuing to await the appearance of the great work on the notion of "no soul" (*anattā*), for example. We are also waiting for that thorough and exhaustive study of the notion of "faith" (*saddhā*).

By the phrase, *in the wake of the* Dhammapada, I wish to indicate that I am not going to attempt a study of *saddhā* in the early phase of the Buddhist movement or to engage in a thorough canonical study of the term and its usage. I will deal with the notion of *saddhā* as it appears in the *Dhammapada* and in the commentarial heritage that has focused on this great text.[2]

I. *SADDHĀ* IN THE *DHAMMAPADA*

The term *saddhā* does not occur frequently in the *Dhammapada*. In fact the term's occurrence is sufficiently rare that one might surmise the notion was considered either of little importance—that is, it was really not worth mentioning—or of such overwhelming significance that its importance was assumed, and hence it was not necessary to mention it. Let us heed what the tradition of the text has averred: "A blessing is faith established,"[3] and begin our very brief textual survey with this observation in mind.

We find a pattern of what one might call "cluster concepts" appearing with "faith" (*saddhā*): one would note "faith" and "insight-wisdom" (*paññā*),[4] "faith" and "virtue" (*sīla*),[5] and "faith" and "enterprise" (*viriya*).[6] There is a delightful pun in one verse, which introduces the idea of a person who has no faith (*assaddho*), who is ungrateful, and so forth, and concludes that such a person is a "person supreme" (*uttamaporiso*).[7] That just about does it for the text: "faith" is a blessing, is associated with insight-wisdom, virtue, and enterprise, and is the kind of thing that, even in clever jest, a person might be considered as not having.

II. *SADDHĀ* IN THE COMMENTARIAL TRADITION

When we come to the commentary on the *Dhammapada*, we find a standard commentarial procedure at work. Drawing widely from different strata of canonical texts a commentator will weave together strands of the heritage in attempts to explain the term or passage of the text at hand. The commentator might work on several levels: presenting only a synonym or an alternative grammatical form, utilizing a series of etymologically associated terms for heuristic-homiletical purposes, or using a term from a verse of the text being commented on in the context of a prose passage to enable one to catch the meaning of the term in the text, placing the term in its customary arrangement in a systematic formula to indicate its location in a comprehensive doctrinal scheme, and so forth.

In conducting a study of the heritage of the commentaries, one could adopt an analytical approach as a method and go backward, as it were, from the later commentaries to the earlier texts to find there the original passages quoted or referred to in the commentaries. However, I will let the commentarial texts themselves represent a creative synthetic attempt of pulling together and "bringing forward," as it were, down to us today, those older passages to present them to the reader in the context of the *Dhammapada* itself. The question about method that I mention here is not one of contradiction, not of opposition, not either one method or another, but, as we are now more and more coming to see as we break through the assumptions of evolutionary orientations, one of complementariness. I make mention of this because the analytic approach tends, surprisingly tenaciously, to be interpreted by some as the only academic approach adequate in itself.

In our brief consideration of *saddhā* here, the point is not to seek to understand what the notion might have meant when the Buddha first spoke it, or how it might have developed in the very early period of the Buddhist movement and thereafter. This, of course, is an important area of inquiry. But our purpose is to understand how *saddhā* has been interpreted *in* the *Dhammapada* and in the commentarial *tradition* that clustered around the *Dhammapada.*

SADDHĀ AND RESTRAINT

The commentary on the *Dhammapada* indicates a relationship between the presence of "restraint" (*saṃvaro/saṃvutam*) and *saddhā.* In locating this relationship, the commentary demonstrates a dynamic quality of *saddhā*, using the term *vīthi*, roughly meaning "process" and, in the particular commentary passage, translated as "stream [of mental events]." When there is this self-control, this restraint, one finds within a "wholesome stream [of mental events]" the presence of faith (*saddhā*) as well as patience, energy or enterprise (*viriya*), heedfulness and understanding. Associated with nonrestraint, one finds "lack of faith" (*assaddhā*), and impatience, sloth (*kosajja*), heedlessness, and ignorance.[8] One notes again the parallelism presented by the presence or absence of restraint in the *Dhammapada* text itself. In verse 7, one who is "in senses unrestrained" (*indriyesu asaṃvutaṃ*)" is noted as being "indolent, inferior of enterprise (*kusītaṃ hīnaviriyaṃ*), whereas in verse 8, one who is "in senses well restrained (*indriyesu susaṃvutaṃ*)" is characterized as being "faithful, resolute in enterprise" (*saddhaṃ āraddhaviriyaṃ*). We are able to discern how the commentary, in commenting on verse 360 in the general context of restraint, is fully consonant with the *Dhammapada* textual position as also found in verses 7–8: *saddhā* is present along with restraint, energy, and resolution in enterprise. With the absence of *saddhā*, there is also the absence of restraint and consequently the presence of indolence or sloth (*kosajja/kusīta*).

ASSADDHO: ONE WITHOUT FAITH

A very interesting form containing our word, *saddhā*, appears in the *Dhammapada*: "one who has no faith," or "one without faith," *assaddho*. I will merely note the *Dhammapada* verse (*Dhp*. v. 97),[9] and present a translation of the gloss provided in the Pāli commentary and an elaboration provided in an old Sinhala text.

> Who has no faith: *assaddho*
> The quality (*guṇa*) that one has attained oneself, one does not take on faith from the word of others: [one is] "not having faith" in that sense.[10]

An old Sinhala text further elaborates this:

> "Who has no faith"—not for one is there faith by the words of another because one knows, having realized for oneself, ordinary and world-transcending virtuous qualities (*laukika lokottara guṇadharmayan*) such as meditative-absorption (*dhyāna*), insight (*vidarśanā*), Path and Fruits, etc., which have been penetrated to by one. Or, ["who has no faith" in the sense that] there is no faith in any teacher other than the Buddha.[11]

We apparently meet some ambiguity when we consider this notion, "one who has not faith" or "one without faith" (*assaddho*). There is a sense in which the absence of *saddhā* brings with it sloth and indolence, as we have seen. Yet, at the same time, we note that the commentarial tradition indicates a line of interpretation that would have one understand "one without faith" (*assaddho*) also to mean immediacy of knowing for oneself, realization, and hence "without faith" in the sense of not relying on the words or reports of others.[12] It also means "without faith" in the teachings of teachers other than the Buddha.

This, then, might lead one to infer that an *arahant* would be a person who is characterized by *assaddho*, as being "one without faith," in the sense of being one who has known for oneself salvific insight. But this does not represent the commentarial heritage of the *Dhammapada*.

There is a line in the *Dhammapada* that says "No fear is there for the wide-awake" (verse 39). The commentary takes this up and notes the following: "What is mentioned is the lack of fear of the [Arahant with] influxes extinct just as of one who is wide-awake. He is said to be *awake* due to being endowed with the five qualities of wakefulness (*pañcahi jāgaradhammehi*), such as faith, and so on."[13]

What are we to make of this term *assaddho*, "one without faith"? Some of the difficulty has to do with the force of the negative preformative *a*, whether it means (1) the opposite of faith or (2) the absence of faith. The Pāli word form and the way the term is used seem to indicate the second sense, "the absence of faith," and this has caused some difficulty for the tradition. It seems that the commentators have said the meaning of *assaddho*, "one without faith" (in the sense of one having realized for oneself) is quite in keeping with a Theravāda Buddhist frame of reference. Yet the commentators seem to have been aware of the necessity to be on their guard in using *assaddho* because of the key importance of faith (*saddhā*).

The commentary on the *Dhammapada* draws one's attention to another canonical passage, found in the *Saṃyutta-nikāya*, a discourse (*sutta*) concerning one of the Buddha's leading disciples, Sāriputta.[14] The commentary on the *Dhammapada* represents that passage well but in the context of its presentation there are important additions. The Sāriputta story or exchange concerns the five spiritual faculties (*indriyas*).

Now this same exchange is also mentioned in another, later, text, the *Mahāniddesa*, a very old commentary considered to be canonical. The *Mahāniddesa*, in commenting on *Sutta-nipāta*, v. 853, includes some key doctrinal points: the three characteristics of life (*tilakkhaṇa*), the description of "Dependent Coorigination" (*paṭiccasamuppāda*), and more. The *Mahāniddesa* concludes by quoting *Dhammapada* v. 97.

However, the commentary on the *Dhammapada* does not include those key doctrinal points. It moves quickly to the Sāriputta story and concludes with an additional comment about volitional activity (*kamma*) and consequences, or "fruits" (*phala*), and the "three gems": the Buddha, Dhamma, and the Sangha. Let us now turn to this commentary's additional elaboration:

> Having heard this [the exchange found in the Sāriputta story], the *bhikkhus* began a discussion. "The Thera Sāriputta has never put aside confusing entanglements. Even today he still does not put his heart[15] on the Perfectly Enlightened One."
>
> Having heard this, the Teacher said "O *bhikkhus*, what is this that you say? In fact I myself asked Sāriputta, 'O Sāriputta, do you trust (*saddahasi*) that without cultivating the five faculties [of which *saddhā* is one], without causing to arise calm and insight, it is possible to realize the Paths and Fruits?' He replied, 'O venerable sir, I do not so trust that there is one realizing it thus.' He does not put his heart on the notion that there is no fruit or consequence of that

which is given or of that which is done. He does not put his heart on the notion that there is no [virtuous] quality of the Buddha and so forth [i.e., Dhamma and Sangha]. Hence this one [i.e., Sāriputta] does not go by faith in others with regard to the qualities of meditative-absorption, insight, Paths and Fruits which have been obtained in and by himself. Therefore he is without fault."[16]

So we find that the commentary is prepared to take *one without faith* (*assaddho*)—in the sense of one who has personally realized, known, the achievements of meditation, insight, that attainment of the Paths and Fruits for, in, and by oneself (*attanā*)—in the sense of one who does not go by means of merely trusting the reports of others.[17] And yet, according to the full account of the commentarial tradition, one, nevertheless, does not transcend faith entirely because the *arahant* continues to be endowed with the faculty of faith (*saddhindriya*).

It would be relatively easy to misread this Sāriputta story (drawing on its presence in the *Saṃyutta-nikāya*, its recounting in the *Mahāniddesa*, and its appearance in the commentary on the *Dhammapada*) to think that there is some kind of fundamental and final contrast between salvific "insight-wisdom" (*paññā*), and "faith" (*saddhā*), that with the rise of "insight-wisdom" (*paññā*) there is no "faith" (*saddhā*), and hence one is known as *one without faith* (*assaddho*).

The point is to understand that when one knows, realizes, that the faculties of faith, enterprise, insight-wisdom, mindfulness, and concentration, when cultivated and made to increase for oneself by means of insight-wisdom, and knows, realizes that they "plunge into ambrosia [that is *nibbāna*]" (*amatogadham*), "culminate in the Deathless [that is *nibbāna*]" (*amatapariyosānam*), one then does not proceed by means of faith in another or in others. One's faith has been *fulfilled*.

"One without faith" (*assaddho*), therefore, is a delicate notion not to be used automatically, as it were, in opposition to theists who might also talk about the centrality of faith, not to be held up as the central articulation of the primary objective within the Theravāda frame of reference, but a term that has been used to stress personal engagement, total involvement in the realization of liberating gnosis or salvific insight-wisdom, the efficacy and fulfillment of faith. One who knows this to be the case does not hold to it on the authority of others. The person who knows, who has realized this salvific insight-wisdom, the fulfillment of faith, does not rely on the instruction or guidance of others. And complementarily, when there is little faith, insight-wisdom does not become full.[18]

LOKIYA-LOKUTTARASADDHĀ

Another intriguing and perhaps very significant interpretation of *saddhā*, in the commentary on the *Dhammapada* as well as within the Theravāda tradition at large, is the standard mode of interpretating faith as twofold: "customary," "ordinary," (*lokiya*) and "transcendent" or "world transcending" (*lokuttara*).[19] The commentary indicates these two dimensions when discussing one who is faithful (*saddho*):

> Faithful: *saddhaṃ*
> Endowed with ordinary faithfulness, which is marked by faith in *kamma* [volitional activity] and *phala* [its consequence], as well as with transcendent faithfulness, which amounts to a firm sense of being pleased (*aveccapasāda*) in the "three objects" [Buddha, Dhamma, and Sangha].[20]

A Sinhala text follows this basic division but leaves some ambiguity whether faith in *kamma* and *phala* is restricted to "ordinary" or "customary" faith (*lokiya saddhā*). "Here, faith means both ordinary faith and transcendent faith. Both of them have the characteristic of being faith in the qualities of the three gems [Buddha, Dhamma, Sangha] and in *karma* and its consequences."[21]

We see clearly in these passages that the so-called karma theory is not adequately understood as long as one interprets it as a theory that might be proven true or false or as an almost foolproof theory to explain inequalities, as "social graphite" or as an old-fashioned way of justifying social injustices. The commentarial passages tell us that this moral order is affirmed by men and women; persons have placed their hearts on this, have averred "this is the context in which human life is to be lived at its best"; namely, that there are cosmic consequences of one's volition.

Faith works through the wholesome deed. Our commentary tells us,

> if one's faith is meager and one's riches ample, one [still] is not able to do a great deal of wholesome (*kusala*) deeds. When faith is meager and riches are also meager, it is indeed not possible [to do much good]; [but] one is capable [of doing this] when faith is ample and riches are also ample. Such a person was Visākhā.[22]

On the basis of the *Dhammapada* commentarial evidence at hand, it seems that the customary expression of faith (*lokiya-saddhā*) pertains only to one's affirmation that volitional behavior (*kamma*) yields consequences (*phala/vipāka*), that this behavior is of cosmic significance, and to one's self-commitment in seeking refuge in the customary way (*lokiya-saraṇa-gamana*) with regard to the three gems.

Regarding world-transcending faith (*lokuttara-saddhā*), we are led by the commentarial tradition to consider the three gems (the Buddha, Dhamma, and Sangha) and the notion of refuge itself. With regard to these three gems, we find this twofold distinction: "ordinary/customary" going for refuge (*lokiyasaraṇagamana*) and "world-transcending" going for refuge (*lokuttarasaraṇagamana*).

The parallelism would then be found, on the one hand, in customary faith and customary going for refuge, and on the other hand, world-transcending faith and world-transcending going for refuge. In the former case, the customary activity occurs, in brief, when a person takes as the object of *emulation* the virtuous qualities of the Buddha and of Dhamma and of those persons who have entered well along the Dhamma way; that is, the "Eight Noble Persons."[23]

In the latter case, the world-transcending realization occurs when one realizes that which the Buddha rediscovered, which enabled one to become the Awakened One, the Buddha, when one realizes *dhamma* that is salvific truth about which *dhamma* that is the teaching teaches, when one realizes that which enabled those who had entered into the "creative receptivity" to realize the first glimpse of *nib-*

bāna, a glimpse that becomes full penetration.[24]

World-transcending faith (*lokuttarasaddhā*), seems to be the calm, quiet, holistic affirmation involved in the realization of salvific truth. Dhamma abides, insight-wisdom arises, and one says with one's mind and heart YES.[25] This yes, on this level, appears to point in the direction in which "world-transcending faith" (*lokuttarasaddhā*) might be found.

Faith is calm; faith is wholesome, faith has as its object *nibbāna*. I quote from a learned writer who stands within the Theravāda Buddhist tradition:

> Faith is a wholesome mental process that causes calm joy in the mind and mental processes with regard to the object that occurs [or arises] with it in the thought procedures themselves. That faith itself is twofold, such as customary and world-transcending. Of the two, the mental process of faith that occurs in thoughts pertaining to Paths and Fruits is called world-transcending faith because it causes calm joy in the thought with regard to the object of *nirvāna*, and that [mental process of faith] itself, when it has to do with customary wholesome thoughts, is called customary faith because it causes calm joy in thoughts with regard to the qualities, *etc.*, of the three gems.[26]

Those of us who are Theravāda Buddhists are not strangers to that quality of life to which the English word *faith* points. In fact, it might be said that this Theravāda Buddhist tradition, this most cautiously measured, methodically reasoned, theoretically analytical of humankind's religious traditions has also, perhaps, one of the most engaging multi-leveled notions of faith it is our enriching pleasure to note.

8

THERE ARE BUDDHISTS LIVING IN SRI LANKA TODAY

The purpose of this chapter is to introduce a person to the Buddhist tradition in Sri Lanka, that lovely island, ancient culture, new nation. In its basic sense, *to introduce,* as used here, means "to lead one into, to bring one within" a perspective held by many Buddhists in Sri Lanka. This, of course, is an immensely difficult task to discharge adequately in a few pages. A person interested in reading sources to gain a comprehensive grasp of the Buddhist tradition or an in-depth competence of a facet of that tradition as it has contributed significantly to Sri Lanka is fortunate to have available a bibliographical essay with which to launch such study.[1]

To introduce, that is, to attempt to bring one within a perspective held by many Buddhists in Sri Lanka is another matter, one requiring interpretation as well as sensitive, empathetic probes into that which is held to be most personal by religious persons, and also critical, reflective observations of one's presuppositions, working assumptions, and the information available. Gaining a perspective requires not only watching and recording and extrapolating in terms of one or another method mutually endorsed, for one reason or another, by one's colleagues, but also listening and reflecting on what one has heard or has been told, reflecting also on what was not said, and why, for what purpose, in what context. To be brought within a perspective implies an activity of another person, whether a fifth-century Buddhist writer or one's patient Buddhist friends living today.

A historian would be less than persuasive, certainly less than perceptive, were he or she to consider a study of history as something inherently other than a study of persons. For that matter, too, a study of humankind's religiousness would tend to ricochet among distorting mirrors of competing theories of method were the focus of one's study something other than persons. Historians have long known the helpfulness of historical sensitivity in attempts to find a reasonableness that provides a pattern in an otherwise erratic occurrence of human events. Similarly, on beginning to read about Buddhists in Sri Lanka, one could do worse than to acquire a sensitive attitudinal orientation to the subject, to discern dimensions of a dynamic process that preserves and engenders anew, creatively, a religious heritage in a person's life, and to note a continuation of a cumulative religious tradition in history within a religious community, a process of change and continuity, of challenge and creative response.

There are Buddhists living in Sri Lanka today. On first blush this might be considered a trite statement, one hardly worth further reflection, certainly obvious and consequently of little import. However, this statement, composed of only eight words, is monumental; it is the kind of statement that is the consequence not only of someone's report but of a cumulative process in history reflecting a deliberate activity of persons, choosing to remember their tradition of a way of life, to endorse that way of life, and to transmit it to their children. This process is not an easy matter, is not inevitable, and could have been otherwise had persons chosen differently, had they found this way of life no longer relevant to their concerns in the course of the past two millennia, had they ceased to find meaning through it, or to form community by it. No, the statement with which we begin is stunning because of the weight of history that stands behind it, bewildering because of the complexity of events, communal and personal, that underpin it, and sobering, too, because of the dedication of unknown millions of men and women who for twenty centuries have remembered, have participated in, and have perpetuated what they found to be supportive.

I

We pause for a moment at the steps of the Temple of the Tooth Relic (Dalada Maligawa, in Kandy, Sri Lanka) to remove our sandals before walking, flower in hand, into the special precincts. Reaching the second floor, we see others placing their flowers on a memorial table before the closed relic chamber. We slow our stride; the space here is not ordinary space and the activity we see—persons on their knees, bowing full forward with heads held in clasped hands—reminds us that one moves gently in delicate moments. Some of us have purchased a closed lotus just outside the temple. Others of us have brought our flowers from our village. We carefully peel back the leaves to open a lotus, sprinkle water on our flower to heighten its freshness and beauty, and take our place, on our knees, to gather our thoughts. Then one by one, when each is ready, we move to place our flower among others, forming a variety of individual hues and shapes and simultaneously a unified arrangement of dazzling diversity. When thoughts become distracted, faint whispers can be heard or one might overhear a prayer that assistance might be forthcoming or perhaps an old verse reminding us that, like these flowers, we, too, will lose our luster and decay; and there is silence.

When each is ready, each walks away and we form our group again as we walk down the stairs and out into the bright sunlight. We do not talk about what we have done, we do not analyze our actions or our thoughts to explain by making piecemeal the action that generates its force precisely because it is integrative.

We have gone to the temple at different times when conch, drums, cymbals, and reed instrument *(horaṇā)* create a din of noise for some, perhaps, and instrumental praise *(śabda pūja)* for others; when we are pressed by the excited devotion of the crowd through the tight passageway to place our flowers before the symbol of the tooth relic, pausing for an extended moment, much too brief, then to make our way out through another passage, an *exit into* our ordinary world.

Persons make their way to this temple for about as many reasons as there are people who come; on a birthday, perhaps, or on the first outing for a newborn babe, or to bring the first portion of a harvest, or when dear friends meet again after being separated for several years, or before making a first trip out of the country, or because it enables one, having come into Kandy for a day's shopping, to sense that one has done something noble that day by calmly being humble, before catching a bus for the village.

The Buddha is being remembered in Sri Lanka.

On another occasion, we are dressed in clean clothes, white if we have it, and step into the cool of an evening—enjoying its refreshing reminder that the pressures of a full day at the office, shop, or factory, the pains of a body bent many hours to the heat of the sun, do pass, if we allow them—prepared to forgo physical rest for something more edifying. Into settings where torches or bottle lamps flicker, or petromax lamps hissingly cast their sharp shadows into the night, or generators grind out light through naked bulbs thoughtfully arranged, or houses with every light fixture aglow, we make our way *in from the dark.*

We remove our sandals in a village hut, in a temple, in urban bungalows because we know that weighty words will be uttered and with us will be monks (*bhikkhus*), men we have decided to support in their pursuits because that support is necessary for them and wholesome for us. We have come for a *pirit* ceremony, an occasion in which monks chant the teachings (*dhamma*) of the Buddha, teachings which, in spite of our foibles, are recognized as being capable of leading one on to full penetration of salvific truth (*dhamma*).

We quietly take our seats, cross-legged, and receive from someone a thread, passing it on to someone else, running it through the fingers of our pressed palms, letting it unravel as it binds us together, an empirical reminder that each individual is really a person grounded in a sacred source and held in balance and buttressed through relationships—between someone and someone else. Some of us know the passages being chanted, a few lips move in cadence with the sound of the monks. Some of us know the general import of the major passages, and others of us are not quite sure of the meaning of the words and the supportive reminder that their meaning communicates, that centuries have not warped the singular message that wholesome living is not measured by rapid gain and clever, quick, acquisition, but by patient giving.

Pāli, the language of *dhamma* being chanted about *dhamma* that transcends language, is not known by many in Sri Lanka. But the ceremony has been structured by the cumulative wisdom of tradition to achieve an objective frequently, but not easily, attained by rituals of humankind's religious traditions—the objective of communicating with each hearer, within his or her life situation, a common theme that what is going on here is momentous, that one is in the presence of that which enables a world-view to have coherence, that for some *empirical reality might be altered* by this activity because, it seems likely, the *lives of persons have been changed*, impressively, by becoming engaged with the meaning of these words.

Throughout the night the chanting continues by monks in pairs, joined after sunrise by the remainder of their brothers in robes in chanting the final stanzas. The hours of the night have passed, and one has talked softly with one's friends, or has walked about to stretch one's legs, or has taken a brief nap here or there, and has heard the chanting of the words continuously, minute by minute, and one meets a new sunrise having been a part of a stitching of the centuries.

Dhamma is being remembered in Sri Lanka.

Not long after dawn, in Colombo, one joins a small group of relatives and friends who have gathered at a small temple for an induction ceremony (*mahaṇa kirīma*) of a young man in his early teens who is seeking to become a novice (*sāmaṇera*) in the monastic order, the Sangha. Dressed in white, the young man has his hair and eyebrows shaved and is rinsed with buckets of cold water drawn from a nearby faucet. He shudders, neither complaining nor joking—the ceremony is much too serious for that. Proud mother and father watch attentively with eyes not without traces of tears.

One listens carefully as this young man, now dressed in the monastic robes and kneeling before the senior monk, in his youthful voice repeats the verses of the threefold refuge and the precepts appropriate for the occasion, each phrase uttered in echo of the full voice of the elderly monk. All are silent except for these two men and the chirping birds, a rejuvenating sound of fresh continuity set against the sounds of the shifting gears of a city yawning itself awake. Receiving a set of robes and a mendicant's bowl, the young man sits aside about to witness something he has never seen before.

Mother and father approach this seated young man, kneel and bow low to him. He sees the top of the heads of the greatest people on earth, his parents, now bent toward him and toward that for which this young life is committed, in humble reverence. An enormously forceful complex of emotions is let loose and this young man is provided with a supportive memory to underpin his motivation as he sets about to live his life in the devout discipline of a monk.

In Kandy, one evening, two men in royal attire ride the backs of richly adorned elephants to the chapter house where they change their attire to that of a monk and sit facing the incumbent monk who is seated at the other end of two rows of solemn elders. One recognizes that one has witnessed a repetition in ritual of the Buddha's great setting out from home on his quest for salvific truth.[2] One takes one's place among the laity from the home villages of these two men, candidates for the ceremony of higher ordinary (*upasampadā*) to become full monks (*bhikkhus*) in the Sangha. The ceremony is brief, words over two millennia old are repeated anew. Two more men have taken their place in the long and noble saffron yellow line of monastic succession.

At the close of the ordination ceremony, wide-eyed children snap up to see the people in the ornately decorated chapter house, older people rise more slowly, more deliberately. A number of gifts (along with "eight requisites," *aṭapirikara*, that a monk is to have) are given to these two *bhikkhus*, newly ordained with the *upasampadā*: umbrellas, notebooks, pillows, suitcases, little of monetary worth. One notes tears in the eyes of villagers, tears suggestive of a proud loss now sealed in this ancient ceremony. Memories of black-haired playful sons now subside before the dignity of two men, heads shaven, seated quietly. Inexpensive gifts, though costly for the givers, become vehicles of inestimable value in this moment of potentiality. Two men, just fully ordained, have placed on them at this moment the ideal aspirations of those who know them best.

The Sangha is being remembered in Sri Lanka.

In these ceremonies, and others, one hears the old and noble formula of the triple refuge uttered, and observing these rituals one sees demonstrated the permeating influence of the Buddha, Dhamma and the Sangha.

When Rome was just becoming established from its early struggles as a young republic, men and women in India were saying the triple refuge:

> *Buddhaṃ saraṇaṃ gacchāmi*
> *Dhammaṃ saraṇaṃ gacchāmi*
> *Sanghaṃ saraṇaṃ gacchāmi*
> I go to the Buddha as refuge.
> I go to Dhamma as refuge.
> I go to the Sangha as refuge.

And, as one reads the Pāli canon, the impressive Pāli commentarial literature, and the great Sinhala classics, one begins to sense the profundity of the notion of refuge (*saraṇa*) in the Theravāda tradition in Sri Lanka.[3] These sources make it quite clear that refuge is not a retreat from the world, a form of escapism. It is not closing one's eyes to the world either to whimper in despair or to delude oneself into illusory compensatory idealism yielding a deceptive sense of security. Refuge, these sources labor to make plain, is deeply personal and replete with cosmic consequences. By discerning this refuge, persons become engaged in a process of deepening understanding of themselves, others, and life in this world and beyond. One is dealing with weighty matters, a lively religious practice and concept, in this notion of refuge, as we have seen earlier, in Chapter 4.

II

But a shift has occurred, a movement somewhat extraneous from these sources and the testimony of the centuries.

We mention again a rather recent Sinhala textbook formally approved for children on an upper kindergarten level and designed, ideally, to acquaint these children with their religious heritage. One reads, in the first three sentences of this little book, "Buddhism is our religion. it is according to Buddhism that we should act. For us, there is nothing more important than Buddhism."[4]

Perhaps this might strike one as an unusual way to introduce children to a religious heritage that has held paramount the importance of responsible, generous living for learning to live well by eradicating personal and communal detrimental behavior. One might have expected a word about kindness and truth speaking in this little reader. What has happened that has contributed to this change in perspective? A great deal has happened over several centuries.

"Change and continuity" is a familiar theme among many who study persons living in societies. Change and continuity is a way of describing the historical process. But it is also a way of describing one's personal life. In considering the Theravāda tradition in Sri Lanka, the notion of change and continuity is hardly new, either from the point of view of the institutional organizations or from the perspective of persons. Something different was happening in each century; something old was being remembered. In *change and continuity,* the conjunction *and* can certainly carry the force of a dynamic cross-reference that reflects a creative response to the new and a creative appropriation of the old.

Creative responses and creative appropriations are, certainly, not inevitable. Over the course of the past two centuries the Buddhist tradition in Sri Lanka has met a series of new ideas stemming from foreign cultural matrixes and, in responding to these ideas, reacting to them, rejecting, fully adopting, modifying, misunderstanding, refining them, Buddhists have acted creatively.

By the early nineteenth century, one complex of ideas came to have significant ramifications for Sinhala Buddhists. About this time, Sinhala Buddhists were becoming acquainted with an idea, "Buddhism," for which, as we have seen, they chose to coin a term, *buddhāgama.* By this time, also, they had become aware of an idea, "religion," for which they chose to utilize, by extending its meaning, an old term, *āgama,* as we have also seen. By this time, Sinhala Buddhists were aware of an institution called *Christianity.* This complex of ideas, weighty in themselves, seems to have permeated the scene in Sri Lanka rather quickly and quite thoroughly because this complex was introduced by Westerners who came to hold political, economic, military, and educational dominance in the country.

What Buddhists had been attempting to do with their lives now came to be called *Buddhism,* and this "Buddhism" was one of a number of things called *religions,* one of which was "Christianity." This triad of ideas—"Buddhism," "religion," and "Christianity"—though widespread in Sri Lanka today and, for the most part, reasonably understood, does not entirely represent the thinking of many Sinhala Buddhists. Once in a while, one can meet an interesting lexical anomaly pivoting on the term *āgama,* an old Sanskrit and Pāli word basically meaning "coming," "approach," "arrival," and also "that which has come down to the present" in the sense of tradition preserved in writing. By further extension the term means "authoritative text" and, further, "established procedure," even "discipline."[5] One listening to a conversation in the Sinhala language might hear *buddhāgama* (*buddha* + *āgama*) used like *Buddhism,* and *āgama,* standing alone, used like *religion;* but occasionally one can hear *āgama,* standing alone, used to designate "Christianity," *āgam kārayā* used to designate a Christian, and *eya āgame* to mean "he is a Christian." These usages suggest the major source of these ideas, namely Christians.

Buddhists had come to see their religious heritage labeled *Buddhism,* designated as one "religion" among several, and affirmed by some to fall somewhere on a spectrum from idolatry to inadequacy. Those who made these affirmations were representatives of a world-view not part of Sinhala culture and were closely associated with a dominating political system.

It might be difficult for a person living today in the United States, for example, to gain a perspective adopted by many Sinhala Buddhists in the early part of this century and even, among some, today. Roughly comparable to that situation would be one in which first Chinese, then Koreans, and finally Japanese had maintained a powerful presence in the United States for approximately 300 years leading to the complete political control by the last of the colonial powers, in this scenario, the Japanese. A knowledge of Japanese language, Japanese classics, attitudes, customs, and preferences would be essential for well-placed employment. One would note the strength of the *yen,* the presence of numerous shrines and temples throughout the country. One would even date one's birth as in, for example, the Showa era, and every letter mailed would be expected to be dated according to imperial reign.

And, further, the most widely used editions of the Bible would be in Japanese syllabaries. Such setting would represent a lively situation; the times would require change, and reflective persons would tend to maintain continuity.

When Buddhists in Sri Lanka came into their new situation, they responded creatively and they responded differently. One discernible response, when self-consciousness is initially thrust on one, is a momentary recoil to gain balance before developing a pattern of relationship with the source engendering that self-consciousness. Often the pattern developed in the early phase of this relationship tends to take a form similar to that of the initiating source, that is, "Buddhism" vis-à-vis "Christianity." And once this move is made, as it was made, one notes a series of debates in the nineteenth century; that is, "Buddhism" vs. "Christianity." These debates took several decades to come about, and the pattern of relationships they and associated procedures of developing and maintaining self-consciousness have tended to educe take decades, perhaps centuries, to transcend.

So, "Buddhism" and "religion" are on the scene in Sri Lanka, as well as "Hinduism," "Islam," and "Christianity," and so, too, one comes to read, "Buddhism is our religion. For us, there is nothing more important than Buddhism."[6] One wonders how a first grade level reader might introduce *dhamma* a century from now.

In rather recent times, since the beginning of this century and continuing today, Sinhala Buddhists in academic circles have tended to adopt a mode of research well entrenched in Western academia, a procedure that searches, through analytical methods, the original teachings of "early Buddhism," or "Primitive Buddhism," or "*Nikāya* Buddhism" (notions strikingly similar to "Early Christianity," "Primitive Christianity," "New Testament Christianity," subject descriptions long in use in the West); and they find the results of their capable scholarship enthusiastically received by readers in Sri Lanka and elsewhere because their studies had made clearer the *original* teachings, or at least the very early teachings, of "Buddhism," that is, it had been assumed, the *true* or *real* teachings of "Buddhism." An international group of scholars has been greatly interested in learning about "Buddhism," and the interest of these scholars has usually followed an "origin and development" view; one has to understand the origin, the early phases, and the subsequent developments before one can understand "Buddhism." And Sinhala Buddhists have made a significant contribution in this study.

Twin movements have occurred in Western scholarship of the Theravāda Buddhist tradition, that strand of the Buddhist heritage which has contributed greatly to the shaping of what has come to be called *Sinhala culture.* Scholars of the Buddhist tradition tend to concentrate their studies in areas containing the greatest number of sources, areas considered of great importance by the largest number of colleagues, and develop this concentration under a conceptual rubric of "origin and development." A student might begin a study of the Buddhist tradition by studying Sanskrit and Pāli. But which way might one move after competence has been achieved in these languages? What other language or languages would tend to enable one to move to the cutting edge of scholarship in tracing the history of the Buddhist tradition? Most frequently, it seems, scholars have tended to move from Sanskrit and Pāli into Buddhist Hybrid Sanskrit to gain access to Indian Mahāyāna Buddhist sources and then to move into Chinese language studies or Tibetan, finding thereby an enormous number of sources at their disposal and an enhanced capability of contributing to our understanding of a number of issues of considerable historical significance for a great number of people over centuries.

Japanese Buddhologists have tended to reverse the process to some extent. Having a knowledge of Japanese and Chinese, a concern for "origin and development" has led many of them into Sanskrit and Pāli sources, perhaps picking up Tibetan along the way.

Western scholars of the Theravāda tradition have tended to keep their focus on the Pāli canonical texts and, to a lesser degree, on the Pāli commentarial literature. The relatively few scholars who have made a move into other languages expressing that tradition have, in general, settled on either Burmese or Thai or Sinhala. There are langauge barriers in scholarship as there are in societies.

There is another movement in academic circles that has yielded remarkable results. Many scholars conducting research and teaching in the social sciences have turned their attention to a study of Buddhists in Sri Lanka, and they have pursued their studies, in the majority of cases, with theoretical models developed within their disciplines. Some have studied Buddhists to corroborate or modify general theories on the role or function of religion in culture and society.

A few scholars of religious studies and many Sinhala young people fall somewhere between these two movements—on the one hand, Buddhologists specializing in the "origin" of "Buddhism" in India and its development in Tibet, China, and Japan or concentrating on the Pāli canon and "early Buddhism," and on the other hand, social scientists studying Buddhists on the contemporary scene in Sri Lanka. After the cut of demythologization on the part of some Buddhologists and the thrust of functionalism on the part of some social scientists, one is left looking for a sculptured form among the fragments.

There is some tension and anxiety among many young men and women in Sri Lanka today.

One notes the stories of the Buddha's former lives (*Jātakas*) and stories of saints of long ago, preserved in the commentaries, long held in the tradition as truth occurring in space and time, likely to have had significant religious meaning for children of our time, discerning within them the truth of living well, are seen by many today as folktales, fables, an example of short stories in comparative literature. One meets medical students in Colombo, who, having sung recently developed devotional songs about the Buddha at an annual festival of lights (*Vesak*) commemorating the birth, enlightenment, and final complete attainment of *nibbāna* by the Buddha, affirm that there really is no footprint of Lord Buddha atop Sri Pada, an awe inspiring mountain peak in central Sri Lanka. And so one hears young Sinhala men and women refer to rituals of their villages, known to these capable young people since childhood, rituals still being held by their seniors in Sri Lanka, as "superstitious"—of course one would hear this in English, their mother tongue has not yet gained a flexibility in using this conceptual misapprehension, "superstitious."

Political ideologies swirl in Sri Lanka. Some people might have used "Buddhism," in a mundane sense, for personal or ideological aggrandizement and in doing so would have overlooked an ancient injunction to overcome inhibiting attachment to material gain or to advancement of opinions. More recently "development" seems to be the most persuasive ideology, and "development" seems to mean a particular kind of development: technological development designed to increase industrial, agricultural, and economic productivity. Buddhists in Sri Lanka appear to have been temporarily jostled by this drive for "development," seen dramatically reflected in the narrowing of streams or cutback in entry quotas for students in cultural studies on the university level. Many are fully aware, however, that for political ideology to become widely endorsed, that ideology must become capable of being communicated with personal relevance to the majority of the population. It is not enough to speak of development of "things": economic, agricultural, national development, viable economic strength and security. One would want to consider *who* is being developed, by whom, for whom, for what purpose, and how? Buddhists in Sri Lanka are developing these considerations and one is not surprised to learn of a group of Buddhist intellectuals grappling from time to time with the possibility of proposing a theory of Buddhist economics.

Some tend to interpret this possibility as one more example of a vestige of traditionalism, one last attempt to hold on tenaciously to an outmoded pattern of collective identity in an international economic system that surpasses such modes of economic theory. Reports suggest that something far more noble is being attempted. Undaunted by an apparent failure in the Western systems to develop a Christian economic theory, some Buddhists appear to be attempting to contain economics within a broader perspective of religious living; to check greed in a profit motive by disciplined rationality; to avoid measuring success by cunning acquisition of rupees, but, rather, to gauge accomplishment by a capacity for maintaining a continuing contribution to human requirements. This is a creative response.

Religious traditions have long been a part of the development of societies, and as these societies become the hosts to a lively interaction with ideologies transmitted by other societies, a dynamic relationship occurs between the religious institutions of the host societies and the newly incorporated ideologies. This process is not peculiar to experiences in the recent years in Sri Lanka. Were one able to search carefully through a massive amount of historical materials, one would spot previous examples in earlier centuries. This process, however, is more apparent on the contemporary scene, more penetrating and pervasive today.

One of the surest ways of contributing to the demise of a religious heritage is to choose to see no relationship between that heritage and the setting in which one is presently living. That there are Buddhists in Sri Lanka today suggests that millions of men and women previously have deliberately chosen otherwise. And because of their decisions, Buddhists today have alternatives for appropriating their religious heritage in their lives as they are living those lives today. The alternatives are, of course, numerous; and personal inclinations, dispositions, are manifold and do vary in different historical phases and social contexts, even in the life of one person.

The so-called "phenomenon of the political *bhikkhu*" represents a creative response in the dynamic relationship between some in the religious institution, the order of monks, and the current drifts in the larger social ensemble. Other Buddhists have differing opinions. For some, these politically inclined *bhikkhus* are betraying an ancient norm of monastic, ascetic life. For others, these *bhikkhus* are keeping faith with an ancient norm of sharing *dhamma* with others in a manner most conducive to their discerning its effectiveness in life. Just as one creatively appropriates one's religious heritage differently at differing phases or moments of one's life, with varying degrees of commitment and intensity, so, too, a collectivity of religious persons will tend to respond differently, but respond those persons will, as they have.

When three citizens of the United States made their voyage to the surface of the moon as the first delegation to that body in space from this planet, a group of Sinhala Buddhists, *bhikkhus*, were chanting *pirit*. How quaint, one might say, that this was being done by *bhikkhus* wishing for the well-being of astronauts from a country halfway round the world—and this just a few years before Sri Lanka was to experience a wrenching moment of introspective self-consciousness with a violent insurgency in 1971. But persons have walked on the moon. Sri Lanka has weathered, though culturally wounded it seems, that insurgency. And *bhikkhus* are still chanting *pirit*.

And now persons in Sri Lanka are experiencing the greatest challenge to national integrity, even existence, in our lifetime. Sinhala boys on behalf of the government and on behalf of a radical movement have been killing each other, and Tamil boys representing differing groups fighting for a separatist movement are killing each other, and Sinhalas on behalf of the government and Tamil separatists are killing each other, and Indian young men have gotten into the act, and have moved on. Hope is beginning, at last, at long last, and in spite of this, to arise again. Perhaps peace will return to this idyllic island nation before the middle of this decade.

However, and marvel one must, that ancient Buddhist norm of human propriety seems to have held—though distraughtingly violated, bewilderingly lacerated, by the eruption of devastating hatred and inexplicable brutality, it seems to have held. And words of truth continue to be chanted by *bhikkhus*.

III

When creative responses are occurring rapidly and moving in multifaceted dimensions, one wonders where to look for signs of continuity. One important area is ritual like the ones we have noted, long a channel through which a religious heritage has been transmitted, a means by which men and women can find their status, their fundamental condition, and their situation in life defined, given meaning, a procedure for collective remembering yielding personal and communal cohesion. In the Theravāda case, one is reminded not to dote on rituals, to think by the mere mechanical act of going through the gestures one automatically achieves a level of profound religious insight. Rituals, of course, as Buddhists have stressed, are not an end. There is more to the process of liberation than rituals, more than meditation, too.

It is in moments of particularly meaningful behavior that a reflective person is no longer *a* Buddhist; one leaves aside a primary sense of loyalty to belief systems, ethnic identities, political power plays by this or that religious organization, language issues of the relative importance of Sinhala, Tamil, and English; and one hits on a reminder of what it means to be *Buddhist*. Buddhist rituals, unlike many treatises written by Sinhala Buddhists today, are not designed for a *Western* audience.

Today, more than ever, we are met with the term *Buddhist,* capable of being used as an adjective and a noun.[7] This term, too, is an outsider's term, used by outsiders quite early in India. I have not yet found the Pāli equivalent of this term (*bauddha*) in either canonical or commentarial literature. It appears that persons who have followed the teachings (*dhamma*) of the Buddha have recognized themselves to be characterized neither by "enlightenment" (*bodhi*) nor by the qualities of the "Enlightened" or "Awakened One" (*Buddha*). The tradition continued to speak of male and female lay monastics (*bhikkhu, bhikkhunī*) and male and female lay devotees (*upāsaka, upāsikā*), not "Buddhists"—and this in spite of having at hand an adjectival form, *bauddha,* "Buddhist," legitimately derived from indigenous languages and present in relatively early Indian sources. This had been the case, it seems, because for one *to claim* that one had fully realized that which enabled a young Indian prince to become the Buddha (*dhamma*) would have been, for most, pretentious and, for some, a clear indication that they had not.

For over 2,000 years the ideal fundamental objectives endorsed by Theravāda Buddhists have been to be characterized as one who has taken refuge in the Buddha, Dhamma, and the Sangha, not only to emulate the virtuous qualities of the Buddha, to manifest the virtuous qualities of Dhamma and reproduce the virtuous qualities of the Sangha—magnificent aspirations in themselves—but also to quest, by following the teachings (*dhamma*) of the Buddha, preserved and shared by the Sangha, for that realization of salvific truth (*dhamma*), which the Buddha and his illustrious disciples attained, for the penetration of which and communication of which the Sangha finds its twofold purpose today. A friend might describe one as being characterized by *dhamma,* as being a righteous, just, person of truth—as being genuinely human. A sensitive person would parry that thought should it arise in one's mind as a description of oneself. Being *a* Buddhist is mundane; being *Buddhist* in the sense of being one characterized by *dhamma* is not.

"Buddhism" is on the scene in Sri Lanka. Children learn to utter the ancient formula of the threefold refuge, of taking refuge in the three gems, so called because they are most precious, are of immense value,[8] the old commentaries tell us, and are told "These are the three gems of Buddhism."[9] And one reads, "It is by means of the moral precept of refuge that one becomes a Buddhist." Without that, we are told, "one is not a Buddhist."[10] "Buddhism" is seen by some in Sri Lanka today; "Buddhism" responding to this or that, undergoing change, becoming "modernized," bifurcated into "lay Buddhism" and "monastic Buddhism," or "popular Buddhism" and "political Buddhism," even "village and urban Buddhism." And *a* Buddhist is frequently understood by reference only to that in which he or she is *seen* to play a part. But aspiring to be *Buddhist* is an entirely different matter, much more personal, much more difficult for one to see, describe, or document, of enormous significance.

To be *a* Buddhist means to be a part of a historical community that has a cumulative religious heritage; a community that has been, is, and will be a part of the historical process, has changed, is changing, and will change. To be *Buddhist* is to strive calmly for a disciplined mind and compassionate heart, to remember *dhamma*, to manifest *dhamma* in one's life in the hope someday fully to penetrate, to realize *dhamma*, salvific truth.

In both senses, as noun and adjective, there are Buddhists living in Sri Lanka today.

9

MUSIC IN THE THERAVĀDA BUDDHIST HERITAGE: IN CHANT, IN SONG, IN SRI LANKA

In this chapter we will explore the legitimation of and foundations for religious music in the Theravāda Buddhist tradition and particularly in Sri Lanka today. Leaving aside technical ethnomusicological considerations for those more competent in these matters and holding for, perhaps, another time an attempt to trace a possible historical development, we will move from text to contemporary context to demonstrate two strands within the Theravāda cumulative heritage: an old admonition about restraint of the senses and an appreciation for, a legitimization of, religious music. These strands are current today in Sri Lanka. Although the former tends to be applied to the monastic form of life and the latter primarily to the laity, the two strands, on occasion separate and parallel, on occasion plaited, tend to converge in a common feature of shifting attention from the self and in developing wholesome dispositions of mind that are conducive in leading one from where one finds oneself to the moment of the first vision of *nibbāna.*

I

Among the precepts that provide the regulatory basis for persons in the Theravāda Buddhist monastic order (*sangha*) is the precept to refrain from seeing performances or shows of dancing, singing, or instrumental music.[1] Moreover, when a text relates how one might praise the moral virtue (*sīla*) of Gotama the Buddha, one finds that he kept aloof, as it were, from performances or shows, dances, singing, instrumental music, stylized lyrical recitations, and rhythmical hand-tapping on the beat, among other things.[2] Singing and dancing are unbecoming to a monk (*bhikkhu*); indeed, singing is called a *lamentation* in the context of the training of a noble disciple, and dancing, further, is considered as going out of one's mind.[3]

Apart from the matter of attending performances or shows involving dancing, music in itself, both vocal and instrumental, has tended to be a matter requiring watchfulness on the part of persons in the Buddhist monastic orders. This should not suggest that Buddhists have merely written off music as base, below one's dignity, a simpleton's enterprise. In an engaging aside, one reads a description given to Ānanda, one of the Buddha's closest disciples, of beautiful gold and silver bells, in a marvelous palace, which produce a sound like that produced by skilled musicians, a sound that is sweet, delightful, charming, and intoxicating.[4] And one becomes alert to the beguiling quality of music, that quality which is a featured characteristic of Māra, the tempter, the one who misleads. It is recorded that Khemā, a nun (*bhikkhunī*) of note, was approached by Māra as a young man who beckons her to come, enjoying the sounds of music.[5] And much the same is recorded elsewhere regarding the experience of another nun, Vijayā.[6]

Yet there apparently is no reluctance to compare the proper exertion or effort in purifying the mind or heart with the skillful tuning of a lute (*vīṇā*),[7] neither overlax nor too taut; hence the example given by the Buddha in a discussion with Sona, who was skilled in playing the *vīṇā* when he was a youth at home prior to becoming a monk (*bhikkhu*).[8] And according to an account in the birth stories (*Jātakas*) about the previous lives of the Buddha, the then Buddha-to-be (*bodhisatta*) was on one occasion Guttila, a master musician, superbly skilled on the seven stringed *vīṇā*.[9]

Could it be that music must be kept in check because it is a hitherto not fully comprehended art of human communication with a heightened capacity to penetrate the psyche, to instill moods and motivations not engendered by conscious processes? Proficiency in music was an accomplishment shared by the monk Sona, as a boy, by the Buddha, as a Buddha-to-be (*bodhisatta*) in a previous life, *and* by Māra, the Bad One, the distorter, the tempter. Did the Buddha, Sona, Khemā, Vijayā, and no doubt others, somehow go beyond an engaging and potentially disorienting charm of music? Is Māra yet to make this move?

Music, of course, if it be communicative relies on the activity of the senses, and Buddhists have left a record over two millennia old that one is to guard one's senses, the five strands of sensual delight and desire (*pañca-kāma-guṇa*).

> These five, O monks, are the strands of sensual delight. What five? [1] Material forms discerned by the eye, wanted, desired, captivating the mind, enticing, comprised of sensuality, alluring, [2] sounds discerned by the ear...[3] smells discerned by the nose...[4] tastes discerned by the tongue...[5] tangible objects discerned by the body....[10]

This is the given condition of the human constitution according to the Theravāda tradition. But also, according to this tradition, the human constitution is not limited by this condition. "And what, O monks, is the exit from sensuality? O monks, the driving out of delight and desire, the putting aside of delight and desire for sensual desires—this is the exit from sensuality."[11]

Dancing, singing, and instrumental music involve sight and sound and the engagement of the eyes and ears. In the context of meditational pursuits, desire and delight in modes of sense impression tend to present formidable obstacles. Discussing such a context, one passage relates how regular tendencies of greed, hatred, and confusion can continue in one's thinking when one has not come to know through immediate insight, as it has actually come about (*yathābhūtam sammāppaññāya*), that sensual desires are of little satisfaction and of much misery; that one is to be aware of the danger of unfortunate consequences related to those sensual desires.[12] And elsewhere in the texts one reads that *greed* is a synonym for these five strands of sensuality;[13] that a *knife and chopping block* are likewise synonymous,[14] so, too, is *fodder for fattening,*[15] and a *whirlpool.*[16]

Hardly have we here casual references to sense desires, minor asides indicating a lighthearted attitude toward sights and sounds, among other sensual impingements. "Watch out! Handle with care!—if at all," seems to be the thrust of the passages.

Some might say that the admonitions related to the perils of sense pleasures, including sounds—and in our concern here, singing and instrumental music—were designed for monastics and not primarily and necessarily for the Buddhist laity. And this observation is for the most part on the mark. However, the perils of sensuality are so often stressed in the tradition that the laity also, when given pause, is not uninformed about the matter.

If one were to arrive today in Sri Lanka and set about to attend as many Buddhist ceremonies as possible, one would hear the sound of drums and reed instruments (*horaṇā*) and be told this is a form of worshipping or paying homage in sound (*śabdapūja*);[17] one would hear rhythmic lyrical chanting performed according to carefully prescribed and learned patterns by monks in their chanting of ancient texts (*pirit*);[18] and over the radio, and elsewhere, on special religious holidays one would hear devotional songs. How does one explain the presence of devotional songs, formal chanting, the sound of drums, cymbals, and horns in this tradition that so clearly stresses the guarding of sense pleasures? Are the ritual activity and song merely soteriologically irrelevant, parallel but dissociate concessions made by the monks for the laity?

Let me suggest that the questions appear to have been answered long ago apparently without necessitating a debate or formal convocation. The bases for this suggestion appear to be rooted in what Westerners might call a mythological stratum of the text, on the one hand, and, on the other, what one might consider a disarmingly commonsense approach to a development within a cumulative tradition represented in the words of the Buddha.

II

We turn again to Māra; this time to Māra who meets the Buddha and attempts to lure the serene one from his meditative endeavors. "You,

O lean one, are pale; you are nigh to death," Māra said. He continued, "Ah, life, sir, life is best!"[19] In short, Māra's point, in the full passage, is that one should enjoy the fullness of life, to draw it all in, including the performance of customary religious rituals in order to acquire merit. Struggles in meditative pursuits are tough, Māra suggests.

The major portion of this passage of verses in the *Sutta-nipāta* constitutes the Buddha's reply to Māra. In describing the tenfold army of Māra, the Buddha mentions that sensuality, that is, sensual desire, is the first army.[20] Seeing that the Buddha was resolute and totally unperturbed, Māra, disappointed, left. The Buddha provides the closing verse of the sequel:

> The lute (*vīṇā*) of that one overcome by grief
> Fell down from under his arm.
> Then that sad spirit
> Vanished right then and there.[21]

The dropped lute (*vīṇā*)—what is one to make of it? In another text,[22] Māra is depicted as carrying a yellow-hued vilva-wood lute—and there, too, he is said to have been dejected and to have dropped it.[23] It appears that the lute (*vīṇā*) is symbolic of the entrancing charm of music and dalliance. Māra, having let fall his lute, has shown his despondency—gone is his power to beguile one into wanton amorous play, gone is his subtle snare of music and song.

But the lute is not grounded for long. The commentary on this *Sutta-nipāta* passage says that this yellow-hued lute of vilva wood (*beluvapaṇḍu-vīṇā*) that fell from under Māra's arm, this lute that, when plucked with the fingers, released sweet music lasting for four months, was picked up by the god Sakka and given to one Pañcasikha,[24] a heavenly musician (*gandhabba*). Now the setting shifts with Pañcasikha in ways that are instructive for our considerations.

In the *Dīgha-nikāya*, one of the collections forming part of the received canon, there is an interesting episode involving Sakka, lord of the gods, Pañcasikha, a heavenly musician or *gandhabba* who attends the gods, the Buddha, and Bhaddā, daughter of the *gandhabba* Timbarū. Sakka and Pañcasikha, who was carrying his lute (*beluvapaṇḍu-vīṇā*), vanished from the celestial realm of the thirty-three gods

(Tāvatiṃsa), and appeared on the Vediya mountain just north of a brahmin village called Ambasaṇḍā to the east of Rājagaha in Magadha. The mountain was said to have become resplendent with the presence of the celestials—even the village of Ambasaṇḍā is said to have become radiant. On that mountain, in a cave called Indasāla, the Buddha (*Tathāgata*) was deep in meditation (*jhāna*). Sakka, wishing to ask questions of the Buddha, but sensing that such meditating ones are hard to approach by the lord of gods, asked, "But if you, Pañcasikha, would first cause the Blessed One (*Bhagavant*) to be calmly disposed, then I might approach to see the Lord, the Worthy One, Fully Enlightened One who first has been made calmly disposed by you."[25]

Being the dutiful attendant that he was, Pañcasikha took his lute and approached the Indasāla cave. Taking a position neither too close to nor too far from the Buddha, but at a distance just adequate for his song to be heard clearly without startling his hearer, he played his special lute and sang a song. Of what did he sing? He sang, the text tells us, of the Buddha, of salvific truth (*dhamma*), of worthy ones (*arahants*), of love (*kāma*).[26]

The song itself is a love song, one in which the suitor praises the beloved's beauty, seeks to be caressed, and pleads to be embraced. The metaphors are rich and powerfully suggestive.[27] Love (*kāma*) is the theme—reference to the key doctrinal elements are by means of analogy. For example, one reads in the fourth line of the verses, "O radiant One, you are dear to me as is truth (*dhamma*) to worthy ones (*arahants*)."[28] And the celestial composer continues by noting how his love for his beloved achieves abundance like that achieved through gifts of honor given to the worthy ones (*arahants*); how, as the Silent Seer, that is, the Buddha, desires to acquire the deathless (i.e., *nibbāna*), he desires his beloved; how, as the Silent Seer would rejoice having attained incomparable full enlightenment, he would rejoice in attaining union with his beloved.

Two other important ideas are present in Pañcasikha's song: the notion of merit (*puñña*) and divine favor (*varam*). "O beautifully proportioned one," the heavenly bard sings, "being with you is the fruition of the merit done by me to such worthy ones (*arahants*)."[29] Indeed, such is considered the fruition of the bard's meritorious action throughout the entire world; so he sings in the immediately following verse. Later, Pañcasikha sings that if the god Sakka were to grant a divine favor to him, would that he grant to him his beloved.

The song then ends as it began, by praising the father of the beloved for his offspring. In the formal structure of the song, the poet-singer, with focal attention given to his beloved, speaks directly of his praise of his beloved's father, of his performance of meritorious action and the consequence, of his wish for a divine boon. Reference to the key doctrinal features by means of which the song is introduced are made by analogy.

The performance of religiously meritorious actions, ideally to be inseparably concomitant with an "interior transformative effect,"[30] and the practice of wishing for a divine favor or boon are customary features of lay Buddhist life today in Sri Lanka, as apparently they were when reflected in the case of the celestial musician Pañcasikha, recorded approximately two millennia ago. The technical term for this religious behavior is *lokiya*, denoting literally "worldly" but in the wider, and deeper, Buddhist frame of reference connoting something like religiously customary practices and orientations circumscribed by our own capacities of conceptualization.

When Pañcasikha completed his song, the Buddha complimented him, noting both the complementarity and balance of the music from the strings of his instrument and from his voice. Then the Buddha asked when Pañcasikha composed this song about the Buddha, *dhamma, arahants*, and love.

The reply by Pañcasikha introduces another story frame within the larger frame. It seems that Pañcasikha was in love with Bhaddā, another *gandhabba*, who was in love with someone else. Not being successful in his attempts to catch her fancy in any other way, Pañcasikha took his special lute and sang the song. When Bhaddā heard it, she said to Pañcasikha that although she had not met the Blessed One (*Bhagavant*), she had heard of him when dancing (*sic*) in the Suddhamma hall in the heavens of the thirty-three gods (Tāvatiṃsa). She suggests that, because Pañcasikha praised the Blessed One, they arrange a meeting that very day. Pañcasikha brings the inner-story frame to a close by doffing his hat to propriety, as it were, and relating to the Buddha that he did not actually meet her on that day, but later. The main story line continues with Sakka telling Pañcasikha to salute the Buddha and to announce the coming of the lord of the gods. The questions of Sakka for the Buddha ensue.

Pañcasikha appears elsewhere in the cumulative accounts in the tradition. He is met again, descending with the Buddha, when the latter descended from the heaven of the thirty-three gods, having there continued his teaching ministry. Pañcasikha, with his special lute, venerated (*pūja*) the Buddha.[31]

What might one conclude about this passage relating to Sakka, Pañcasikha, the Buddha, and Bhaddā? It is possible that one has, in this account, a continuation of a kind of old, "all-India" motif of a god beseeching a *gandhabba* to tempt a meditative ascetic whose psychic powers were beginning to rival those of the god or gods concerned. If this were the case originally, one would be confronted with a reworking of the passage by a redactor or redactors. Pañcasikha, by his singing, brings the Buddha out of his deep meditation, but he does so by a song carefully introduced, in the prose portion of the text, as having to do with the Buddha, Dhamma, worthy ones, and love. The first three ideas, representing the core concepts in the Buddhist heritage, have made legitimate the presence of this song at this place in the text. In the full passage, Pañcasikha gets his wish, his beloved's willingness to be with him, not as a result of his having tempted or tricked the Buddha and not as a result of receiving a divine favor. Although such notion of a divine favor (*varam*) would have been entirely fitting in the cultural context, it might have led to ambiguity about Pañcasikha's motive and role. His wish is fulfilled as a consequence of his having revered (*pūja*) the Buddha in song.

Sensual desire (*kāma*) is a means by which Māra ensnares, whereas romantic love (*kāma*) is an emotion among humans and gods made legitimate. According to the tradition, the lute, with which Māra sang of sensual desire (*kāma*) in attempting to seduce disciples and the Buddha, has fallen to the ground. Yet the lute has been lifted again and sounds again in a song of romantic love (*kāma*) that is now wholly accepted by the Buddha, because that emotion has been placed into the proper context. The expression of romantic love once considered beguiling, deceiving, ensnaring, now receives illustrative, explicative, additional force by means of analogy with fundamental religious orientations among Buddhists, orientations to the Buddha, Dhamma, and the *arahants*.[32]

Music that can pervert oneself or another, song, which has the subtle capacity to turn one aside, can now be utilized in expressing the sentiment of romantic love, can now also be a part of manifesting reverent praise. Buddhists would agree with the adage of romance—"love makes the world go round." *Saṃsāra*, the whirl (*vaṭṭa*) of existence through many life cycles, is kept spinning, as it were, by sensuality, even the long acknowledged emotion of romantic love. This kind of love, Buddhists have attested, is applauded in its ideal expression but is inadequate in itself as a means for transcending *saṃsāra*, that is, as a means of transcending itself. So, too, is reverent praise (*pūja*) of the Buddha, Dhamma, and *arahants* or other noble disciples. For Buddhists more is involved in the soteriological process. There is that dimension of human experience, that ineffable realization, which is not religiously customary (*lokiya*), not circumscribed by our own capacities of conceptualization, is higher (*uttara*) than all of this (*loka*), goes beyond this (*lokuttara*); that moment when the world-transcending path arises before one's mind and in one's consciousness and one gains one's first vision of *nibbāna*.

Music and song, when placed into the proper context, are customarily considered to be religiously supportive. When songs contribute to the arising of wholesome (*kusala*) dispositions that provide the predominating bent of one's thoughts (*citta*), those songs are fitting.

III

Quite consonant with this strand of the cumulative tradition are the contemporary modes of expressing religiousness in music and in song in Sri Lanka. That the music and song be recognized as Buddhist, as religious, does not necessitate their incorporation into liturgy or ritual, but a recognition that they are anchored by themes fully consonant with the Buddhist religious heritage.

The songs that have made the register of the most popular, most appreciated, most meaningful, are those that point the hearer to the existential reality of a dimension of the teachings passed down in the tradition and to the efficacy of those teachings, when personally appropriated, to enable one to discern salvific truth—the abiding reality of which provides the *raison d'être* of the teachings.

In communicating what Buddhist laity are doing religiously with music and song today in Sri Lanka, one can note three general modes, only the first and third of which will receive our attention in the body of this chapter: (1) sung chant either in Pāli or Sinhala, in a ritual setting or while on pilgrimage, usually corporate in nature; (2) *kavi* or sung Sinhala verse;[33] and (3) contemporary Sinhala musical compositions. The themes are didactic, hortatory, and expressive of personal insights or wonder. In most cases, the songs engage the hearer in a commonality of shared experiences by repeating teachings sanctioned by tradition or by evoking mutually recognized moments of personal religious awareness.

To the first category, sung chant, belong the "Verses of Wonderful Victory" (*Jayamaṅgala Gāthā*), numbering approximately nine verses in the Pāli language, sung on auspicious occasions and regularly at weddings, often by young girls. Among the laity, perhaps there is no group of verses that carries a greater sense of invoking corporate supportiveness to mingle with one's wishes for good fortune. Each verse recounts a marvelous accomplishment of the Buddha and closes with a repeated refrain wishing one joyous or wonderful victory by the power of the Buddha's illustrious accomplishment.[34]

One of the most popular Pāli verses in the Theravāda heritage, known by heart by laity and monks alike, has been put to music and sung by W. D. Amaradeva, one of the leading contemporary composer-singers in Sri Lanka. The verse, often heard over the radio on religious holidays, might be considered the core statement of the Buddhist tradition.

> Refraining from all that is detrimental,
> The attainment of what is wholesome,
> The purification of one's mind:
> This is the instruction of Awakened Ones.[35]

In a moving Sinhala rendition of an old theme, the threefold refuge, a group of men and women musicians have recorded a song, replete with instrumental accompaniment (chimes, *śruti*, flute and drums), long associated with pilgrimage to Śrī Pāda, or Adam's Peak. In a particular recording of only three verses in length, the opening verse, sung by women, indicates a totality of personal involvement.

> Bearing on my head the refuge that is the Buddha,
> Cleansing the mind, the refuge that is Dhamma,
> Donning the robes, the refuge that is the Sangha,
> I will live, having faith in the threefold refuge.[36]

The second verse, sung by men, by mentioning the three times of day, dawn, midday, and evening, each being indicative of a dimension of the threefold refuge, suggests the totality of commitment in the process of human existence. The third verse is culminative in religious affirmation, although this might not be readily communicated here in English:

> Refuge, refuge, Buddha is refuge.
> Refuge, refuge, Dhamma is refuge.
> Refuge, refuge, Sangha is refuge.
> Refuge, refuge, these three are refuge.[37]

An interesting rather recent development in ritual procedures performed at the temple on religious holidays is a form of corporate sung chanting in which both monks and laity chant melodiously together in Sinhala. Although the customary procedure is for the laity to listen attentively while the monks chant canonical passages in Pāli, and although one occasionally hears some criticism of this new form,[38] those who participate in the form in Sinhala speak very highly of it and will go to considerable inconvenience to be present for it. Venerable Panadure Ariyadhamma has created some chanting patterns and composed many verses in Sinhala for such purposes. The following, from a recording,[39] provides an example:

> May there be wholesome thoughts in every mind.
> May they be bathed with loving kindness and compassion.
> May concord, community, and loving kindness spread afar.
> May all persons on earth attain well-being.[40]

To the third category, contemporary Sinhala musical compositions, belong a variety of works that draw on religious themes but are not particularly associated with religious holidays or corporate ritual settings. In a Sinhala motion picture, *Anklets* (*Kiṇkiṇi Pādā*), a song begins by quoting, in a sung chant mode, a Pāli canonical passage, with a repetition of the second phrase, thereby focusing sharply the religious context. An English translation of the Pāli is

> Death destroys one's human form;
> It destroys not one's name and lineage.[41]

The two singers, a man and a woman, then move into Sinhala. Representative phrases are

> Everything that is beautiful
> Gives but brief satisfaction;
> Sorrow is at the end of it,
> Sorrow is at the end of it.[42]
>
> If with both eyes one can see,
> If one can smell,
> If one's ears are not deaf;
> There is the advantage of enjoyment—
> Yet, misfortune is near.
> What's the benefit of the fivefold sense desires?[43]

The last verse says,

> While the lamp of Dhamma true is burning,
> Why become immersed in the darkness of wrong?
> Without Buddhadhamma, there is no welfare;
> Without Buddhadhamma, there is no welfare.
> That is the highest gain.[44]

From the soundtrack of another movie, *Seven Seas* (*Sat Samudura*), one hears W. D. Amaradeva sing,

> Unstable is the ocean of *saṃsāra*;
> No calmness there, so turbulent.
> Ten thousand times within
> One nudges death.[45]

And the song continues,

> This filthy body is pithless; it does not last.
> Only the good that was done remains in this world.
> There is poverty, helplessness, sickness, and sorrow
> For us, us human beings.
> Why does one not think of this,
> In the unstable ocean of *saṃsāra*?[46]

Victor Ratnāyake, a leading contemporary composer-singer, in one of the most famous, most appreciated performances called *Sa* (the first note of the musical scale), begins the evening of song with an introduction not unlike an invocation,

> By the power of the Sambuddha and Dhamma true,
> With the peace of Viṣṇu and Śrī Skanda,
> With the blessing of Sarasvati,
>   Who sits on the lotus seat,
> For the purpose of your enjoyment
> In this beautiful night that gives birth to joy,
> May twenty-four thousand ears
> Be uplifted with delight,
> Be uplifted with delight.[47]

In this concert, Victor Ratnāyake sings a song representing one's longing to have been alive at the time when the Buddha was residing at a monastic dwelling called Devārama (the song title is "Devram Veherā" [Pāli: Devārama Vihāra]). But, apparently, since insufficient meritorious acts had been done, and consequently one was not living then in the presence of the Buddha, one takes one's place before a statue of the Buddha, there to meditate in hopes of being reborn in the future in the presence of the next Buddha, Maitreya. With subtlety of voice and insight, Ratnāyake sings,

> Among a thousand fires of lamentations and sorrows,
> In the darkness of fires burning in my heart and mind,
> O Lord, by simply seeing your statue,
> They become completely extinguished—
>   What is the mystery?[48]

Addressing the complex of human emotions and cluster of ideas that are present in one who stands reflectively before a stature of the Buddha, W. D. Amaradeva sings of a famous statue in the ancient city of Anurādhapura and concludes with the following:

> Like a mighty flood that overflowing moves,
> Like a cooling cascade flowing down,
> That soothes the weariness
> Of this desert of existence,
> The majesty of Buddha's virtues
> That gives *nibbāna.*
> The Samādhi Buddha Statue in Mahāmevunā Park,
> The Samādhi Buddha Statue.
>
> Falling currents of loving kindness, gentleness,
> Compassion,
> Flowing from eyes half-closed,
> Falling currents of loving kindness, gentleness,
> Compassion,
> Flowing from eyes half-closed.[49]

We have already mentioned Śrī Pāda, or Adam's Peak, in relation to an old refrain sung by pilgrims and recently performed by musicians and singers for radio broadcast. W. D. Amaradeva sings a brief song, well known and often heard, about Śrī Pāda. Omitting the refrains, the words are

> At the blessed feet of the Sage
> Where a world-transcending sound spreads afar,
> There comes a breeze extinguishing fatigue,
> Which gives a silver calm,
> Which pacifies the heart.[50]

Music whether in liturgical or nonliturgical settings has a place in the Theravāda Buddhist tradition. Although it has no formal place in long established ritual procedures, except for drums and reed instruments (*horaṇā*) to inaugurate auspicious moments, its presence appears to have been long assured insofar as its legitimization derives from the religious themes on which it focuses. Music is accepted in this tradition as an authentic form of religious expression insofar as it points beyond itself as an art form.

IV

From the incipient phase of the Buddhist movement there has been a contrast between the regulated living patterns established for those in the monastic life and the guidelines proposed for the laity. What is not acceptable behavior for a monk is clearly enunciated to assist a monk in the movement through training and mental discipline nearer to a state of clarity and purity of mind, and so to be poised for an arising of the first vision of *nibbāna*. Beware of what might detract and distract from this movement, the monastic regulations exhort.

Recommendations about guarding the senses, about putting at a distance the adhesive weight of sensuality, including attachment to sound, are part of the monastic regimen of disciplined reflection. The ancient text that provides the major guidelines for monastic living includes an admonition by the Buddha against singing in the ordinary manner:

> O monks there are five disadvantages for one singing the teaching in an extended sung intonation. [1] He is attached to himself regarding that sound, [2] and others are attached to that sound, [3] and even householders are irritated, [4] there is a dissolution of concentration on the part of one straining to lock in on the sound, and [5] people who follow after [this procedure] undergo an adherence to opinions.[51]

The Buddha is here recorded as establishing a stylistic difference between the chanting of the monks[52] and the singing of the laity. Rather than chant, he might tend to focus on the sound and not on the meaning of the teachings, might think the sound of his voice to be beautiful, in vibrato or pitch or tone, might think of himself as skilled, might think of himself. Also, others might find their attention turning from the meaning of the teachings to the sound of the singing. And the laity might consider such singing as not proper for a monk, as being undecorous. Such a singer could lose his focused concentration since the focal awareness could shift from meaning and purpose to notes and scales. And, further, people would tend to endorse one mode over others, would begin to become attached to their opinion about which mode is the most beautiful. Straightforwardly, resolutely, the statement is that the meaning is in the message, set apart in metrical chant from the commonplace, but otherwise unadorned.

Institutionally, therefore, the distinction between monastic and lay modes of conduct has tended to produce two different approaches to music. Ideally, the mainstream position of the tradition avers, although a layperson might compose songs about the religious life, a monk is to meditate on the fundamentals of religious truth and to compose his life as an expression of that truth. The laity creates musical compositions; the monks enter into meditation and concentration. Not all laypersons are composers, and it is widely held in Sri Lanka, not all monks excel in their exacting discipline.

What, for Buddhists in Sri Lanka, would constitute good religious music?[53] The tradition has recorded that music that evokes passion is to be put aside—Māra dropped his lute. Music that is discerned as heavenly is acceptable—Sakka picked up the lute and gave it to Pañcasikha, a heavenly *gandhabba*. Heavenly music, as the old texts say, which is beautifully rendered in quality of instrument and voice, in harmonious balance of instrument with voice, and utilized in reverent praise of religious themes, symbolized in the reference to the Buddha, Dhamma, and the *arahants* and other noble ones, is acceptable and is positively endorsed.

But is not there still a fundamental dichotomy, a fundamental cleavage between creating, performing, sharing, hearing, and appreciating religious music and the higher pursuits of meditation and quiet contemplation? Institutionally and behaviorally, yes.[54] But existentially, as a dimension of human experience, the matter is much too fluid and subtle for one to categorize in terms of dichotomy or cleavage.

Just as institutionally there are two dimensions, so the soteriological process within the Buddhist context of faith is spoken of as having two dimensions: *lokiya*, what is customary, that which is limited by agential conceptualization; and *lokuttara*, that which is not limited by what is humanly customary, that which transcends even what one might consider heavenly. We have touched on these two ideas earlier and return now to them to reinforce the point of the legitimation of music and song in the soteriological process in the contemporary setting.

It would misrepresent, by being stunningly inadequate, the subtlety of Buddhist religious insight to equate *lokiya* with the life of the laity and *lokuttara* with the monastic life. The latter form of living is considered more conducive to a quest for or a realization of *lokuttara* wisdom. But confusion occurs when one takes what is conducive to a pursuit, or the quest itself, as synonymous with the realization itself. Both modes of life, the lay and the monastic, are to be interpreted from the perspective of each particular person involved; and as a fundamental religious aspiration of Theravāda Buddhists, it is wished that each person live well within the *lokiya* frame of reference in the hope that the *lokuttara* salvific occurrence will arise.

The primary concern of this cumulative religious tradition is not to have everyone enter the monastic order, obviously. It is to contribute to a religiously meaningful orientation of one's life within the *lokiya* dimension of human existence by providing a context broader, deeper, higher (*uttara*) than that existence (*loka*), a context assured to be available to human awareness both because of the testimony of those noble ones (*sāvakasangha*) who have seen through to it and because this availability is inherent in the order of reality (*dhammatā*).

Music of praise for the Buddha, Dhamma, and the Sangha (*sāvakasangha*, the noble witnesses, and, symbolically, the *bhikkhusangha*, the order of monks) is *lokiya*, but it is properly and consistently oriented when it turns one away from self-focus and enhances, by a *lokiya* medium, a message that the *lokiya* is not all there is to human life. All human effort, creations of the human mind, exertions of the will, even compositions of religious music, must fall away at a moment of the mind's "creative passivity"[55] when the first vision of *nibbāna* occurs.

The monastic regimen (*vinaya*), by making more restricted the day-to-day processes of life, keeps sharply highlighted an awareness of a broader, more meaningful context of human living. And in this regimen (*vinaya*) religious music plays no part. Persons of the laity, who are met with day-to-day contingencies and uncertainty, might not keenly discern the stability of an awareness of a broader, more meaningful context of human living. And in this setting of lay life, religious music plays a substantial role. For monks well along the way of contemplative discipline, religious music might be a distraction. For other monks and for the laity, it might provide direction.

The soteriological process, although fused in customary interpretations in Sri Lanka with the act of entering the monastic order, is not to be confused with it, as being synonymous with this shift in institutional status.[56] The monastic discipline (*vinaya*) and the religious utilization of the lute (*vīṇā*) are *lokiya*, limited. Both can be means for one who seeks a further goal; both can be obstacles for one who clings to them.

Like everything else that is *lokiya*, limited to the whirl of life that is *saṃsāra*, religious music is also, finally, unstable, fleeting. At the dawning of world-transcending (*lokuttara*) salvific insight (*paññā*), even the strings of the lute fall silent, for it is in mental quietude that the mind becomes poised with a spontaneously alert receptivity to the arising of the first vision of *nibbāna*. Those who have realized this moment are neither tempted by religious music, nor are they disturbed by it. Music, for them, has lost its delight:

> For such a one there is no delight
> In music's fivefold sound,
> Like that for one discerning truth fully,
> Who has one-pointedness of mind.[57]
>
> Some delight in *mutiṅga*-drums,
> In lutes (*vīṇās*) and *paṇa*-drums.
> But I at the base of a tree
> Delight in the instruction of the Buddha.[58]

In commenting on a phrase, "The delight in *dhamma* prevails over every delight," occurring in verse 354 of the *Dhammapada*, the commentary on that text says:

> The delight in sons and daughters, in wealth, in women, and the numerous [other] kinds of delight, such as that of dance, song, music, and so forth, are [ultimately] causes for suffering alone, making [one] to fall into the whirl of *saṃsāra*. But this joy that arises within one who either speaks dhamma or hears dhamma, produces a sense of elation, brings out tears and makes hairs to stand on end. It puts an

> end to the whirl of *saṃsāra*; it is [a state] having [its] end in the Fruit of Arahantship. Hence, of all delights, this kind of delight in dhamma is the best.[59]

V

The Theravāda Buddhist tradition takes the position that music that might contribute to the arousal of sensuality, even music that might call attention to itself as a noteworthy human creation, must be put aside. In its place is to be religious music that is put into the service of communicating Dhamma, an old and historically successful Buddhist enterprise; and our references to the contemporary setting in Sri Lanka have demonstrated the continuing response through faith of Buddhists in placing their musical talents into this service. Even when put into this service, religious music still might draw attention to itself, pull focal awareness from the message to the medium. However, religious music among Buddhists in Sri Lanka is considered at its best when it tends to efface itself in the presence of the message. In this way, religious music becomes fully consonant with the religious activity of renouncing the cosmic centrality of the self, a mode of renunciation with which Buddhists are familiarly conversant, even to the extent of renouncing the self completely in the presence of salvific truth to which the message points.

In conclusion, and speaking metaphorically, the lute of ordinary music and song is to be dropped, and then to be picked up again to be played in praise, and finally to be put aside, appreciatively, when one hears the sound not produced by human creativity or, as the point is more frequently put in English, realizes that vision which arises uncaused by human agency.

The institutional dichotomy of *vinaya* vs. *vīṇā* formally remains. Practically, meditative concentration on psychic processes is difficult when in a musical concert. Hence, *vīṇā* yields to *vinaya*; but both at their best are not in themselves conclusive, but are conducive to a more noble event, not at all synonymous with entering the monastic order.

Of the arising of the path on which one can walk through this world (*lokiya*) in a process of transcending this world (*lokuttara*), a contemporary Buddhist has written:

> Thus the *magga* [path] event, swiftly arising after a moment of the mind's creative passiveness, regenerates and makes a new person of the pilgrim and gives him his first vision of Nibbāna. It is the true blessed event of the religious life of the Theravāda Buddhist. What is infused into mind at that moment is *lokuttara pañña*: "world-transcending insight."[60]

10

THE SOTERIOLOGICAL PROCESS AND ITS SOCIOLOGICAL RELEVANCE IN THE SINHALA THERAVĀDA BUDDHIST TRADITION[1]

For quite some time sociologists and cultural anthropologists have been analyzing the Sinhala Theravāda Buddhist case past and present, and in some instances, their work has been remarkably successful in assisting their readers to rationalize the interrelations of religiocultural strands discerned in the subject they have chosen to study. Utilizing analytical methods, the tendency in these works has been to isolate levels, strata, spheres, fields, and so on and attempt to explain their purposive presence. We have been made aware of correspondences and tensions or torsions between systems of meaning, of the function of religious world-views in society as a whole through legitimation and compensation, by mitigating opposition and engendering conflict resolution, by contributing to cohesiveness and continuity, even change. We have learned a great deal.

Some scholars have made the point that we are dealing, in the case of Sinhala Buddhists, with an integral religious system from the point of view of some religious actors; a system, nevertheless, composed of sharply differentiated component parts, specialists, belief systems, rituals with differing historical origins. Attempts have been made to discern the processes by means of which those sharply differentiated component parts cohere in a meaningful whole. Such attempts have yielded an interpretation stressing a complementariness of a predominant literary religious tradition with "otherworldly" emphasis, on the one hand, and widespread local and also traditional religious practices expressive of "this-worldly" concerns, on the other, or, from another perspective, a complementariness of a cognitive awareness of traditional doctrine (text) with an affective expressiveness in practice (context).

In this chapter, I will attempt to move in a middle course between, on the one hand, developing sharply differentiated elements, factors, or strands and, on the other, merely reporting what Buddhists in Sri Lanka are doing. Perhaps, for some, what I have to say might appear "fuzzy," might suggest that I am attempting, without clear analysis, to treat a subject "subjectively"; that this work does not reflect a discipline.[2] Nevertheless, I am attempting to move in an exploratory venture to gain a clearer understanding of *Buddhists* in Sri Lanka today.

In this venture empathy is fundamental, as is the case with one's seeking to understand another person, even one's spouse or sibling. On the need for empathy (*Einfühlung*) in our study, Gerardus van der Leeuw has written,

> Not a critical analysis, therefore, is in the foreground here: a dissection into segments, however necessary it may be at an analytical preliminary stage, constitutes an insuperable obstacle for empathy. Whoever dissects the whole kills it, and we have to do with living things here.[3]

This study aspires to move on what might represent a new stage in Western attempts to understand Buddhists in Sri Lanka, a stage highlighted by Wilfred Cantwell Smith, who, when he referred to stages in Western understanding of India, said,

> there has been a clear advance through successive stages: first, ignorance; second, impressionistic awareness of random parts of the culture (an outside subjective stage); thirdly, a growingly systematic and accurate yet insensitive and externalist knowledge of facts (an objective stage); and more recently, and richly promising, the beginnings

> of serious and even profound humane understanding of the role and meaning of those facts in the lives and the culture of the persons involved.[4]

The last stage Smith called *personalist.* And I agree with him when he immediately continued,

> I hope that it is hardly necessary to insist that by "personal" I do not mean "individual." Personality is profoundly social. The opposite of individual is social; the opposite of personal is impersonal. The earlier stage was of an impersonal knowledge of facts (it aimed at impersonal knowledge). The newer stage is of a personal knowledge, an understanding, of the meaning of those facts, in the cultural life of Indians [and in our present case, in the cultural life of Sinhala Theravāda Buddhists].[5]

I hardly propose to provide resolutions, or even to proffer explanations, but rather to elucidate a dynamic complexity in the religious life of Buddhists in Sri Lanka by (I) placing aside some standard heuristic paradigms, (II) by stating once again, in order to stress, the importance of the laity and by noting a process by which the faith of Buddhist laypersons is engendering anew the Buddhist tradition today (both in our today and into our tomorrow), (III) by illustrating more particularly a dynamic and deeply personal interaction between the laity and the Sangha, and (IV) by providing an interpretation of a fundamental, comprehensive notion that has enabled Sinhala Buddhists to allow for a variety of religious orientations in a cumulative tradition and also to perceive in those orientations not irresolvable contradictions within a religious world-view but patterns for purposive social behavior.

In trying to work from *within* a cumulative religious tradition that is qualified by being Buddhist, characterized by being Theravāda, and modified by being Sinhala, I am seeking to understand religious *persons* engaged in a soteriological process that is qualified by being Buddhist, characterized by being Theravāda and modified by being Sinhala. It is to ramifications of this soteriological process that I wish to point in an attempt to communicate from *within* the Sinhala Theravāda Buddhist tradition a fundamental orientation that allows for a variety of religious orientations and practices and relevance for the situation in life experienced by the laity.

In this procedure, I will attempt to suggest the sociological relevance of this soteriological process primarily from the point of view of laypersons who are immediately and dramatically involved in shaping their society today in Sri Lanka.

I

In the study of men and women living within the Buddhist heritage in Sri Lanka a number of brilliant scholars have proposed several heuristic paradigms. We have read of "Buddhism and society" and "religion and social change" and are familiar with the notions of "this worldly" and "otherworldly," and have seen a pattern in presentations whereby a dichotomy is placed before a reader and then an explanation of interrelations is provided, usually following in one form or another a kind of functionalism. Although in some cases these heuristic paradigms are demonstrably catalytic in analytic inquiries conducted by splendid social scientists, often these studies do not take us far enough, are capable of misleading us, tend to oversimplify.

Rather than speaking of "Buddhism and society" it would be preferable to speak of the Sinhala Buddhist tradition because, as we have discussed the matter in Chapter 1, "Buddhism" is a problematic concept, one not always used with consistent precision by a scholar in different phases of scholarly development and writing, or even within the pages of one book; indeed it is a term not readily yielding definitional precision and is itself, as a concept, an important factor to be recognized and carefully considered in any attempt to analyze the interpretation of life endorsed by religious persons in Sri Lanka. Heinz Bechert has well indicated a sense among Buddhists in Sri Lanka that their religious tradition was under serious threat of disappearing under the sustained and permeating impact of Western thought. In an attempt to gain balance, there was, as Bechert noted, a "necessity of a compromise with Western civilization."[6] Discussing briefly some key indicators of this process, he notes a movement to represent the Buddhist tradition as "the 'Religion of Reason',"[7] a development of lay organizations,[8] a self-consciousness developed as a result of Western Indological studies, some parallel developments, of sorts, with the West in which progress in natural and physical science challenged traditional conceptions, and a number of other matters. Bechert does not, however, analyze the significance of the incorporation of the concept "Buddhism" in this process; for with the adoption of this notion, and that other weighty Western notion, "religion," the stage was set in Sri Lanka for what some have called the fragmentation of an integral society.

Once the concept "Buddhism" came on the scene in Sri Lanka, one could then speak of "early Buddhism," "Neobuddhism," "distortion of Buddhism," "traditional Buddhism," even "*Urbuddhismus*"; and further, one could then speak of "Buddhism and Society," "Buddhism and the legitimation of power," "Buddhism and modernization," and even "contradictions in Sinhalese Buddhism." Once the concept "religion" came on the scene in Sri Lanka, one could then speak of "Religion and Politics," "Religion and Social Change," and so forth.

Now both the concepts "Buddhism" and "religion," having recently appeared, are on the scene in Sri Lanka. The more familiar with English discourse a Sinhala man or woman tends to be, the more often these two notions appear. In my understanding of the situation, notions like "Buddhism" and "religion" are what one might call "cross-cultural contact notions"; that is, the way of thinking a Sinhala Buddhist might develop in attempting to converse with Westerners. In my judgment, these are not primary categories for self-understanding, personal evaluations of one's life, for most Sinhala Buddhist men and women, although they might have some hold on the personal thinking of Buddhist men and women whom some have tended to call the Western-educated urban elites.

Another popular paradigm is the juxtaposition of "this worldly" and "otherworldly." On first blush, such paradigm appears neat, and by picking it up one would be enabled to draw readily on the work of a number of fine scholars. One could thereby move swiftly within a recognized vocabulary and within a frame of reference of a shared method, surprisingly tempting for one preparing brief presentations. But, on reflection, such paradigm is beguiling—it appears sound but is remarkably perplexing because of the definitional cross-directionality involved in the concepts. *This world* is defined by "the other world" and so also *the other world* is defined by "this world." So to understand *this world* as *this* world that Sinhala Buddhists see, one has to know what is meant by *the other world* as Sinhala Buddhists consider it.

The problem is complicated. Which account of *this world* is one to follow when analyzing interpretations? Does one, in the name of social science, have to assume an ontological underpinning for *this world* before one says that other people "deny this world" or stress "otherworldly" pursuits and thereby attempt to assert something more than merely a trivial observation?

Some have suggested that the Sinhala term *laukika* (Pāli: *lokika/lokiya*) means "the worldly" and "refers to things that are mundane, secular, profane."[9] Apparently, for some Sinhala Buddhists, *laukika* carries such meanings. But this usage appears recent. If *laukika* had carried this sense through the centuries then one would want to note that both propitiation of the gods *and also* taking refuge (*saraṇa*) in, attempting to emulate the virtuous qualities of, the Buddha, to follow *dhamma* and to hold as an ideal a form of living in accord with *dhamma*, with lifelong commitment, which is called in Pāli, *lokiya-saraṇa-gamana*, is a "mundane, secular, profane" act.[10] Obviously, the world-transcending mode of going for refuge, *lokottara-saraṇa-gamana*, is other than the *laukika/lokiya* mode, the customary mode of expressing one's religiousness, as we have seen. But to speak of this latter as worldly, mundane, secular, profane, demonstrates, also obviously, that something has gone awry, that new meaning has forcibly entered old word forms, meaning derived jostlingly from a foreign cultural source.

A problem one might confront in attempting to understand the multifaceted orientations in the Theravāda tradition by using a "this worldly and otherworldly" heuristic paradigm is that at best one might end up reporting what is obvious and, at worst, distorting subtle dimensions of Buddhist religiousness. Given a religious tradition, such as the Theravāda Buddhist, that has maintained the centrality of the monastic life in the soteriological process, one would anticipate there being a peripheral valuational orientation toward other forms of communal relationships. This much seems clear. But the paradigm, "this worldly" and "otherworldly," because it has appeared generally accepted by some of us working in this subject, might lead one to move too quickly conceptually.

Ernst Troeltsch spoke of "flight from the world"[11] in the rather early Christian case and Max Weber spoke of "authentic ancient Buddhism"[12] as "this only really consistent position of world-flight."[13] This way of looking at things does not discern the subtle inner dynamics *within* the Theravāda perspective. Buddhists *do not* speak of the procedure of entering monastic life as a "flight" from the world. Although they have interpreted this procedure as "going out from the household life," that is, going out from the customary institutions of ordinary social relationships,[14] they have chosen to make formal a slightly different interpretation of this procedure—it is an act of "going forth."[15] Viewing this procedure as "going out" with connotations of renunciation represents primarily a monastic perspective. "Going forth" with connotations of going onward reflects a twin dimension, the purpose of the *bhikkhu and* the perspective of the laity.

Ambiguity abides in the "this worldly and otherworldly" paradigm when used by Western scholars in studies of the Theravāda tradition. Consider Figure 1. In short, what some have meant by "this worldly

The Western (theistic) Case	The Sinhala Buddhist Case
("Concept-transcending notion of God"?)	*lokuttara* "world-transcending" — *Dhamma/nibbāna*
"Otherworld" God heaven next life	*paraloka* ("Otherworld") *devas* ("gods") *svarga* ("heaven[s]") *devaloka* ("realm[s] of gods") *lokiya* *lokika* *laukika*[16]
"This World"	*ayam loka* ("This World") (or *idhaloka* or *melova*)

Figure 1

and otherworldly," Sinhala Buddhists have called *lokiya*, or, "pertaining to this world" or "customary." For Sinhala Buddhists, there is also *lokuttara*, meaning "*other* than 'this worldly and otherworldly'," "transcending *both* 'this worldly *and* otherworldly'."[17]

And so we place aside these paradigms and turn our attention to a dynamic complexity in the religious life of Buddhists in Sri Lanka—the role of the laity.

II

The laity has been a part of the cumulative religious tradition.[18] A cumulative religious tradition is dynamic; it changes, develops, suffers setbacks, incorporates some things new, forgets, or allows to ossify some things old—and all this occurs as a consequence of persons, one by one, numbering in the tens of millions, who have participated in and have thereby perpetuated that cumulative religious tradition. And there is a reliable tendency on the part of persons grappling with current issues, whether in the third century B.C. or the twentieth century A.D.[19] to respond creatively, to remember, to explore, to put aside, and to do all of this religiously.

Of course, the contribution of the Sangha in the history of the Theravāda tradition is inestimable; those persons who have committed their lives to the pursuit of a holistic realization of *dhamma* and who have served, in the memory of Buddhists, as channels, vessels, preservers, custodians of the teachings of the Buddha about salvific truth.

Yet, it would seem that rather early in the history of the Buddhist cumulative tradition, the laity, men and women devotees (*upāsakas* and *upāsikās*), began to outnumber those engaged in monastic pursuits. And ever since the laity has constituted the majority of those persons who found in *dhamma* a means of becoming meaningfully oriented to their daily activities. Also the laity has experienced a fluid development with regard to expressions of religiousness within their local settings. Laypersons in Sri Lanka had received a cumulative tradition, and they did not search for an analytical distance to enable them to separate strands in their heritage, nor did they find in that heritage an "evangelical triumphalism" that might have led them to speak harshly or degradingly about religious practices that others—in most cases other people known to them—found supportive in getting on in life. Until rather recently, perhaps, they have not had an orientation to their religious understanding reflecting exclusive loyalty to a system of beliefs as has developed in the Jewish, Christian, and Islamic traditions.[20]

So often scholars, who have studied the Theravāda tradition, have made their mark and their contribution by sharply delineating a strand in that tradition or by focusing solely on one part of that tradition or working singularly with one method—ancient text or contemporary context, idea or institution, view or village—that it has been unusually difficult to discern the pictures seen by Buddhist laypersons. Buddhist laypersons have had the pictures; we academics seem to have been holding fragments.

Now, for over a decade, aware of the results to which an unrelenting analytical method tended to lead them, scholars have also introduced synthetic interpretations of the Sinhala Buddhist case, which, in my judgment, has brought us closer to an understanding of the general perspective of the laity. Within the same year, two anthropologists, Michael Ames and Gananath Obeyesekere, made important statements on this matter. Ames wrote, "In Ceylon, Buddhism and magical-animism have always remained quite distinct from each other, forming two separate, but complementary, subsystems of a more general religious system which may be termed 'Sinhalese Religion'."[21] And Obeyesekere said, "some aspects of Sinhalese behavior which on the surface seem contradictory are really not so from the actor's viewpoint." Following up on this observation, Obeyesekere continued, "But Sinhalese Buddhism cannot be equated with Theravāda. Instead it should be seen historically as a fusion and synthesis of beliefs derived from Theravāda with other non-Theravāda beliefs to form one integrated tradition." And, he proposed, "In other words, individual identifications and actions have significance only in relation to a single system—Sinhalese Buddhism."[22] Obeyesekere also spoke of "the Sinhalese religious tradition."[23]

Both Ames and Obeyesekere were moving along lines of inquiry I am attempting to develop in this chapter. Ames added together (1)

"Buddhism" and (2) "magical-animism" and came up with "Sinhalese Religion." Obeyesekere took (1) "Theravāda" and (2) general religious behavior of the populace and came up with "Sinhalese Buddhism." Further, Obeyesekere made an important advance on two counts: (1) his sensitivity to what he notes "from the actor's viewpoint,"[24] and his notion, which I will consider later, of the "salvation idiom" (*karma/ kamma*) drawn from the Theravāda.

It is in this synthetic sense that I tend to see a cumulative religious tradition that relates primarily to Sri Lanka, to this country's past and now, today. For this reason I use *Sinhala* to modify, to restrict, to suggest a particular modality of the tradition. Although the "salvation idiom" is drawn from the Theravāda heritage, as Obeyesekere notes, I tend to place that particular "salvation idiom" (*karma/kamma*) into a broader context, *dhamma*, within the Theravāda tradition, consequently preferring to use *Theravāda* as an adjective suggesting the characteristic mark of that tradition and soteriological process. And, of course, I consider both the Theravāda tradition and the soteriological process to possess the quality of being religious, of being Buddhist.

A cumulative religious tradition changes, of course, as all things historical have made manifest. A topic frequently addressed by scholars observing contemporary changes of the tradition is "the crisis confronting" the Sinhala Buddhist tradition today—can it endure the process of political, economic, educational, and social changes with, sadly, the wrenching evidence of bloodshed, that is presently swirling on the scene in Sri Lanka? Analyses of the contemporary case have shown us particular movements, responses, and developments, have described for us isolated trends. On a more general level, in a synthetic manner, let me suggest that the Sinhala Buddhist tradition will weather "the crisis confronting" it, will continue, and this for several reasons.

First, the laity is not by any means cut adrift from ethical teachings that can provide a basis for getting along well in their life situation.[25] Nor, second, are lay leaders unaware of an integral religious activity of what Robert McAfee Brown calls "the creative appropriation of an open past."[26] Nor, third, would one want to interpret the presence of a degree of doubt, on the part of some lay leaders, about the relevance of their apprehension of *dhamma* for living in the pace of the twentieth century in Sri Lanka as a lack of faith—lack of faith, rather, tends to yield indifference, as Tillich has suggested in a not entirely dissimilar context, in his *Dynamics of Faith*.[27]

Without getting involved in the complex relationship of the delicate and subtle notions of faith (*saddhā*) and salvific insight-wisdom (*paññā*) in the Theravāda Buddhist perspective, one might suggest that Robert McAfee Brown and Paul Tillich, Christian theologians not very thoroughly informed about the Theravāda tradition, in their respective notions of faith being in part "the creative appropriation of an open past" and a dynamic of experiential participation and a sense of separation, have touched on a dimension of personal religious dynamics, shared by Sinhala Buddhists today, that tends to provide a *personalist parallel* to some concerns expressed by Robert N. Bellah about what he considered religious and societal progress in modern Asia. With the notion of "the creative appropriation of an open past," compare Bellah's statement,

> To the liberal Westerner or Asian, there is little doubt that a syncretic ideology, stressing continuity with the best of the past and progress toward a better future, preferably underpinned by a reformist religious position and a commitment to liberal values, seems the best solution for Asians to follow.[28]

With the general notion of "tension" in Tillich's "dynamics of faith," compare Bellah's observation,

> Two conditions seem especially unfavorable for the religious encouragement of progress: too close a fusion between religious symbolism and the actual world and too great a disjunction between them.[29]
>
> The situation in which progress is most likely to be advanced seems to be that in which transcendent ideals, in tension with empirical reality, have a central place in the religious symbol system, while empirical reality, itself, is taken very seriously as at least potentially meaningful, valuable, and a valid sphere for religious action[30]

I should think that this personal dynamic of creatively appropriating an open past, of experientially participating in *dhamma* living yet sensing a separation from the goal, which many have noticed among Sinhala Buddhists, compellingly expressed by the more highly educated laypersons, will continue with renewal and reform in the "tension" suggested by Bellah. That there is uncertainty, even doubt, that there is tension, that there are attempts at reform, that questions of relevance of a religious tradition in today's settings are being seriously considered—all those are signs both of faith and of strength.

III

The relevance of the monastic community for the laity has long continued in Sri Lanka, and the multifaceted ramifications of that relevance have been far more pervasive and subtle than the usual comments about "merit making" would suggest; the monastic community is important for the laity because the laity, by giving to the monks, by caring for the community, "gains merit."

Analyses of the Sinhala Theravada Buddhist tradition have often reflected a monastic institutional orientation, and we are indebted to this general approach for the results it has yielded. It is clear that the monastic setting has been maintained consistently as an institutional expression of a living situation most readily conducive to a holistic penetration of *dhamma* or, put another way, to the attainment of *nibbāna.* With little difficulty we could adduce a series of canonical passages that prescribe the "going forth" procedure as a significant activity in the soteriological process. However, I know of no passage that *equates* this "going forth" with "entering the stream" (*sotāpatti*),[31] that monumental moment when one is assured that the whirl of the world(s) will be transcended. Consequently, the prescriptions for this "going forth" are not to be interpreted primarily as proscribing the life of the laity, but, rather, as a moving forward from a form of personal living most often met in the ordinary transactions of relationships in the setting in which the laity finds itself, unlike, of course, the setting ideally arranged for the *bhikkhus*.

It is because a *bhikkhu* is to *reject* a form of personal living—hatred, envy, slander, and on and on, impressively so—and not, conceptually, to reject a context of living, that the laity, and a *bhikkhu*, too, can interpret this "going forth" as a *step forward*, not a jump over an abyss of sorts.

What is that without which there would be no Theravāda Buddhist tradition today? Obviously, as Buddhists have said, the Buddha, Dhamma, and the Sangha (*sāvakasangha* and *bhikkhusangha*). But just as obvious, one must add because it is often overlooked in spite of what Buddhists have demonstrated, manifestly, are mothers and fathers.[32]

One is reminded of an old passage in the *Mahāvaṃsa*, that has Moggaliputta say to King Aśoka,

> Even a person of great generosity like you
> Is not an heir (*dāyāda*) of the *sāsana*:
> Only a giver of means (*paccayadāyaka*) he is called,
> O ruler of men.
>
> But one who leads son or daughter to
> Go forth into the *sāsana*
> Is an heir (*dāyāda*) of the *sāsana*;
> Not so [in the case of] a giver (*dāyaka*).[33]

And the *bhikkhu* remains his mother's son, his father's son, and, perhaps, a sibling. Some have interpreted this "going forth" as renunciation, and this it is, in part. But it is a renunciation of the "hold" on one that "the household life" involves and not of one's parents and siblings. This "going forth" ideally is a gift made by parents in being supportive of a child, it is an expression of faith on their part. Parents now become relatives, kinsfolk of those wholly committed to the *sāsana*, the Buddha's guiding instruction, of those *in* the *sāsana*, become kinsfolk not through a blood line, not at all through status reflected in kinship structures—this has been severed; the tradition is quite clear about this—but, rather, by means of inheritance, of receiving that originally not one's own, but now acquired because of a deeply personal experience expressed in this gift. And Sinhala Buddhist parents of men now become *bhikkhus* would not find particularly opaque a Pauline Christian notion that inheritance, the state of being heirs, as a religious category, does not depend on blood lines (Greek: *sperma*) but on faith (Greek: *pistis*).

Parents have often experienced the remarkable discovery of observing a child growing into adulthood, finding his or her own personhood, becoming his or her own person. Occasionally, this might be a difficult process for some parents, letting a son become a man, a daughter become a woman. When compared with the activity of being supportive for a son in his "going forth," parental procedures in supporting a child through adolescence to adulthood appear rather easy. And further, the continuity of these heirs, the idea that sons do "go forth," that a parent *gives most* to a son by supporting him *in losing him* would tend to be instructive to all parents in Sri Lanka, and elsewhere, as they set about to assist their children to move wholesomely through adolescence into adulthood.

Parents who look on the development of their children with a concern for what would be most beneficial for them have before them a possibility that a son, some day, might "go forth." An awareness of this possibility, whether or not a son "goes forth," whether or not the possibility is clearly articulated, it would seem, is a paradigm by which a parent might be motivated to instill in a child a wholesome purposiveness in living life.

The relevance of the monastic community for the laity extends beyond parents whose son "goes forth." The reasons for a person's "going forth" are manifold, much too complex for us to consider here. That young men have "gone forth" *and* continue to do so, even today, has had enormous ramifications in Sinhala Buddhist society; indeed, without these recurring events, Sinhala Buddhist society would be other than it is, empirically. (This is another way of saying that "this world" that a Sinhala Buddhist sees is the world that *he* or *she* sees precisely because of that which is beyond both "this world" and the "other world" for which his or her fellows are questing.) That there are *bhikkhus* is of weighty consequence for society. This is obvious, but needs stressing.

Further, in this relevance of the monastic community for the laity there is a conceptual interrelationship of considerable importance: the fact that there are *bhikkhus* provides a frame of reference for the laity in their life setting. This frame of reference is not endorsed primarily because it relegates the lay life to a secondary mode of existence.

Rather, the *idea of the bhikkhu*, reinforced by empirical manifestation, can set moving a wholesome tension in the life of a layperson. Let me try to elaborate this.

Why have persons *not* "gone forth" into the monastic order? That this question might be raised, might have been raised by laypersons, is of enormous social consequence, I should think. What might have been some factors that led a person not to become a *bhikkhu?* As a young man, perhaps, one factor might have been a desire for technical education—and the *idea of the bhikkhu* could remind him that there is more to life than "engineerism." He comes to be a lively consumer in the economic system—and the *idea of the bhikkhu* might suggest prudence.[34]

Later, perhaps, a layman might raise again the question of entering the order but his love for wife and children might lead him to continue living in the context of relationships with which he is familiar. The *idea of the bhikkhu* could lead a person (1) to say that he could not care less about the question of "going forth," and such person would not have become engaged with either the question or related issues and would have recognized this; (2) to refrain from entering the order because life is too much fun, and such a person would thereby hit on his controlling purpose for living; (3) to decide not to enter the order because he has important obligations—to parents, siblings, wife, children, and so on—and such a person would note thereby that he lives not for himself.[35]

In short, the possibility of a layman raising the question is significant. That he raises it or seriously ponders it at some stage in his life is momentous. In choosing not to become a *bhikkhu*, if this decision is carefully weighed and seriously made, a person at least is led to take stock of his life, discern his values for living as he is (values placed into perspective by the *idea of the bhikkhu*), and thereby to perceive the purpose of his priorities and through all of this *to accept himself*, his aspirations, and his inadequacies. Psychiatrists would recognize this as no mean accomplishment.[36]

There appears to be another dimension of the relation between the monastic institution and the laity. Gananath Obeyesekere has drawn our attention to a recent development in the Sinhala Buddhist tradition; a "spatial shift" has occurred in which the Buddha image has entered the "marketplace" and the home, and monks have entered the political arena.[37] In the process of developing his argument, Obeyesekere educed evidence from sociopolitical dimensions to substantiate his observations and interpretations and in the process alerted his readers to behavior patterns of Sinhala Buddhists, particularly those in the urban settings, in response to a dynamic interaction with Western cultural elements and the pressures of urban living. I found Obeyesekere's interpretations of some underlying factors responsible for this spatial shift[38] to be a significant contribution to our understanding of the case. However, I sense that a more fundamental shift had occurred among Sinhala Buddhists *before* the "spatial shift," of which Obeyesekere spoke, could have occurred. Let me quote Obeyesekere.

> Traditionally the ideal way of building a temple or any religious edifice is to ensure a spatial separation of the religious edifice from the human community. Analogously the incumbents of these temples—the Buddhist monks—were spatially separated from the peasant laity. For religious worship the peasant went to the temple: for certain parish tasks like participation in almsgiving rites, recital of texts (*parittas*) and funeral rites the monks went to the village. The spatial separation of the edifice and the incumbent from the human community reflects a behavioural manifestation of a central Buddhist doctrinal value. Briefly stated, the Buddha and rites associated with him deal with the other-worldly interests of the masses. Furthermore, salvation (*nirvana*) involves as its prerequisite an emancipation from the social structure, i.e., emancipation from the attachment to the world. These ideal doctrinal postulates are manifest in the spatial separation of monk and temple from the peasant and the village.[39]

It is with this interpretation of the "tradition" as a background that Obeyesekere wrote, "In the urban context...a spatial shift has occurred—the Buddha is being brought into the hub of events."[40] I should think, rather, from a less recent point of view, one might say that the Buddha (i.e., statues of the Buddha) was being brought into the *hubbub* of events.

In working with a "this worldly" and "otherworldly" paradigm[41] it appears that Obeyesekere was presenting a parallel structure of sorts in which there had been a shift from one to the other. Not only is this shift recent, but I am coming to suspect that a conception of this parallelism itself is also recent within the Sinhala Theravāda Buddhist tradition.

Let me put it this way. Within the Protestant Christian churches, from which Weber drew so much of his data, there has been, by and large, a strand of ecclesiastical interpretation that has viewed the Christian monastic tradition as in some cases, at best, peripheral, in some cases as an outmoded addendum to Biblical teachings. Some Protestants might interpret a young person's entering the Christian religious orders to become a monk or a nun as "*fleeing from* the world" whereas, I should think, the persons involved might interpret their action as a "deliberate, reflective *move toward*" the fulfillment of their lives. There has been a traditional Protestant perspective that interprets the celibate contemplative life of the religious as on the periphery, "out there," "spiritual," not primarily concerned with "this world," not "where the action is," in short, "otherworldly." It would appear that Sinhala Buddhists are coming to endorse this parallel perspective primarily through Protestant Christian orientations,[42] but also, perhaps, through the institutional conceptualization of the secular and religious orders in the Roman Catholic Church, which has long grappled with Augustine's emphasis on the contemplative life *and* loving service.

I suggest that an older Sinhala Theravāda Buddhist perspective was otherwise, one that was hierarchical and concentric. I trust that this will become clearer as we move to our third consideration, that of a soteriological process. Here, let me note that a person "going forth" into the order is making a behavioral-institutional manifestation of a movement toward a center, toward the source of understanding. I suggest that for centuries, and perhaps among the more reflective today, the Sinhala Buddhist laity has conceptualized *themselves* as living on the periphery. In spite of the spatial structuring in establishing a monastery *outside the village*, in a setting ideally conducive to the contemplative life, it seems that once a monastery became established, a conceptualization had occurred that interpreted the villager, the layperson, as being on the *outside of the monastery*. So, although the monastery is "out there" it is, I suggest, nevertheless, nearer "the center out there."[43]

The "spatial shift" that Obeyesekere has documented would, in a traditional perspective, seem to represent an extension from a point nearer the center of a sociosoteriological cosmography to positions more immediate for the laity on the outside. It is not a matter of a shift from the sacred to the profane, from otherworldly emphasis to this-worldly concerns, from the periphery to the center, from the "out there" to "the hub," but, rather, that which is central has been extended, disseminated, and made more visible.

IV

Theravāda Buddhists have said a great deal about process and much of what has been said in this context has to do with soteriology. Some commentators have equated salvation within the Theravāda context as the attainment of *nibbāna.* This, unless qualified as "ultimate salvation," tends to misrepresent not only the Western theistic usage of the notion but also the Buddhist case. If one means by *salvation* an assurance that one is no longer subjected to ultimate failure, to continual meaningless sorrow, to a course leading to perdition, then salvation is enormously comprehensive in the Buddhist case, is closer to hand than one might think. One who attains the stream (*sotāpatti/sotāpanna*) might have seven more life sequences ahead, but such a person is assured, nevertheless, that he or she will not fail. One who has not attained the stream, yet has taken refuge in the Buddha, Dhamma, and the Sangha is told these three gems are called *refuge* because they "slay *dukkha*," undercut the arising of *dukkha* in a future life sequence. A person who sets his or her mind to living a considerate life, alert to the need to ameliorate the suffering of others, will not go to perdition.

Of course, the notion of *karma/kamma* looms large in this consideration. Modern (Western) existentialists have discerned the meaningfulness of a notion of choosing and thereby coming to be what one chooses oneself to be. But Buddhists have at their disposal an added dimension that obviates an existentialist's sense of associated forlornness and despair. There is, and has been, *dhamma.* A life lived (volitional activity: *kamma*) in accordance with *dhamma* will lead to wholesome consequences (*kamma-vipāka*). Just as there are many levels of meaning in the notion of *dhamma*, so also are there levels in the soteriological process. A holistic penetration of *dhamma* is synonymous with the attainment of *nibbāna*. Truth speaking, apparently seen by some as ordinary, rather mundane, lies at the foundation of any social cohesiveness and, for Buddhists, is not off the soteriological track. It is awry to speak of something called *Nibbānic Buddhism* over against *Kammatic Buddhism* because the soteriological modality is uniform, is *dhamma*, and is a process.

Obeyesekere has discerned a dynamic interrelationship in "one integrated tradition," which he calls *Sinhalese Buddhism*. He noted the way an event might be explained by an appeal to notions of astrological, demonological, and divine causality. Ultimately, he mentions, the integrative principle is the notion of *kamma*.[44] The tradition of the monk and that of the villager are "linked" for Obeyesekere, are "fused" but not "confused" for Ames.[45] Both of these scholars have recognized a hierarchical structure in the Sinhala Buddhist pantheon, a structure with the Buddha placed at the apex and deities, benevolent and malevolent spirits subordinated, ranked, variously, below.

Both Obeyesekere and Ames provide a functionalist explanation for the linkage or fusion of what they discern as religious systems. They hold that the Theravāda or Great Tradition or Buddhism has an "otherworldly" interest and the village religious practices, propitiation of the deities and spirits, and healing rituals have a "this-worldly" focus. Setting aside this Weberian paradigm, we can still appreciate the positions of these scholars by noting their interpretations of the way the local rituals tend to relieve anxieties precipitated by numerous factors ranging from ill health to the pressures of exams and urban living.

I understand Obeyesekere and Ames to have said that the rituals related to the deities and spirits in the Sinhala pantheon are, and have been, a continuing part of the religious heritage of Sinhala Buddhists because of the frame of reference that allows for the particularity of events/issues/occurrences for which the rituals can be related, the immediacy of the sensed power of the deity and spirits, and the temporal proximity of an alteration of the status of affairs resulting from the ritual procedure. Of course, one should add, even stress, the assurance on the part of some Sinhala Buddhists that these procedures are efficacious.

There is another dimension to consider in treating the integration of what has been seen as a dual system. Obeyesekere was on the mark when he spoke of a "salvation idiom" being derived from the Theravāda and mentioned the integrative force of the notion of *kamma*. The notion of *kamma* would have a bewildering effect were it not for a conceptual rubric that enables one not only to discern how it has come to be that one is confronted with the present general situation in one's life but also how one is to determine proper motivation for behavior that will yield wholesome and not detrimental consequences. Of course, this conceptual rubric is the notion of *dhamma*.

Dhamma, we have already seen, has many meanings and several levels of meaning. Some meanings are technical, related specifically to the teachings of the Buddha (*buddhabhāsita, desanā*). *Dhamma* also carries less technical connotations, that is, meanings that do not presuppose a thorough acquaintance with the learned tradition; for example, "merit" (*puñña*), "proper conduct" (*ācāra/sucarita*), "proper manner, propriety" (*nāya*), "that which is customary" (*vyavahāra*), "custom, fitness" (*yutti*), "virtuous moral quality" (*guṇa*). The remarkable integrative force of this very comprehensive concept is that, traditionally at least, it can carry meanings from "salvific truth," "four paths, four fruits, and *nibbāna*," "that to be known," "inherent nature," to "the texts that are the three *piṭakas*," to "reason, cause," and "that which is customary."[46]

The linkage or fusion of an integrated religious system is attributable not only to functional utility but also to the absence of a sense of exclusive loyalty to a syllogistic belief system, characteristic of some strands within the Christian tradition. Along with this functional utility, and in place of this syllogistic exclusivity, lies the general notion of *dhamma* that allows for a variety of religious behavior as long as that behavior is supportive of the well-being of persons and, correspondingly, also allows for a variety of behavior in other dimensions of human relationships as long as that behavior, too, is supportive of the well-being of persons.

The soteriological process can be conceptualized as hierarchical and concentric, with a holistic penetration of *dhamma*, that is, the attainment of *nibbāna*, forming the common center with circular spheres representing stages within that process extending outwardly to a perimeter marked by socially established patterns of propriety. This graphic representation depicts no carefully defined, rigidly demarcated, discrete spheres but a dynamic process of an inward and higher movement replete with accomplishments and failures, doubt and anxiety, faithfulness today and forgetfulness tomorrow, advance and slippage, in short, religious faith and human foibles. Within this pattern of concentric circles a Sinhala Buddhist finds himself or herself, recognizing that there is more to be done in this soteriological process and knowing that he or she, too, is found, is given personal, individual and collective, identity.

Two points need to be clear in this connection. First, there is a moment in the movement through this concentric pattern when one is assured that one will not fail, that the Center "out there" will be reached. This has been called the stage of *entering the stream*: "It is the true blessed event of the religious life of the Theravāda Buddhist. What is infused into mind at that moment is *lokuttara paññā*: world-transcending insight."[47] Just as important for our considerations is the recognition, "this side" of that "moment," that *a person living religiously* within a world-view in which the Buddha is held superior to the gods and humankind, within the frame of reference of that religious environment, a person *not contradicting dhamma* in its general sense and thereby not engaging in behavior that will yield detrimental consequences, *is a person in the soteriological process.* Wherever this person chooses to live, however this person chooses to act, whether or not this person chooses to become engaged in ritual acts, liturgy or ceremony, this person's motives and intentions in relationship are not without sociological ramifications and soteriological significance.

Second, and finally, Sinhala Buddhists are generally aware of a difference between institutionalized rituals and beliefs associated with the canonical strand of the Theravāda tradition (that is, the institutes of the Buddha [*buddhasāsana*] that form the basis of what has developed into the Buddha's institution [also *buddhasāsana*]) over against some of the more extraordinary practices associated with propitiation of the gods and spirits. But, it appears, they have not found it particularly compelling to differentiate, through analytical reification, a cogent coherence that they have patently discerned. They have not been engaged in an analysis of comparative belief systems seeking for some explanation for a synthesis of sorts. They have found, I venture to suggest, that integrating factor to lie elsewhere; not in belief systems, not in rituals, but *in persons*, in the intentionality of behavior, whether persons act for the well-being of others, behavior that we might call *agathopoietic*, as characterized by doing what is good for oneself and for others, as an individual and in community, which is a fundamental dimension of *dhamma* living.

11

THE ROLE OF THE AMERICAN SCHOLAR IN BUDDHIST STUDIES IN SRI LANKA

I

For a number of years, persons in Sri Lanka have been talking a lot about "development," and they have been doing something about it, too. One occasionally asks oneself, "What is generally being understood by *development*?" "What are the models for development?" "Where might someone look to find one or several?" Usually, by "development," most people tend to mean economic development—and this is due in large measure to a willingness to adopt, rather quickly it seems, a technocratic view of the life context. One is occasionally perplexed on hearing the phrase *developed country*. Often *developed country* refers to the United States—but one thinks of the robbery, assault, and murder in Miami, along the docks of Houston, in Los Angeles, Detroit, New York City, and Washington, D.C. And one notes the growing number of illiterate persons, of men and women, and children too, with no shelter, and growing malnutrition, of urban riots, the continuation of nagging racism, the rise of chemical dependency, the epidemic of AIDS, and on and on one might readily go. What constitutes a "developed country"?

Of course, one will tend to say, a great deal hinges on precisely what is meant by *development*, depends on how far one wants to extend the meaning of the term. And here I broach my introductory point—we hardly have our bearings if we think there is a foundation, a basic principle, a fundamental frame of reference for economic development, industrial development, agricultural development, political development, social or cultural development, other than the development of persons.

It is a happy occasion for us formally to express our deep appreciation for an agreement between the government of what some might call a developed country and the government of a so-called developing country (heaven forbid that we continue to use the terms *underdeveloped,* or *backward*), an agreement that has enabled many Americans to live in Sri Lanka, seriously to study and to become enabled sincerely to share an understanding of a religious heritage replete with insight into the development of persons.

With this expression of gratitude is coupled a word of admonition. Although we have not forgotten the significance of this personalistic sense of development in America, we all might tend to remember it less frequently and should we do so, the obstacles we might erect in cross-cultural understanding could be enormous.

Let me approach this general observation somewhat negatively and indirectly. For some of us today, the educational exchange program of the United States Educational Foundation in Sri Lanka might appear analogous to a sophisticated rubber-rice agreement, Sri Lankan rubber for China's rice. One might say, "Let America export her technological expertise by sending scientists and engineers to us and by our sending students in these disciplines there, and let us 'export' facets of our Buddhist tradition by sending Buddhist scholars there as visiting lecturers and by welcoming scholars and students in Buddhist studies here." This looks like a fine arrangement, one might suggest, for this particular exchange program and the Educational Foundation to adopt—everyone seems to benefit and, assuredly, benefit we do. But the benefits do not seem to be equal. Americans are learning more about the cultural fabric of this country—in a seriously disciplined academic way that can be shared with generations of students—than Sri Lankans are learning, in a similar fashion, about America. Sri Lankan students and professors who have studied, conducted research, and have taught in America under the auspices of this exchange program have left a splendid record. But this record has been made overwhelmingly in the study of education, administration, economics, science, and technology.

The one or two Sri Lankan scholars who have specialized in religious studies and have gone to America under the sponsorship of this program have gone to lecture in Buddhist studies or to work in comparative religious studies. No one, it appears, has gone from here under the sponsorship of this program to study religion in America, to study Americans, to study us in that nebulous zone in our lives that we tend outwardly to keep a private matter, yet knowing all along that it sets the tone for and brings quality to those fundamental decisions and pivotal acts that concern us most in both the individual and social dimensions of our lives.

The complex and subtle influence that the American religious heritage has had on the shaping of American public opinion would not be understood were one, for example, to interpret the American government's concern for peace and stability in the Middle East (as Americans tend to call that area you know as West Asia) as merely a desire to assure oil imports, on the one hand, and to placate a strong Jewish lobby, on the other. Furthermore, the profound decision by Martin Luther King, Jr., who received his theological education in the American North, in Rochester and Boston, to make his dramatic commitment to the civil rights movement in the American South is not fully grasped if one were to think he did so because racism was only in the South. Obviously, racism was there, but this is part of the point; it was obvious there, unlike elsewhere. But something else was there in the South about which King was familiar. It was there, powerfully so, pervasively so; namely, the Christian church, and this is the other part of the point. King brought to the surface the inherent contradiction between the personal faith of Christians and racism, and thereby brought about impressive change—not for greater racial discrimination, but for greater freedom.

Just as one frequently hears it stressed that one cannot grasp the intricacies of life, the complexities of the social context in Sri Lankan culture and civilization without having some in-depth comprehension of the function or significance of the religious heritages of Sri Lanka as they were maintained and now are being expressed by persons living here today, so also the case is as compellingly established that one cannot grasp the subtleties of the culture and civilization of America without some awareness, at least, of the crucial role religious orientations have played and are playing there. For the All Ceylon Buddhist Congress, the point is that more Buddhists need to study the religiously plural context in the United States, particularly American Christians, Jews, and secularists, too, insofar as secularism, a Western phenomenon, provides a buttressing, total orientation to life.

It might seem strange, at first blush, that an American who teaches Buddhist studies would suggest at the beginning of an address to a predominantly Buddhist audience that more Buddhists in Sri Lanka should be studying Christians and Jews in America. Not entirely strange, I should think, because our task is to broaden our horizons of knowledge by studying persons in the dimension of their lives that they, in the final analysis, take most seriously. It is just complicated, certainly, and stimulating, exhilarating.

The point at issue is straightforward: the study of humankind's religious life is the study of persons; what they have said, and how they have chosen to say it, what they have done, and the purpose for which they have done it; their history, and the quality of life as they lived it in history, in the past, and now, today.

Buddhist Studies, then, is the study not of "Buddhism"—a recent Western concept—but of Buddhists. And the American scholar in Buddhist studies, if he or she is able to rise to the task, regardless of professional rank, remains a student among Buddhists and of Buddhists. He or she continues to learn from Buddhists.

II

The role of the American scholar in Buddhist studies is gradually unfolding internationally, in the United States, and in Sri Lanka. First, on the international scene, at the dawn of Buddhist studies in the West, American scholars in Buddhist studies were relatively few.

French scholars took a very early lead to be joined within a few years by German and British scholars. Until the twentieth century, American scholars, less under the sway of the impetus that colonial rule gave to international scholarship, by and large were not counted among the internationally leading scholars in Buddhist studies. An outstanding Sanskritist certainly was on the scene relatively early: William Dwight Whitney of Yale.

When American scholars began to participate in earnest in Buddhist studies, they were in the wake of the monumental work of the Pali Text Society based in London. The work by Americans won early and widespread recognition for introducing in English some of the texts of the Pāli canon (as in the case of William Clarke Warren in the latter half of the nineteenth century and thereafter Eugene Watson Burlingame, both of Harvard) and for providing sensitive, insightful interpretations of Theravāda Buddhist life to an international audience (as in the case of the philosopher-psychologist, James Bisset Pratt of Williams College). But once the movement began, the early trend in American scholarship focussed mainly on the early Buddhist tradition in India, on the one hand, and on the Mahāyāna Buddhist tradition in China and Japan, on the other. That trend remains even today. I think it is fair to say that, except for the Japanese, more work is being done by American scholars in Mahāyāna Buddhist studies than by any other national group. But there is now coming on the scene a younger generation of American scholars in Theravāda Buddhist studies.

On the international scene, it is becoming clearer today that the great scholars who have preceded us have left much ground unplowed. More scholars are now beginning to turn afresh to Theravāda Buddhist studies, and among this group of scholars, Americans are moving into position to play a very significant role. It is now true to say that whenever there is an international gathering of leading scholars dealing with Buddhists Studies—Mahāyāna and Theravāda—American scholars will be there with enthusiasm and with substance.

Second, within the United States, American scholars in Buddhist studies are active in several arenas. Besides supporting the International Association for Buddhist Studies and being published in its journal, these scholars are active in the Association for Asian Studies, a professional organization for scholars who have a special interest in Asian studies. Within this association, which regularly exceeds 3,000 participants at its annual meeting, there is a major program committee on Buddhist studies and a recognized committee on Sri Lankan studies. Theravāda studies are occasionally featured on the annual program and all Americans engaged in Sinhala Theravāda Buddhist studies are members of the Sri Lankan Studies Group. Over fifty scholars are listed with this committee on Sri Lankan studies, representing several areas of specialization: political science, economics, anthropology, development studies, linguistics, literature, art, Buddhist studies and history. This group of fifty or so scholars represents the most impressive concentration of talent in Sri Lankan studies in the world, outside of Sri Lanka.

Another professional organization in the United States is the American Academy of Religion, whose delegates at the annual meetings number over 4,000. At these annual meetings regular panel sessions have been devoted to Buddhist studies, Mahāyāna, and I am happy to say, Theravāda, too. And, from time to time, sessions devoted to Buddhist studies are held in conjunction with the annual meeting of the American Oriental Society.

There are also regional conferences within the United States sponsored by the Association for Asian Studies and the American Academy of Religion, and in almost every one of these regional conferences, Buddhist studies has consistently held a place.

All this about associations and committees, annual meetings and regional conferences might strike one as a bit complicated. Give Americans half a chance and they will tend to make things more complex, but with an operating ideal—to provide an opportunity for everyone to have a go.

Now what can we infer about all this activity? The American scholars in Buddhist studies have ample opportunity to share the results of their research and learn from their colleagues. They have continued to demonstrate a keenness to share their findings and a willingness to be tested openly by their peers. The present status of Buddhist studies in the United States is healthy, vibrant, continuing to grow.

The role of the American scholar in Buddhist studies in the United

States is not only to advance our knowledge in Buddhist studies globally but also to assist Americans in learning of the religious tradition of a sizeable portion of humankind. One of my tasks at Colgate University was periodically to compile a list of professors in the United States and Canada who teach the religious traditions of Asia and the colleges offering courses in those religious traditions. Our recent records indicate that 2,248 professors in the United States and Canada were teaching the religious traditions of Asia, and 1,083 colleges or universities offered such courses. This information hardly supports a contention that religious traditions no longer matter and that an understanding of the religious traditions of other people is really of little significance in the education of persons living today, whether in the United States, Canada, or in Sri Lanka.

Third, the role of the American scholar in Buddhist studies is of significance in Sri Lanka itself. In this dimension of one's activity, the work is delicate, challenging, and exacting. Sri Lanka is one's laboratory, it is the catalytic field for one's study and interpretation. But there is something additional in this dimension of one's work, the scholarly activity in Theravāda Buddhist studies in Sri Lanka, something additional that is weighty and of monumental significance in the history of Theravāda Buddhist studies, in the history of Buddhist studies generally and, indeed, even in the history of humankind's religiousness.

Insofar as the work of a foreign scholar in Buddhist studies is read and found to be significant, found helpful and meaningful by Sinhala Buddhists living in Sri Lanka today, that scholar, whether he or she intends it to be so, whether he or she be Buddhist, Christian, Jew, or secularist, is participating in the history of the Theravāda Buddhist tradition. Scholars who have not lived and worked in the culture nurtured by the religious tradition being studied might find this notion of participation somewhat difficult to accept. But American scholars in Buddhist studies are learning of this sense of participation, conceivably of momentous consequence in humankind's religious history, and the agreement between our governments that established the United States Educational Foundation in Sri Lanka, in 1952, has enabled a number of American scholars in Buddhist studies to come to recognize this point.

The role of the American scholar in Buddhist studies is to participate in the history of the Buddhist tradition and for the American scholar who has done work in Buddhist studies in Sri Lanka that role is to participate in the history of the Theravāda Buddhist tradition in Sri Lanka. One's role is also to participate in the history of the Buddhist tradition in America, and thereby to participate in the history of the Buddhist tradition internationally and in the history of humankind's religiousness generally.[1] To participate in the history of the Buddhist tradition in this way—whereby an American might help a Sinhala Buddhist to gain a greater appreciation of his or her own religious heritage, might assist a Sinhala Buddhist in catching a wider vision of his or her own religious aspirations—does not require slipshod sentimentalism, but exacting scholarship, does not require conversion, but a genuine sense of community, does not require a radical change in faith, but deep and abiding friendship.

The American scholar in Buddhist studies has known that what one says about the subject must withstand rigorous scrutiny. But one is beginning to recognize that the matter is now no longer completed with that; just as important as achieving factual accuracy is how one has chosen to express it. No longer is the gathering of information and marshalling of evidence of sole importance, but also the purpose for which one has done it, said it, written it.

III

What might be a constructive conclusion in all of this for all of us? The role of the American scholar in Buddhist studies in Sri Lanka is to participate in the history of the Theravāda Buddhist tradition in this country and internationally. But one's role in cross-cultural understanding and in humankind's religious history, although conceivably highly significant, of momentous consequence, nevertheless remains incomplete. It remains incomplete not insofar as we are waiting for more American scholars to join us—they are on their way—but insofar as Sinhala Buddhists have not studied American Christians and Jews, and authentic secular humanists, have not, as Buddhists, taught their students about American Christians and Jews and others.

When Sinhala Buddhists study American Christians, Jews, and secular humanists, when you share your insights about us, with us, when we learn from you and discern ourselves afresh in your scholarly work and in your abiding friendship, you, as Sinhala Theravāda Buddhists, will be participating in the history of the Christian, Jewish, and the secular humanist traditions in America and internationally. And in a new way you will be participating in humankind's religious history.

Participating in each others religious history today will lead our children, and their children, too, to come to see that we, in our lifetimes, were laying foundations for community, globally, because an abiding sense of global community will develop when our children, if not we ourselves, recognize that humankind's religious history is *our history.*[2]

It might seem strange, at first blush, that an American who teaches Buddhist studies would suggest at the conclusion of an address to a predominantly Buddhist audience that more Buddhists in Sri Lanka should study the religiously plural context in the United States, particularly American Christians, Jews, and secular humanists in American.

Not entirely strange, I should think, as our task is to study each other and ourselves in that dimension of our lives that, in the final analysis, we take most seriously; to understand each other and ourselves taking our places in humankind's religious history. This study and understanding of each other and ourselves in our religious history, humankind's religious history, is squarely based on a principle expressed long ago in our Latin past: "I count nothing that is human as foreign to me." This is a principle, which is, after all, a fundamental thesis for human understanding, an unerring foundation for personal and communal development, long endorsed by the humanities in the Western Academic tradition and penetratively taught by the Buddha.

ABBREVIATIONS

A. *The Aṅguttara-nikāya*, Part I, ed. Rev. Richard Morris, 2d ed., revised by A. K. Warder (London: Published for the Pali Text Society, Luzac & Co., 1961), Part II, ed. Rev. Richard Morris, 1955, Parts III–V, ed. E. Hardy, 1958.

AA. *Manorathapūraṇi: Commentary on the Aṅguttara Nikāya*, Vol. I, ed. Max Walleser, Vol. II, ed. M. Walleser and Hermann Kopp, Vols. III–IV, ed. H. Kopp (London: Published for the Pali Text Society, Oxford University Press, 1924, 1930, 1936, 1940).

AdprD. *Abhidhanappadīpikā: or, Dictionary of the Pali Language*, ed. Waskaḍuwe Subhūti, 2d ed. (Colombo: Frank Luker, Acting Government Printer, 1883).

AdprP. *Abhidhānappadīpikā nam Pālinighaṇduva*, ed. Moragallē Siri Ñāṇobhāsatissa Thera (Colombo: M. D. Gunasena, 1960)

AdprS. W. Subhūti, *Abhidhānappadīpikāsūci: A Complete Index to the Abhidhānappadīpikā* (Colombo: H. C. Cottle, Acting Government Printer, 1893).

AmāV. *Amāvatura*, ed. Wälīvitiyē Sorata Nāyaka Thera (Mt. Lavinia, Ceylon: Abhaya Prakāśakayō, 1960).

Bu. *The Buddhavaṃsa and the Cariyā-Piṭaka*, ed. Rev. Richard Morris, (London: Published for the Pali Text Society, Oxford University Press, 1882).

BuA. *Madhuratthavilāsinī nāma Buddhavaṃsaṭṭhakatha of Bhadantācariya Buddhadatta Mahāthera*, ed. I. B. Horner (London: Published for the Pali Text Society, Oxford University Press, 1946).

Cūl. The *Cūlavaṃsa*, being the second part of *The Mahāvaṃsa*, ed. Wilhelm Geiger (London: Published for the Pali Text Society, Oxford University Press, 1908).

Cūl. Tr. *Cūlavamsa: Being the more recent Part of the Mahāvaṇsa*, Parts 1 and 2, tr. Wilhelm Geiger and from the German into English by C. M Rickmers (Colombo: Ceylon Government Information Department, 1953).

D. *The Dīgha Nikāya*, Vols. I–II, ed. T. W. Rhys Davids and J. Estlin Carpenter (London: The Pali Text Society, Oxford University Press, 1949, 1947), Vol. III, ed. J. Estlin Carpenter (London: Published for the Pali Text Society, Luzac & Co., 1960).

DA. *Sumaṅgala-vilāsinī: Buddhaghosa's Commentary on the Dīgha-Nikāya*, Part I, ed. T. W. Rhys Davids and J. Estlin Carpenter (London: Published for the Pali Text Society, Oxford University Press, 1886), Parts II–III, ed. W. Stede (London: Oxford University Press, 1931, 1932).

DAG. 1967—*Dahampiyā Aṭuvā Gäṭapadaya*, ed. Mäda-Uyangoḍa Vimalakīrti Thera and Nähinnē Sominda Thera (Colombo: M. D. Gunasena, 1967)

1974—*Dhampiyā-aṭuvā-gäṭapadaya*, ed. D. E. Hettiaratchi (Sri Lanka: The Press Board of the Sri Lanka University at the University Press, 1974).

Dhp. *The Dhammapada: A New English Translation with the Pali Text and the First English Translation of the Commentary's Explanation of the Verses with Notes Translated from Sinhala Sources and Critical Textual Comments,* by John Ross Carter and Mahinda Palihawadana (New York Oxford Univeristy Press, 1987).

DhpA. *The Commentary on the Dhammapada*, New edition, Vol. I, Part I, ed. Helmer Smith (London: Published for the Pali Text Society, Oxford University Press, 1925), Vol. I, Part II, Vols. II–IV, ed. H. C. Norman (London: Published for the Pali Text

Society, Oxford University Press, Vol. I, Part II, 1909, Vol. II, 1911, Vol. III, 1912, and Vol. IV, 1914).

Dhpr. *Dharmapradīpikāva*, ed. Baddēgama Vimalavaṃsa Thera, 2d ed. (Colombo: M. D. Gunasena & Co., 1967)

DhsA. *The Atthasālinī: Buddhaghosa's Commentary on the Dhammasaṅgaṇī*, ed. Edward Müller (London: Published for the Pali Text Society, Oxford University Press, 1897).

DS. *Daham Saraṇa*, ed. Kiriällē Ñāṇavimala Thera (Colombo: M. D. Gunasena, 1965)

Itv. *Iti-vuttaka*, ed. Ernst Windisch (London: Published for the Pali Text Society, Oxford University Press, 1948).

Jā. *The Jātaka: Together with Its Commentary*, Vols. I–VI, ed. V. Fausbøll (London: Published for the Pali Text Society, Luzac & Co., Vol. I, 1962, Vols., II–V, 1963, Vol. VI, 1964).

JāA. *Jātakatthavaṇṇanā*, the commentary on the *Jātaka*, as published in *The Jātaka: Together with its Commentary*, Vols. I–VI, ed. V. Fausböll.

JāAg. *Jātaka Aṭuvā Gäṭapadaya*, ed. Mäda-Uyangoḍa Vimalakīrti Thera and Nähinnē Sominda Thera (Colombo: M. D. Gunasena & Co., 1961).

Khp. *The Khuddaka-Pāṭha: Together with Its Commentary Paramatthajotikā I*, ed. Helmer Smith from a collation by Mabel Hunt (London: Published for the Pali Text Society, Luzac & Co., 1959).

KhpA. *The Khuddaka-Pāṭha: Together with Its Commentary Paramatthajotikā I*, ed. Helmer Smith from a collation by Mabel Hunt (London: Published for the Pali Text Society, Luzac & Co., 1959).

M. *Majjhima-nikāya*, Vol. I, ed. V. Trenckner, Vols. II–III, ed. Robert Chalmers (London: Published for the Pali Text Society, Luzac & Co., Vol. I, 1963, Vols. II–III, 1960).

MA. *Papañcasūdanī Majjhimanikāyaṭṭhakathā of Buddhaghosācariya*, Parts I–II, ed. J. H. Woods and D. Kosambi, Parts III–IV, ed. I. B. Horner (London: Published for the Pali Text Society, Oxford University Press, Part I, 1922, Part II, 1923, Part III, 1933, and Part IV, 1937).

Mhbv. *The Mahā-Bodhi-Vaṁsa*, ed. S. Arthur Strong (London: Published for the Pali Text Society, Oxford University Press, 1891).

Mhv. *The Mahāvaṃsa*, ed. Wilhelm Geiger (London: Published for the Pali Text Society, Oxford University Press, 1908).

MhvT. *Vaṃsatthappakāsinī: Commentary on the Mahāvaṃsa*, Vols. I–II, ed. G. P. Malalasekera (London: Published for the Pali Text Society, Oxford University Press, 1935).

Miln. *The Milindapañho: Being Dialogues Between King Milinda and the Buddhist Sage Nāgasena*, ed. V. Trenckner (London: Published for the Pali Text Society, Luzac & Co., 1962)

Nd.1. *Niddesa I: Mahāniddesa*, Vols. I–II, ed. L. de La Vallée Poussin and E. J. Thomas (London: Published for the Pali Text Society, Oxford University Press, Vol. I, 1916, Vol. II, 1917).

Netti. *The Netti-pakaraṇa: With Extracts from Dhammapāla's Commentary*, ed. E. Hardy (London: Published for the Pali Text Society, Luzac & Co., 1961).

Pm. *Paramatthamañjūsā of Bhadantācariya Dhammapāla Thera: Or The Commentary of the Visuddhimagga*, Vols. I–III, ed. Morontuḍuwē Dhammānanda Thera (Colombo: Mahabodhi Press, Vol. I, 1928, Vol. II, 1930, Vol. III, 1949).

Psbp. *Purāṇasiṃhalabaṇapota*, ed. Jinavara Dharmakīrti Śrī Ratanapāla Thera (Colombo: Mahabodhi Press, 1929).

PTS. The Pali Text Socity, London

PTSD. *The Pali Text Society's Pali-English Dictionary*, ed. T. W. Rhys Davids and William Stede (London: Luzac & Co., 1966).

PugA. *Puggala-paññatti-aṭṭhakathā From the Pañcappakaraṇaṭṭhakathā (Ascribed to Buddhaghosa)*, ed. Georg Landsberg and Mrs. Rhys Davids, *Journal of the Pali Text Society* (1914), pp. 170–254.

PūjaV. *Pūjavaliya*, ed. Kiriällē Ñāṇavimala Thera (Colombo: M. D. Gunasena & Co., 1965).

Pv. *Petavatthu*, ed. [J.] Minayeff (London: Published for the Pali Text Society, Oxford University Press, 1888).

S. *Saṃyutta-nikāya*, Parts I–V, ed. M. Léon Feer (London: Published for the Pali Text Society, Luzac & Co., 1960).

SA. *Sārattha-ppakāsinī: Buddhaghosa's Commentary on the Saṃyutta-nikāya*, Vols. I–III, ed. F. L. Woodward (London: Published for the Pali Text Society, Oxford University Press, Vol. I, 1929, Vol. II, 1932, Vol. III, 1937).

SdhAl. *Saddharmālaṅkāraya*, ed. Kiriällē Ñāṇavimala Thera (Colombo: M. D. Gunasena, 1954).

SdhRk. *Saddharmaratnākaraya*, ed. Kalupaluvāvē Devānanda Thera (Colombo: Ratnākara Pot Velanda Sālāva, 1955).

SdhRv. *Saddharmaratnāvaliya*, ed. Kiriällē Ñāṇavimala Thera (Colombo: M. D. Gunasena, 1961).

Sdhs. *Saddhamma Saṃgaho*, ed. Nedimāle Saddhānanda, *Journal of the Pali Text Society* (1890), pp. 21–90.

SdhSS. *Saddharma Sārārtha Saṅgrahaya*, ed. Kiriällē Ñāṇavimala Thera (Colombo: M. D. Gunasena, 1957).

Sdpj. *Saddhamma-pajjotikā: The Commentary on the Mahā-Niddesa*, Vols. I–II, ed. A. P. Buddhadatta (London: Published for the Pali Text Society, Oxford University Press, Vol. I, 1931, Vol. II, 1939).

Sn. *Sutta-Nipāta*, new edition, ed. Dines Andersen and Helmer Smith (London: Published for the Pali Text Society, Oxford University Press, 1948).

SnA. *Sutta-Nipāta Commentary: Being Paramatthajotikā II*, Vols I–II, ed. Helmer Smith (London: Published for the Pali Text Society, Oxford University Press, Vol. I, 1916, Vol. II, 1917).

ŚsdhAv. *Śrī Saddharmāvavāda Saṃgrahaya*, ed. Vēragoḍa Amaramoli Thera (Colombo: Ratnākara Mudranālayaya, 1956).

Śssk. Wälivitiyē Sorata Thera, *Śrī Sumaṅgala Śabdakoṣaya* (Colombo: Anula Pres, 1956)

Thag. *The Thera- and Theri-gāthā: (Stanzas Ascribed to Elders of the Buddhist Order of Recluses)*, ed. Hermann Oldenberg and Richard Pischel, 2d ed. (London: Published for the Pali Text Society, Luzac & Co., 1966).

ThagA. *Paramattha-Dīpanī Theragāthā-Aṭṭhakathā: The Commentary of Dhammapālācariya*, Vols. I–III, ed. F. L. Woodward (London: Published for the Pali Text Society, Vol. I Oxford University Press, 1940, Vols. II–III, Luzac & Co., 1952, 1959).

Thig. *The Thera- and Theri-gāthā: (Stanzas Ascribed to Elders of the Buddhist Order of Recluses)*, ed. Hermann Oldenberg and Richard Pischel, 2d ed. (London: Published for the Pali Text Society, Luzac & Co. 1966).

Ud. *Udāna*, ed. Paul Steinthal (London: Published for the Pali Text Society, Oxford University Press, 1948).

UdA. *Paramattha-Dīpanī Udānaṭṭhakathā (Udāna Commentary) of Dhammapālācariya*, ed. F. L. Woodward (London: Published for the Pali Text Society, Oxford University Press, 1926).

Uj. *Upāsakajanālaṅkāra*, ed. H. Saddhatissa (London: Published for the Pali Text Society, Luzac & Co., 1965).

VbhA. *Sammoha-vinodanī Abhidhamma-Piṭake Vibhangaṭṭhakathā*, ed. A. P. Buddhadatta (London: Published for the Pali Text Society, Oxford University Press, 1923).

Vin. *The Vinaya Piṭakam*, Vols. I–V, ed. Hermann Oldenberg (London: Published for the Pali Text Society, Luzac & Co., 1964).

Vism. *Visuddhimagga of Buddhaghosācariya*, ed. Henry Clarke Warren, revised by Dharmananda Kosambi, Harvard Oriental Series, 41 (Cambridge, Mass.: Harvard Unversity Press, 1950).

Vv. *The Vimāna-Vatthu: of the Khuddaka Nikāya Sutta Piṭaka*, ed. Edmund Rowland Gooneratne (London: Published for the Pali Text Society, Oxford University Press, n.d. [1886?]).

VvA. *Dhammapāla's Paramattha-Dīpanī*, Part IV, Being the Commentary on the *Vimāna-Vatthu*, ed. E. Hardy (London: Published for the Pali Text Society, Oxford University Press, 1901).

NOTES

INTRODUCTION

1. Willard G. Oxtoby, "Editor's Introduction," *Religious Diversity: Essays by Wilfred Cantwell Smith* (New York: Harper and Row, 1976), p. vii.

2. Wilfred Cantwell Smith, *The Meaning and End of Religion: A New Approach to the Religious Traditions of Mankind* (New York: Macmillan Company, 1963), p. 22. Smith notes that with Cicero (106–43 B.C.) one finds *religio* used in a personalistic way. "Here," Smith writes, "*religio* is an attitude" (ibid., p. 23). This work has been reprinted as a Mentor Book (published by The New American Library, 1964), see pages 24–25; and by Harper and Row (1978, with the subtitle changed on the paperback cover to "A Revolutionary Approach to the Great Religious Traditions" and dropped on the title page), see pages 22–23.

3. So the impressive arguments advanced by Smith in ibid., Chapter 5, "Is the Concept Adequate?" Chapter 6, "The Cumulative Tradition," and Chapter 7, "Faith."

4. Particularly with regard to Sri Lanka, until recently an idyllic setting for the flourishing of the Theravāda tradition including, of course, modifications and new ventures in the latter part of this century, one is at something of a loss in finding an explanation for the recurring, lacerating upheavals and apparently unrelenting, vicious reprisals erupting between Tamils and Sinhalas and among Sinhalas of differing political leanings during these times. With a broken heart one seeks more immediately to heal, to find a basis for contributing

to the arising of peace and faithfulness. Another time, one trusts—profoundly so—will provide a less disruptive, more engaging, occasion for reflection in a quest for understanding what has occurred in the history of the Theravāda tradition in this island nation and what has transpired in the life of Buddhist men and women living there during the decade of the 1980s and into the closing decade of this century.

5. Ibid. (1963 ed.), p. 189; (1964 ed.), pp. 170–171; (1978 ed.), p. 189.

6. Wilfred Cantwell Smith, "Objectivity and the Humane Sciences: A New Proposal," in *Religious Diversity,* p. 171.

7. Smith has also considered this case of disciplined self-consciousness, which he has also called *corporate critical self-consciousness*. He writes,

> By corporate critical self-consciousness I mean that critical, rational, inductive self-consciousness by which a community of persons, constituted at a minimum by two persons, the one being studied and the one studying, but ideally by the whole human race, is aware of any given particular human condition or action as a condition or action of itself as a community, yet of one part but not of the whole of itself; and is aware of it as it is experienced and understood simultaneously both subjectively (personally, existentially) and objectively (externally, critically, analytically; as one used to say, scientifically). (Ibid., p. 163)

8. Smith has written, "Students would do well to ask themselves, concerning any account or any project that they meet [or initiate], in which category it falls: impersonal/it [as one might study Buddhism], impersonal/they [as one might study them], we/they [as we might study Buddhists], we/you, we-both, or we-all." Wilfred Cantwell Smith, "Comparative Religion: Whither—and Why?" *The History of Religions: Essays in Methodology,* ed. Mircea Eliade and Joseph M. Kitagawa (Chicago: University of Chicago Press, 1959), p. 57. Our study will attempt to move in the area of "we/they" in the broader context of "we-both," "we-all."

CHAPTER 1

1. Wilfred Cantwell Smith, *The Meaning and End of Religion: A New Approach to the Religious Traditions of Mankind* (New York: Macmillan Company, 1963; Mentor Book, 1964; republished by Harper and Row, 1978).

2. Ibid., Chapter 5.

3. Ibid., Chapter 3.

4. Ibid. (1963 ed.), p. 58; (1964 ed.), p. 56 (1978 ed.), p. 58.

5. In 1896, the following sentences were published: "But what is meant by religion? The word, *as is well known* [my italics], is not found in languages not related to our own, and its derivation is uncertain" (T. W. Rhys Davids, *Buddhism: Its History and Literature*, American Lectures on the History of Religion, First Series, 1894–1895, New York: G. P. Putnam's Sons, 1896, p. 1).

6. See ibid., p. 38, where T. W. Rhys Davids, having decided to continue using the term *religion* and in the process to attempt to broaden its meaning in the light of the data drawn from other religious traditions, says: "But I have considered it my duty to bring out into as clear a relief as possible the points most essential to a right understanding of what we [*sic*] call Buddhism, and what the founder of that religion called the Dhamma, that is the Law, or the Norm." In 1903, T. W. Rhys Davids reminded his readers that "the people we now call Buddhists (they did not call themselves so) were concerned so exclusively with the Dhamma...that their doctrine was called the Dhamma" (*Buddhist India*; London: T. Fisher Unwin, 1903, p. 294). C. A. F. Rhys Davids, in 1932, noted that around 1802, about the time of the Treaty of Amiens, "the words Buddhism, Buddhist [she is speaking of English words knowing quite well that the Sanskrit term *bauddha* carries the force of "Buddhist"] came into use. It took some time before the spelling of these terms was settled" (*A Manual of Buddhism: For Advanced Students*; London: The Sheldon Press, 1932, p. 5).

7. A discussion of the term *samaya* occurs at *DhsA*., pp. 57ff. See *The Expositor* (*Atthasālinī*), vol. 1, trans. Pe Maung Tin, ed. and rev. Mrs. Rhys Davids (London: The Pali Text Society, 1958), pp. 76–82.

8. *The Dhammapada: A New English Translation with the Pali Text and the First English Translation of the Commentary's Explanation of the Verses with Notes Translated from Sinhala Sources and Critical Textual Comments,* by John Ross Carter and Mahinda Palihawadana (New York: Oxford University Press, 1987), v. 183, pp. 44, 243–244. It is possible that this verse constituted a part of what might have been an early form of the *pāṭimokkha*, the disciplinary code of monastic rules. The verse also occurs in the *Mahāpadānasutta, D*.II.49.

9. See, for example, *Thag*., vv. 24, 181, 204, 212, 220; *Ud*., p. 57.

10. *Bu.*, III.23; See *ThagA.*, II.84 (on *Thag.*, v. 220); *ThagA.*, I.85 (on *Thag.* v. 24); *SA.* III.200. See also *Sdpj.*, I.147 (on *Nd.1.*, I.i.40 [on *Sn.*, 775]); *AA.*, III.170 (on *A.*, II.185).

11. *Sn.*, 933, 1084. *Nd.1.*, I.ii.399 (on *Sn.*, 933) glosses *sāsane Gotamassa* by noting "*Gotamasāsane buddhasāsane jinasāsane tathāgatasāsane devasāsane arahantasāsane*...."

12. See, for example, *UdA.*, p. 309 (on *Ud.*, p. 57). Note also that when *dhamma* is used as a designation for the thirty-seven "qualities that are constituents of enlightenment" (*bodhipakkhiyadhammā*), as at *S.*, III.96, the commentary (*SA.*, II.306) glosses *dhamma* as *sāsanadhamma*, and at *SA.*, III.200, *dhammavinaya* is considered a term designating the *sāsana* of the Teacher. See also *UdA.*, p. 309, where *sāsana* is glossed by reference to moral virtue, concentration, and salvific wisdom (*sīla, samādhi*, and *paññā*).

13. See, for example, *Thag.*, v. 181.

14. See *SnA.*, II.591 (on *Sn.*, 1056) where the commentator glosses "right here" with "in just this *sāsana* or in just this present existence." See also *SnA.*, II.433 (on *Sn.*, 536) where the gloss is "who, in this *sāsana*...."

15. Some Sinhala Buddhists have suggested that *brahmacariya* parallels the notion "religion." See Smith, *The Meaning and End of Religion*, note 19 to Chapter 3 (1963 ed.), p. 249; (1964 ed.), p. 240; (1978 ed.), p. 249.

16. See *SnA.*, II.489 (on *Sn.* 693).

17. *SnA.*, I.163 (on *Sn.*, 87): "'*idh' eva sāsane ayam dhammo na ito bahiddā' ti.*" The commentary takes *dhamma* as both *nibbāna* and the path, *magga*.

18. *Mhv.*, XI.34. This passage is quoted at *PūjaV.*, p. 759. See *MhvT.*, pp. 307–308.

19. "...*budusasnehi śraddhāvanta upāsikāvarun*...." *PūjaV.*, p. 365. On the notion of demonstrating a quality of faith in the *sāsana*, see also *Cūl.*, I.54, v. 17, "...*so rājā pasanno buddhasāsane*...." and *Cūl.*, II.90, v. 36. See Rērukāne Candavimala, *Pāramitā Prakaraṇaya* (Maradana, Colombo: Anula Press, 1966), p. 232, where he notes the *buddhasāsana* is composed of *bhikkṣus*, *bhikṣunīs*, *upāsakas*, *upāsikās*.

20. See *Mhbv.*, p. 86, and also *Cūl.*, II.89, v. 70.

21. See the parallel glosses for "honors *dhamma*" and "delight in the *sāsana*" at *DAG.*, (1967), p. 12; (1974), pp. 12–13 (on *DhpA.*, I.17).

22. As at *DAG.*, (1967), p. 29 (1974), p. 31 (on *DhpA.*, I.56) and *DAG.*, (1967), p. 37 (1974), p. 39 (on *DhpA.*, I.92).

23. *Mhbv.*, p. 91; *Sdhs.*, p. 24.

24. I am aware that the *Mahāvaṃsa* is the technically correct title for the entire work but, because the references are to the PTS edition, I have kept W. Geiger's divisions of *Mahāvaṃsa* and *Cūlavaṃsa.*

25. This, of course, is not to say such tendencies are met at every occurrence of the term *sāsana.* At *Cūl.*, I.44, v. 110, a king gives an order, *sāsana,* and four verses later, v. 114, it is said he went forth into the *sāsana.*

26. *Mhv.*, XXV.1–3.

27. *Cūl.*, I.38, v. 37.

28. Wilhelm Geiger, *Cūl. Tr.*, Part I, note 1, p. 32. Burlingame was also aware of some shift in the import of *sāsana* and chose to translate it with "religion" in *Buddhist Legends* (Cambridge, Mass.: Harvard University Press, 1921, reprinted in 1969), I.149, and on page 151 he proposed "the Religion of the Buddha" for *buddhasāsana.* He was translating from *DhpA.*, I.7 and *DhpA.*, I.11, respectively. Walpola Rahula, *History of Buddhism in Ceylon* (Colombo: Gunasena, 1966), p. 104, interprets the cleansing of the *sāsana,* as mentioned in the *Mahāvaṃsa* (*Cūlavaṃsa*), I.39, v. 57; I.44, v. 46, as "the purification (*sodhana*) of the *Sāsana* (religion)."

29. See his *Cūl. Tr.*, Part I, p. 78 (a translation of *Cūl.*, I.44, v. 46).

30. See *Miln.*, pp. 133–134; *DA.*, III.898 (on *D.*, III. 114); *SA.*, II.201–202 (on *S.* II.224); *AA.*, I.87ff; *VbhA.*, pp. 431–432; *ThagA.*, III. 89 (on *Thag.*, v. 977).

31. See *M.*, I.374.

32. *D.*, II.125. The commentary, *DA.*, II.566, provides no gloss on the term. For other references see under *āgama* in *PTSD.*, 95a.

33. *DhpA.*, III.272: *āgamādhigamasampannam.* The *DAG.*, the tenth-century Sinhala commentary on the *Dhammapada* commentary (1967), p. 2 (1974), p. 2, clearly treats *āgama* as authoritative texts.

34. *VvA.*, as quoted in the *Vimāna-vatthu* ed. E. R. Goonaratne (London: PTS edition, 1896), p. vii. See *Dhammapāla's Paramattha-Dīpanī*, Part IV, *Being the Commentary on the Vimānavatthu*, ed. E. Hardy (London: PTS edition, 1901), p. 3. One would want to note, also, the use of *āgama* at *Cūl.*, I.44.109, *sajjhāyitva ca āgamam*, "and having recited the authoritative texts" (Geiger, at *Cūl. Tr.*, Part I, p. 84, takes it here as "sacred texts").

35. His title at this time was Atapattu Mudaliyār.

36. E. R. Goonaratne's translation of the opening section of *VvA.* in his edition of *Vv.*, p. xi.

37. *Journal of the Pali Text Society*, ed. T. W. Rhys Davids (London: Published for the Pali Text Society by Henry Frowde, 1982), p. 21.

38. Ibid., p. 25: "*Garu kata yutu āgama dharmayak....*" It is difficult to determine the precise meaning of this compound, *āgama* + *dharma*, so used over a century ago. I think the *bhikkhu* was working from the context of *pariyattidhamma*, "*dhamma* that is to be taken up, learned and held in mind," that is, the authoritative text, as he was writing to the president of the Pali Text Society and also because *pariyatti* and *āgama* can be used interchangeably. The use of the Sinhala indefinite form, *-dharmayak*, rather than the definite, can be explained by the context in which he wrote the letter, that is, to European scholars. However, it is possible that *āgamadharmaya* might represent an early attempt to catch the concept "religion."

39. I refer to the 1966 reprint, *PTSD.*, p. 95a. The work was first published in fascicles 1921–1925, and Part II of fascicle A–O was first published in 1922.

40. Charles Carter, *A Sinhalese-English Dictionary* (Colombo: Gunasena, 1965), p. 87a. This work was first published by the Baptist Missionary Society, 1924. Rev. Carter died in 1914.

41. Some of the more famous debates were those held at Vāragoḍa (1865), Baddēgama (1865), Liyangēmullē (1866), Udanviṭa (1866), Gampala (1871), Pānadura (1873), and Urugoḍavattē in Colombo (1899).

42. See, e.g., *Udanviṭa vādaya hā baddēgama vādaya* (Vällampitiya: T. S. Dharmabandu, Navajīvana Press, 1947); *Gampala vādaya* (Vällampitiya: T. S. Dharmabandu, Navajīvana Press, 1947); *Pānadurē vādaya* (Maradana, Colombo: Lanka Free Press, n.d.); *Buddhism and Christianity: Being an Oral Debate Held at Panadura...Introduction and Annotations*, J. M. Peebles (Colombo, n.d.).

43. See, e.g., *Udanviṭa vādaya*, pp. 11, 20; *Gampala vādaya*, pp. 19, 41; *Pānadurē vādaya*, pp. 24, 81.

44. See, e.g., *Udanviṭa vādaya*, p. 11; *Pānadurē vādaya*, pp. 24, 81.

45. *Udanviṭa vādaya*, pp. 10, 12, 14, 15, 17–24, 26, 27. Forming the second part of this same volume, with pagination beginning again, is the account of *Baddēgama vādaya*. See this section, pp. 1, 2, 4, 5, 16. *Gampala vādaya*, pp. 9, 11, 12, 14, 21, 22, 25–31, 35–41. *Pānadurē vādaya*, pp. 1, 2, 4–5, 7–8, 13–16, 18–19, 21–22, 24–25, 29, 34–37, 40–43, 49–51, 54–56, 58, 60, 64, 66, 68–69, 73, 79–80, 82–85, and possibly elsewhere.

46. *Pānadurē vādaya*, pp. 21, 41 (*buddhāgamē asatyakama*).

47. Ibid., pp. 14, 15, 16, 18 (*kristiyāni āgamē asatyatāva*).

48. Ibid., p. 19 (*buddhāgamē...satyatāvat....*).

49. Ibid., pp. 35, 83 (*boru āgamak*).

50. Ibid., p. 58 (*kristiyāni āgama säbä āgamak*).

51. Ibid., p. 83 (*buddhāgama satyāgamak*).

52. Ven. Pandit W. Sorata Nayaka Thera, *Śrī Sumaṅgala Śabdakoṣaya*, Part I, second edition (Colombo: Anula Press, 1963), p. 123b.

53. Ibid., p. xlii (*kathāvyavahārayehi eyi*).

54. Ven. Pandit W. Sorata Thera, *Śrī Sumaṅgala Śabdakoṣaya*, Part II (Colombo: Anula Press, 1956), p. 657a.

55. Jayasēkara Abēruvan, *Buddhāgama: Ihaḷa bālāṃsaya* (Colombo: M. D. Gunasēna, 1963); Jayasēkara Abēruvan, *Buddhāgama: Tunvana śrēṇiya* (Colombo: M. D. Gunasēna, 1968); S. F. de Silvā, E. R. Eratna, S. Vanigatunga, *Buddhadharmaya: Ihaḷa bālāṃsaya* (Colombo: Sri Lanka Prakāśaka, 1964). Of course there are others, but these three texts might provide an adequate example.

56. Abēruvan, *Buddhāgama: Ihaḷa bālāṃsaya*, p. 1. (*Buddhāgama apē āgama yi. Apa kata-yutu karannē buddhāgama anuva yi. Apata buddhāgamata vadā usas deyak nä.*)

57. Abēruvan, *Buddhāgama: Tunvana śrēṇiya* (third level), p. 1. (*Bauddhayangē usas ma vastuva budun, daham, sangun. E tamā apagē ruvan tuna hevat tunuruvana....*)

58. De Silva, Eratna, and Vanigatunga, *Buddhadharmaya: Ibaḷa bālām-saya*, p. 1. (*Api teruvan yayi kiyannē* (i) *apē budu hāmuduruvanta* (ii) *unva-hansēgē dharmayata yi* (iii) *sanghayā vahansēta yi. Mē tamā buddhāgamē teruvana.*)

59. I find it disquieting that the two booklets by Abēruvan seem to introduce a child in the first grade to something called *Buddhism* rather than something called *compassion* (*karuṇāva*) or *gift* (*dānaya*); that before children recite in unison the three gems, they become aware wherein they differ from other children in Sri Lanka.

60. Walpola Sri Rahula, *What the Buddha Taught*, 2d and enlarged ed. (Bedford, England: Gordon Fraser, 1967), p. 5. This work was originally published for a Western audience, in English, in 1959. Two years later it appeared in French, and in 1963 there was a German edition. Not until 1965, six years after the first publication, did the work appear in Sinhala.

61. I should point out that the question Rahula often asked probably has been raised more frequently in the West than in Sri Lanka. During a three year stay in Sri Lanka, and more recent visits, I have heard the question asked a few times and on every occasion by schoolchildren. A leading Buddhist philosopher today was stunned when he, in 1970, was asked, at the close of a talk at a *pansala*, whether *buddhadharma* was an *āgama* or a *darśana*. He replied that it was neither and both. Rahula's book will probably continue to give rise to the question. In spite of his comments in the passage under consideration, he uses the phrase "according to Buddhist philosophy," ibid., p. 23, which his translator takes as *bauddha darśanayata*. Walpola Rahula, *Budun vadāla dharmaya*, 3d ed. of the work first published in Sinhala in 1965 (Colombo: M. D. Gunasēna, 1970), p. 34. See also p. 31, *Bauddha darśanayē* for "in Buddhist Philosophy," English ed., p. 21.

62. Rahula, *What the Buddha Taught*, p. 5; Rahula, *Budun vadāla dharmaya*, p. 8.

63. *The Ceylon Government Gazette*, Extraordinary, No. 14, 1947/3—Saturday, 27 February 1971, p. 102/9. Basic Resolution 5 (iv) reads: "Every citizen shall have the right to freedom of thought, conscience and religion. This right shall include freedom to have or to adopt a religion or belief of his choice, and freedom, either individually or in community with others and in public or private, to manifest his religion or belief in worship, observance, practice and teaching" (ibid., p. 102/10). Under Proposed Amendments to the Basic Resolu-

tions, J. R. Jayewardene and Dudley Senanayake proposed the addition of "(a) the words 'inviolable and be' between the words 'shall be' and 'given' in line 2; (b) the words 'its rites, Ministers and places of worship' immediately after the words 'foster Buddhism' and before the words 'while assuring'" (ibid., p. 102/11). S. J. V. Chelvanayakam proposed an alternative resolution, that the "Republic of Sri Lanka shall be a secular State but shall protect and foster Buddhism, Hinduism, Christianity and Islam" (ibid.). The Sinhala word used to translate Chelvanayakam's "secular" is *lokāyata*, which is probably more recent, in this usage, than Sinhala terms for *religion* and *Buddhism*. See *Andukrama sampādaka maṅḍalayē tyāya patraya*, 30 March 1971, p. 22. The word *lokāyata* traditionally meant "having to do with the mundane, the world" and has designated the Carvaka school of materialistic thought.

64. A portion of the Sinhala translation of S. J. V. Chelvanayakam's substitute proposal mentioned in the previous note reads "*bauddhāgama hindu āgama kristiyāni āgama saha islām āgama.*"

CHAPTER 2

1. I refer to the third edition of the *Encyclopaedia Britannica*, vol. 3, p. 762b.

2. See the parallel note by Wilfred Cantwell Smith, *The Meaning and End of Religion: A New Approach to the Religious Traditions of Mankind*, note 36 to Chapter 3 (New York: Macmillan Company, 1963), p. 253; (New York: Mentor Books, New American Library, 1964), pp. 245–246; (New York: Harper and Row, 1978), p. 253.

3. Isaac Jacob Schmidt, *Ueber die Verwandtschaft der gnostisch-theosophischen Lehren mit den Religionssystemen des Orients vorzuglich dem Buddhaismus* (Leipzig, 1828). See Smith, ibid.

4. Brian Houghton Hodgson, *Sketch of Buddhism, derived from the Bauddha Scriptures of Nepal* (London: J. L. Cox, 1828).

5. Edward Upham, *The History and Doctrine of Buddhism, popularly illustrated; with notices of the Kappooism, or Demon worship, and of the Bali, or planetary incantations of Ceylon* (London: R. Ackermann, 1829).

6. E. Burnouf, *Introduction à l'histoire du buddhisme indien* (Paris: Imprimerie Royale, 1844). Note that in 1831 Jean Jacques Bochinger wrote a

book entitled *La vie contemplative, ascetique et monastique ches les Indous et chez les peuples bouddhistes* (Strasbourg, 1831), and the way he chose a title to reflect a way of life among people.

7. Felix Neven, *De l'état présent des études sur le Bouddhisme et de leur application* (Ghent, 1846).

8. Robert Spence Hardy, *A Manual of Buddhism in its Modern Development*; translated from Sinhalese MSS. (London, 1853).

9. Felix Neven, *Le Bouddhisme, son fondateur et ses écritures* (Paris, 1853)

10. See V. Vassilief (Vasily Pavolovich Vasiliev), *Der Buddhismus, seine Dogmen, Geschichte und Literatur...aus dem Russischen übersetzt* (St. Petersburg, 1860). This work was also translated into French as *Le Bouddhisme ses dogmes, sa histoire et sa littérature*, trans. M. G. A. La Comme (Paris, 1865).

11. T. W. Rhys Davids, *Buddhism: Being a Sketch of the Life and Teachings of Gautama Buddha* (London, 1877).

12. Reginald Stephen Copleston, *Buddhism, Primitive and Present in Magadha and in Ceylon* (London: Longmans, Green, 1892).

13. Joseph Dahlmann, *Nirvāna. Eine Studie zur Vorgeschichte des Buddhismus* (Berlin, 1896).

14. T. W. Rhys Davids, *Buddhism. Its History and Literature* (London: G. P. Putnam's Sons, 1896).

15. H. C. Warren, *Buddhism in Translations*, Harvard Oriental Series, vol. 3 (Cambridge, Mass.: Harvard University Press, 1896).

16. J. L. Sawyer, *Buddhisme populaire* (Paris, 1897).

17. Paulo Emilio Pavolini, *Buddhismo* (Milano, 1898).

18. A. Lillie, "Buddha and Buddhism," in *The World's Epoch Makers*, ed. William Henry Oliphant (Edinburgh: T. & T. Clark, 1900).

19. Manmathanatha Datta, *Buddha: his life, his teaching, his order, together with the history of the Buddhism* (Calcutta: Society for the Resuscitation of Indian Literature, 1901).

20. P. Lakshmī-Narasu, *The Essence of Buddhism* (Madras: Srinivasa Varadachari and Co., 1907).

21. Daisetz Teitaro Suzuki, *Outlines of Mahāyāna Buddhism* (London: Luzac and Co., 1907).

22. Warren, *Buddhism in Translations.*

23. Lakshmī-Narasu, *Essence of Buddhism.* See also Edward [Eberhard Julius Dietrich] Conze, *Buddhism: Its Essence and Development* (Oxford: Bruno Cassirer, 1951).

24. Bhikkhu Ñānatiloka, *The Quintessence of Buddhism...A Lecture etc.* (Colombo: Sinhala Samaya Press, 1913).

25. Kenneth James Saunders, *The Heart of Buddhism: an anthology of Buddhist verse* (London: Oxford University Press, 1915).

26. Hari-Simha Gauda, *The Spirit of Buddhism: being an examination of the life of the founder of Buddhism, his religion and philosophy* (London: Luzac, 1929).

27. Theodor Ippolitovich Shcherbatskoi [Stcherbatsky], *The Central Conception of Buddhism and the Meaning of the Word "Dharma"* (London: RAS [The Royal Asiatic Society] of Great Britain and Ireland, 1923).

28. T. R. V. Murti, *The Central Philosophy of Buddhism: A Study of the Mādhyamika System* (London: George Allen & Unwin, 1955).

29. For some, the term *Pāli Buddhism* has been used to demarcate the scope of their work. See H. H. Tilbe, *Pāli Buddhism* (Rangoon: American Baptist Mission Press, 1900); Carl Seidenstuecker, *Pāli-Buddhismus in Übersetzungen* (Wroclaw, 1911); and note S. Tachibana, "The Ethics of Pāli Buddhism" (Oxford, Ph.D. thesis, 1922); E. R. de S. Sarathchandra, "The Psychology of Perception in Pāli Buddhism, with Special Reference to the Theory of Bhavanga" (London, Ph.D. thesis, 1948).

30. J. Bird, *Historical Researches on the Origin and Principles of the Bauddha and Jaina Religions* (Bombay: American Mission Press, 1847). See also de Alwis, *Buddhism: Its Origin, History and Doctrines, Its Scriptures, and Their Language, the Pali* (Colombo, 1862–1863).

31. Léon de Milloue, *Le bouddhisme dans le monde. Origine-dogmas-histoire...* (Paris, 1893); H. Oldenberg, *Die Lehr der Upanishaden und die Anfänge des Buddhismus* (Göttingen, 1915); C. A. F. Rhys Davids, *Śakya; or Buddhist Origins* (London: Kegan Paul, Trench, Trübner and Co., 1931); and the same author's *What was the Original Gospel in Buddhism?* (London:

Epworth Press, 1938); Govind Chandra Pande, *Studies in the Origins of Buddhism* (Allahabad: University of Allahabad, 1957).

32. See T. W. Rhys Davids, *Lectures on the Origin and Growth of Religion as Illustrated by Some Points in the History of Indian Buddhism* (London: Williams and Norgate, 1881); and note. A. J. Dadson, *Evolution and Its Bearing on Religions* (London, 1901); J. Buchan, *The First Things: Studies in the Embryology of Religion* (Edinburgh, 1902); K. D. Doyle, *The Real Origin of Religion* (London, 1902); F. Bierer, *The Evolution of Religions* (New York: Putnam's, 1906); A. E. Crawley, *Origin and Function of Religion* (London, 1907); R. Kreglinger, *Études sur l'origine et la developpement de la vie religieuse* (Brussels, 1919). Now, note the way the following works reflect a common orientation. R. Kimura, *The Origin and Developed Doctrines of Indian Buddhism, in Charts* (Calcutta, 1920); E. W. Hopkins, *Origin and Evolution of Religion* (New Haven, Conn., 1923); G. F. Moore, *The Birth and Growth of Religion* (Edinburgh, 1923); A. Churchward, *Origin and Evolution of Religion* (London: Allen and Unwin, 1924); Jean Przyluski, "Origin and Development of Buddhism," *The Journal of Theological Studies* (October 1934).

33. I refer to the ninth edition of the *Encyclopaedia Britannica* (1876), vol. 4, p. 432a. This was nearly fifty years after the works of I. J. Schmidt, *Ueber die Verwandtschaft...dem Buddhaismus* and B. H. Hodgson, *Sketch of Buddhism,* were published in 1828. And note that "Buddhism" occurred in the seventh edition of the *Encyclopaeia Britannica* (1842), vol. 5, p. 637a, and again in the eighth edition (1854), vol. 5, p. 724a.

34. Arthur Lillie, *Buddha and early Buddhism* (London: Trübner and Co., 1881).

35. Elizabeth A. Read, *Primitive Buddhism: Its Origin and Teachings* (Chicago: Scott and Foresman, 1896). See also Reginal Stephen Copleston, *Buddhism, Primitive and Present in Magadha and in Ceylon* (London: Longmans, Green, 1892).

36. G. de Lorenzo, *India e Buddhismo antico* (Bari, 1904). See also L. de La Vallée Poussin, *The Way to Nirvāna: Six Lectures on Ancient Buddhism as a Discipline of Salvation* (Cambridge: Cambridge University Press, 1917).

37. T. W. Rhys Davids, *Early Buddhism* (London: Archibald Constable and Co., 1908).

38. Sukumara Datt [Sukumar Dutt], "The Vinayapitakam and Early Bud-

dhist Monasticism in Its Growth and Development," *Journal of the Department of Letters*, Calcutta University, no. 10 (1923), *Early Buddhist Monachism, 600 B.C.*–100 B.C. (London: Kegan Paul, 1924).

39. Nalinaksha Datta [Dutt], *Early History of the Spread of Buddhism and the Buddhist Schools* (London: Luzac and Co., 1925).

40. I. B. Horner, *Women under Primitive Buddhism: Laywomen and Almswomen* (London: Routledge, 1930).

41. Vimalā-Charana Lāhā [B. C. Law], *Geography of early Buddhism* (London: Kegan Paul, Trench, Trübner, 1932).

42. Vimalā-Charana Lāhā [B. C. Law], *Caste in early Buddhism* (Guernsey, England, 1934), originally published in an article by the same title in *Buddhism in England*, later *The Middle Way* (1933), vol. 8.

43. E. J. Thomas, *Early Buddhist Scriptures* (London: Kegan Paul, 1935).

44. I. B. Horner, "An Aspect of Becoming in early Buddhism," *The Indian Historical Quarterly*, Calcutta, 12, no. 2., (June 1936): 282–286.

45. I. B. Horner, *The Early Buddhist Theory of Man Perfected: A Study of the Arahan* (London: Williams and Norgate, 1936).

46. D. N. Bhāgavata, *Early Buddhist Jurisprudence: Theravāda Vinaya-Laws* (Poona, 1939).

47. J. Kashyap, *The Abhidhamma Philosophy: The Psycho-Ethical Philosophy of early Buddhism*, 2 vols. (Sarnath: Maha Bodhi Society, 1942, 1943).

48. I. B. Horner, "Some Aspects of Movement in early Buddhism," *Artibus Asiae* 10, no. 2 (1947): 138–141.

49. I. B. Horner, "Early Buddhist Dhamma," *Artibus Asiae* 11, nos. 1–2 (1948): 115–123.

50. W. S. Karunaratne, "The Development of the Theory of Causality in Early Theravāda Buddhism," Ph.D. thesis, University of London, 1956. See also David J. Kalupahana, "A Critical Analysis of the Early Buddhist Theory of Causality as Embodied in the Pāli Nikāyas and the Chinese Agamas," Ph.D. thesis, University of London, 1967.

51. Anagarika Brahmacari Govinda, *The Psychological Attitude of Early Buddhist Philosophy*... (London: Rider and Company, 1961).

52. I. B. Horner, ed., *Early Buddhist Poetry; An Anthology* (Colombo: Ananda Semage, 1963).

53. Kulatissa Nanda Jayatilleke, *Early Buddhist Theory of Knowledge* (London: George Allen and Unwin, 1963).

54. J. W. de Jong, "The Background of early Buddhism," *Journal of Indian and Buddhist Studies*, Tokyo, 12, no. 50 (January 1964): 34–37.

55. A. K. Warder, "On the Relationship Between early Buddhism and Other Contemporary Systems," *Bulletin of the School of Oriental and African Studies* 18 (1965): 43–63; see also Kashi N. Upadhyaya, *Early Buddhism and the Bhagavadgita* (Delhi: Motilal Banarsidass, 1971).

56. Donald Swearer, "Knowledge as Salvation: A Study of Early Buddhism," Ph.D. thesis, Princeton University, 1965.

57. B. G. Gokhale, "Early Buddhist Kingship," *Journal of Asian Studies* 26 (1966–1967): 23–36.

58. B. G. Gokhale, "The Early Buddhist View of the State," *Journal of the American Oriental Society* 89, no. 4 (October–December 1969): 731–738.

59. James P. McDermott, "Developments in the Early Buddhist Concepts of Kamma/Karma," Ph.D. thesis, Princeton University, 1971.

60. Note the title of Frank Reynolds's important bibliographical essay, "From Philology to Anthropology: A Bibliographical Essay on Works Related to Early, Theravāda and Sinhalese Buddhism," in *The Two Wheels of Dhamma: Essays on the Theravāda Tradition in India and Ceylon*, ed. B. L. Smith (Chambersburg, Pa.: American Academy of Religion, 1972).

61. See William Peiris, *The Western Contribution to Buddhism* (Delhi: Motilal Banarsidass, 1973).

62. Since first writing this, I have had the delightful opportunity of being associated with responses to this and closely related questions made by leading Sinhala Buddhist scholars. See W. S. Karunatillake, "The Religiousness of Buddhists in Sri Lanka through Belief and Practice," in *Religiousness in Sri Lanka*, ed. John Ross Carter (Colombo: Marga Institute, 1979), pp. 1–34; the late S. L. Kekulawala, "The Religious Journey into *Dharma* (*Dharmayātrā*): Pilgrimage as an Expression of Buddhist Religiousness," ibid., pp. 35–65; G. D. Wijayawardhana, "Literature in Buddhist Religious Life," ibid., pp. 67–77; L. P. N. Perera, "The Significance of the Sangha for the Laity," ibid., pp. 79–100;

Hevanpola Ratanasara, "'Reaching Out' as an Expression of 'Going Forth'," ibid., pp. 101–111; Kannimahara Sumangala, "The Tradition Needs Review: An Examination of Possibilities of Refining Theravāda Interpretation," ibid., pp, 113–127; Mahinda Palihawadana, "*Dhamma* Today and Tomorrow," ibid., 129–147.

63. The book *Religiousness in Sri Lanka*, with which I had the delightful opportunity of being associated, some chapters from which were mentioned in the immediately preceding note, was the first attempt in which persons from the Buddhist, Hindu, Islamic and Christian communities in Sri Lanka wrote self-consciously and for each other about themes dealing with their own religious involvement. The book was translated into Sinhala by the translation staff of Marga Institute, as *Śrī Lankāvē Āgamika Bhāvaya* (Colombo: Marga Institute, 1985). Sensitive studies of the religious life of Hindus by Buddhists and of Buddhists by Hindus, and so forth, a series of colloquia involving religious persons from the several communities, are yet to appear in Sri Lanka. And, alas, with the lamentable strife in the country now one doubts we will soon see such a necessary process of understanding.

64. Heinz Bechert, *Buddhismus, Staat und Gesellschaft in den Ländern des Theravāda-Buddhismus*, Band XVII/1–3, der Schriften des Institute für Asienkunde in Hamburg (Berlin: XVII/1, Alfred Metzner Verlag, 1966; Wiesbaden: XVII/2–3, Otto Harrassowitz, 1967, 1973).

CHAPTER 3

1. John Ross Carter, *Dhamma: Western Academic and Sinhalese Buddhist Interpretations—a study of a religious concept* (Tokyo: Hokuseido Press, 1978).

2. Eugene Burnouf, *Introduction à l'histoire du buddhisme indien* (Paris: Imprimerie Royale, 1844), vol. 1 p. 80, n. 2. See also ibid., p. 283.

3. R. Spence Hardy, *Eastern Monachism: An Account of the Origin, Laws, Discipline, Sacred Writings, Mysterious Rites, Religious Ceremonies, and Present Circumstances of the Order of Mendicants founded by Gotama Budha* (London: Partridge and Oakey, 1850).

4. Robert Caesar Childers, *A Dictionary of the Pāli Language* (London: Trübner & Co., 1875), p. 118b.

5. T. W. Rhys Davids, *Buddhism: Being a Sketch of the Life and Teachings of Gautama, the Buddha,* Twentieth Thousand, a new and rev. ed., with map (London: Society for Promoting Christian Knowledge, 1903 [first published, 1877]), p. 45.

6. Hermann Oldenberg, *Buddha: sein Leben, seine Lehre, seine Gemeinde* (Berlin: Verlag von Wilhelm Hertz, 1881), "Lehre oder Wahrheit," at note 1, p. 256. This work was translated into English relatively quickly after its first German appearance by William Hoey as *Buddha: His Life, His Doctrine, His Order* (London: Williams and Norgate, 1882).

7. Caroline A. F. Rhys Davids, trans., *A Buddhist Manual of Psychological Ethics: Of the Fourth Century* B.C., a translation of the *Dhammasaṅganī*, Oriental Translation Fund, new series, vol. 12 (London: Royal Asiatic Society, 1900), p. xxxiii.

8. Mrs. Rhys Davids, *Buddhism: A Study of the Buddhist Norm,* Home University Library (London: Williams and Norgate, n.d. [1912?]).

9. Hermann Beckh, *Buddhismus: Buddha und seine Lehre,* 2d ed. (Berlin: G. Göschensche Verlagshandlung, vol. 1, 1919; vol 2, 1920; first published in 1916 [vol. 1] and 1919 [vol. 2]), vol. 1, p. 20, n. 1.

10. Magdalene und Wilhelm Geiger, *Pāli Dhamma: vornehmlich in der kanonischen Literatur,* Abhandlungen der Bayerischen Akademie der Wissenschaften; Philosophisch-philologische und historische Klasse (Munich: Verlag der bayerischen Akademie der Wissenschaften, 1920), vol. 31, p. 1.

11. Ibid., p. 7.

12. Ibid.

13. Wilhelm Geiger, "Dhamma und Brahman," *Zeitschrift für Buddhismus* 3, no 2 (March 1921): 73–74.

14. P. Masson-Oursel, "Note sur l'acception, à travers la civilisation indienne, du mot dharma," *Journal Asiatique* 29, no. 2 (1922): 269–275.

15. Paul Oltramare, *L'histoire des idées théosophiques dans l'Inde,* vol. 2, *La théosophie bouddhique*, Part. III, Chapter 1, "Le Dharma bouddhique," vol. 31, Annales du Musée Guimet: bibliothèque bouddhique d'études (Paris: Librairie orientaliste Paul Geuthner, 1923), pp. 462–478.

16. Otto Rosenberg, *Die Probleme der buddhistischen Philosophie,* Mate-

rialien zur Kunde des Buddhismus, nos. 7–8, herausgegeben von M. Walleser (Heidelberg and Leipzig: Kommission bei O. Harrassowitz, 1924); trans. from the Russian [published originally in Russian in 1918] Frau E. Rosenberg).

17. Theodor Ippolitovich Shcherbatskoi [Stcherbatsky], *The Central Conception of Buddhism and the Meaning of the Word "Dharma"* (London: Royal Asiatic Society, 1923).

18. Mrs. Rhys Davids, *A Manual of Buddhism: For Advanced Students* (London: Sheldon Press, 1932), p. 166.

19. Mrs. Rhys Davids, *Buddhism: Its Birth and Dispersal*, The Home University Library of Modern Knowledge (London: Thornton Butterworth, 1934), p. 229.

20. Robert Lawson Slater, *Paradox and Nirvana: a study of religious ultimates with special reference to Burmese Buddhism* (Chicago: University of Chicago Press, 1951), p. 114.

21. Ibid., p. 63.

22. Ibid., p. 63, n. 76.

23. Winston L. King, *Buddhism and Christianity: Some Bridges of Understanding* (London: George Allen and Unwin, 1963), p. 38. King used the Sanskrit forms: Dharma, Karma, Nirvana.

24. Ibid., p. 45.

25. Ibid., p. 227.

26. Winston L. King, *A Thousand Lives Away: Buddhism in Contemporary Burma* (Oxford: Bruno Cassirer, 1964), p. 171.

27. Wilfred Cantwell Smith, "Religious Atheism? Early Buddhist and Recent American," *Milla wa-Milla*, no. 6 (December 1966), p. 10. This work has been reprinted in *Comparative Religion: The Charles Strong Trust Lectures 1961–70*, ed. John Bowman (Leiden: E. J. Brill, 1972), pp. 53–81. See also Smith's Chapter 2, "The Buddhist Instance: Faith as Atheist?" in *Faith and Belief* (Princeton: Princeton University Press, 1979), pp. 20–32.

28. Smith, "Religious Atheism?" ibid., pp. 10–11.

29. Ibid., p. 12.

30. See the *Sumaṅgala-vilasinī*, the commentary on the *Dīgha-nikāya*

(PTS edition; hereafter, *DA.*), I.99; the *Atthasālinī*, the commentary on the *Dhammasaṅganī* (PTS edition; hereafter, *DhsA.*), p. 38; *The Commentary on the Dhammapada: Dhammapadaṭṭhakathā* (PTS edition; hereafter, *DhpA.*), I.22; *Papañcasūdanī Majjhima-nikāyaṭṭhakathā;* the commentary on the *Majjhima-nikāya* (PTS edition; hereafter, *MA.*), I.17; *Madhuratthavilāsinī nāma Buddhavaṃsaṭṭhakathā* (PTS edition; hereafter, *BuA.*), p. 13.

31. See the preceding note and include the following: *Abhidhānappadīpikā nam Pālinighaṇḍuva*, ed. Moragallē Siri Ñāṇobhāsatissa Thera (Colombo: M. D. Gunasena, 1960), p. 156 (hereafter, *AdprP.*); *Abhidhānappadīpikā: or, Dictionary of the Pali Language*, ed. Waskaḍuwe Subhūti, 2d ed. (Colombo: Frank Luker, Acting Government Printer, 1883), p. 220 (hereafter, *AdprD.*); *Dharmapradīpikāva*, ed. Baddēgama Vimalavaṃsa Thera, 2d ed. (Colombo: M. D. Gunasena & Co., 1967, pp. 236–237 (hereafter *Dhpr.*).

32. See the previous two notes and include the following: W. Subhūti, *Abhidhānappadīpikāsūci: A Complete Index to the Abhidhānappadīpikā* (Colombo: H. C. Cottle, Acting Government Printer, 1893), pp. 183–184 (hereafter, *AdprS.*); Wälīviṭiyē Sorata Thera, *Śrī Sumaṅgala Śabdakoṣa* (Colombo: Anula Press, 1956), Part I, p. 481b (hereafter, *Śssk.*). I have presented these thirty-four definitions in "Traditional definitions of the term *dhamma*," *Philosophy East and West: A Quarterly of Asian and Comparative Thought* 26, no. 3 (July 1976): 329–337.

33. *BuA.*, p. 13.

34. *Dhpr.*, pp. 236–237.

35. See, for example, *DA.*, I.76, II.377, III.701; *MA.*, II.232; *Sāratthappakāsinī*, the commentary on the *Saṃyutta-nikāya* (PTS edition; hereafter, *SA.*), II.200; *Manorathapūranī*, the commentary on the *Aṅguttara-nikāya* (PTS edition; hereafter, *AA.*), I.52; *Paramatthadīpanī Theragāthaṭṭhakathā*, the commentary on the *Theragāthā* (PTS edition; hereafter, *ThagA.*), I.58; *DhpA.*, I.230.

36. *MA.*, I.163 (on *Majjhima-nikāya* I.34; hereafter, *M.*); see also *Puggala-paññatti-aṭṭhakathā*, the commentary on the *Puggalapaññatti* (PTS edition; hereafter, *PugA.*), pp. 197ff.

37. *Visuddhimagga of Buddhaghosācariya*, ed. Henry Clarke Warren, rev. Dharmananda Kosambi, Harvard Oriental Series 41 (Cambridge, Mass.: Harvard University Press, 1950), Chapter 7, paragraph 83, p. 179 (hereafter, *Vism.*).

38. *AA.*, III.325; *Paramattha-Dīpanī Udānaṭṭhakathā*: the commentary on the *Udāna* (PTS edition; hereafter, *UdA.*), pp. 293, 326; *SA.*, III.253; *ThagA.*, II.153; *Sutta-Nipāta Commentary: Being Paramatthajotikā II* (PTS edition; hereafter, *SnA.*), I.329.

39. *Dahampiyā Aṭuvā Gäṭapadaya*, ed. Mäda-Uyangoḍa Vimalakīrti Thera and Nähinnē Sominda Thera (Colombo: M. D. Gunasena, 1967), p. 2 (hereafter, *DAG.*); *Dahampiyā-aṭuvā-gäṭapadaya*, ed. D. E. Hettiaratchi, (Colombo: Press Board of the Sri Lanka University at the University Press, 1974), p. 2 (hereafter, *DAG.*).

40. *DA.*, III.898; *DhpA.*, II.31. See also *Niddesa 1: Mahāniddesa* (PTS edition; hereafter, *Nd. 1*), I.143; *SnA.*, II.536; *Saddhama-Pajjotikā*, the commentary on *Nd. 1.* (PTS edition; hereafter, *Sdpj.*), II.270, where the word *instruction* (*sāsana*) is interpreted in a parallel manner as "authoritative teaching" (*pariyatti*) and "practice" (*paṭipatti*).

41. See, for example, *Saddhamma-Saṃgaho*, ed. Nedimāle Saddhānanda, *Journal of the Pali Text Society* (1890): 65 [ca. fourteenth century A.D.]; *Saddharmaratnāvaliya*, ed. Kiriällē Ñāṇavimala Thera (Colombo: M. D. Gunasena, 1961) p. 458 (hereafter, *SdhRv.*) [ca. thirteenth century A.D.]; *Saddharmaratnākaraya*, ed. Kalupaluvāvē Devānanda Thera (Colombo: Ratnākara Pot Veḷaňda Śālāva, 1955), p. 63 (hereafter, *SdhRk.*) [ca. fifteenth century A.D.]; *Saddharmālaṅkāraya*, ed. Kiriällē Ñāṇavimala Thera (Colombo: M. D. Gunasena, 1954), pp. 20–22 (hereafter, *SdhAl.*) [ca. fourteenth century A.D.]; see also *Śrī Saddharmāvavāda Saṃgrahaya*, ed. Vēragoḍa Amaramoli Thera (Colombo: Ratnākara Mudraṇālayaya, 1956), pp. 2, 10, 249 (hereafter, *ŚsdhAv.*). This threefold structure is also applied in a parallel manner to "instruction" (*sāsana*). See *Vaṃsatthappakāsinī*, the commentary on the *Mahāvaṃsa* (PTS edition; hereafter, *MhvT.*), I.151 [ca. tenth–eleventh century A.D.].

42. *SdhAl.*, p. 20.

43. See my brief entry on this very interesting and important figure, "Buddhaghosa," *The Encyclopedia of Religion*, Mircea Eliade, editor in chief (New York: Macmillan Publishing Company, 1987), vol. 2, 332–333.

44. *Vism.*, Chapter 7, p. 176, paragraph 68; see also pp. 176–180, paragraphs 69–88.

45. *Upāsakajanālaṅkāra* (PTS edition; hereafter, *Uj.*), Chapter 1, paragraph 66.

46. See, for example, *Amāvatura*, ed. Welīviṭiyē Sorata Nāyaka Thera (Mt. Lavinia, Ceylon: Abhaya Prakāśakayō, 1960), p. 64 (hereafter, *AmaV.*) [ca. 1200 A.D.]; *Jātaka Aṭuvā Gäṭapadaya*, ed. Mäda-Uyangoḍa Vimalakīrti Thera and Nähinnē Sominda Thera (Colombo: M. D. Gunasena and Co., 1961), pp. 207, 422 (hereafter, *JaAg.*) [twelfth century A.D.]; *Daham Saraṇa*, ed. Kiriällē Ñāṇavimala Thera (Colombo: M. D. Gunasena, 1965), pp. 45, 91, 207 (hereafter, *DS.*) [twelfth century?]; *SdhRv.*, pp. 34, 138–139, 386–387, 458, 520, 712, 746, 1037 [thirteenth century?]; *SdhAl.*, pp. 19, 93, 105–106, 229, 418, 780 [fourteenth century A.D.], *SdhRk.*, pp. 61, 212, 266, 298, 531 [ca. 15th century A.D.]; *Purāṇasiṃhalabaṇapota*, ed. with a glossary Jinavara Dharmakīrti Śrī Ratanapāla Thera (Colombo: Mahabodhi Press, 1929), pp. 11, 50 (hereafter, *Psbp.*) [date uncertain]; *Saddharma Sārārtha Saṅgrahaya*, ed. Kiriällē Ñāṇavimala Thera (Colombo: M. D. Gunasena, 1957), pp. 42, 353, 442, 469 (hereafter, *SdhSS.*) [1726 A.D.]; *ŚsdhAv.*, pp. 2, 143, 468 [1773 A.D.].

47. See, for example, *SdhRv.*, pp. 34, 520; *SdhAl.*, pp. 19, 93, 106, 229, 418, 780; *SdhRk.*, pp. 61, 212, 266, 298, 531; *SdhSS.*, pp. 352–353, 442; *ŚsdhAv.*, pp. 2, 468.

48. Mapalagama Siri Somissara, *Bauddha Dharma Mārgaya*, 2d ed. (Colombo: Vijayasēna saha Sahōdarayō, 1967 1st ed., 1965?]), pp. 185–186; Rērukānē Candavimala, *Pohoya Dinaya* (Colombo: Anula Press, 1966), pp. 30, 32. Also see the following works by this same author: *Bauddhayāgē At Pota*, 5th ed. (Colombo: Anula Press, 1966 [fifth impression of the work first published in 1949]), p. 22; and *Sūvisi Maha Guṇaya* (Colombo: Anula Press, 1969 [1st ed., 1964]), pp. 429 *passim*. See, further, Kiriällē Ñānavimala, *Bauddha Ädahilla* (Colombo: M. D. Gunasena, 1957), p. 66. See further the article, "Dhamma Saraṇam Gacchāmi," signed Buddhaputra, in *Budusaraṇa, śrī bu. varṣa* 2514 *vū navam masa ava atavak pohoda*, no. 7, (Wednesday, February 17, 1971), p. 6. See, further, *Siṃhala Upāsaka Janālaṅkāraya*, ed. D. P. R. Samaranāyaka (Colombo: M. D. Gunasena, 1961), p. 51.

49. *MA.*, I.131. See also *AA.*, II.107–108; *Uj.*, Chapter 1, paragraph 66.

50. As have Mrs. Rhys Davids, *Buddhism: A Study of the Buddhist Norm*, p. 36, and Magdalene and Wilhelm Geiger, *Pāli Dhamma*, p. 7.

51. As did Wilfred Cantwell Smith, "Religious Atheism?" p. 11.

52. *DS.*, p. 1

53. Ibid., pp. 45, 56, 58, 64, 77.

54. Ibid., p. 48.

55. Ibid., p. 60: *Esē māgē svāmidaruvan visin aneka yatnayen sādhāgat saddharmaya mama ayatnayen ladimi.*

56. Ibid., p. 43: *Mahatun visin mē sā mahat yatnayakin patanalada saddharmaya apa visin ayatnayen pämiṇena lada....*

57. *Rasavāhinī*, ed. Kiriällē Ñāṇavimala Thera (Colombo: M. D. Gunasena and Co., 1961), p. 2. On page 94 of the *SdhAl.*, a Sinhala text of the fourteenth century, the three prosperities are noted with the foremost example of each: "human prosperity, such as a world ruling monarch (*cakravartin*), etc.; heavenly prosperity, such as Śakra's [Lord of the gods], etc.; the prosperity of *nirvāna*, that is, the attainment of perfect full enlightenment (*samyak-sambodhi*), etc."

58. *DS.*, pp. 189, 194, 196, 229, 244, 256, 264, 285; *Rasavāhinī*, ibid., p. 237.

59. *DS.*, pp. 68, 235, 238, 277–278, 299; *SdhAl.*, pp. 114, 147; *SdhRk.*, pp. 61, 62; *SdhRv.*, p. 961.

60. *Sutta-Nipāta* (PTS edition; hereafter, *Sn.*), v. 884: *Ekam hi saccam na dutīyam atthi...*

61. *Nd. 1.*, II.292.

62. *Vism.*, Chapter 16, p. 422, paragraph 26.

63. *Paramatthamañjūsā of Bhadantācariya Dhammapāla Thera: Or The Commentary of the Visuddhimagga*, ed. Morontuḍuwe Dhammānanda Thera, 3 vols. (Colombo: Mahabodhi Press, 1928, 1930, 1949), II.526 (hereafter, *Pm.*).

64. *Vism.*, chapter 7, p. 177, paragraph 74.

65. *DA.*, II.652, commenting on the *Dīgha-nikāya* (PTS edition; hereafter, *D.*), II.233.

CHAPTER 4

1. *Buddhaṃ saraṇaṃ gacchāmi*
dhammaṃ saraṇaṃ gacchāmi
samghaṃ saraṇaṃ gacchāmi (*Khp.*, p. 1)

I am aware that the absence of the definite article before the term *Dhamma* in the English translation will tend to strike an English reader, at first blush, as being somewhat unusual, possibly because of its presence before the other nouns in the threefold refuge and also because of its near standard presence in almost all books in English of and about Buddhists.

The main point at issue in my refraining from using the definite article here is that, within the English context, the definite article tends a little too directly toward specificity when used as the sole adjectival modifier of the term *Dhamma*. Part of the subtle and important force held in this term is that it becomes a notion that is discerned in nuance, in delicate connotations that are evoked when a Buddhist becomes engaged with an idea that points beyond itself. Further, *the Dhamma* might suggest particularization in the sense that *the Dhamma* becomes something that Buddhists have or that Buddhists do. However, Buddhists tend to avoid implications of possessiveness while averring that following Dhamma is eminently worthwhile. They have discerned through the term, idea, concept, notion, that which is universal and available to all persons, that which is not readily particularized.

The point might be seen rather quickly by drawing to our attention what others, who have written in English, have already sensed about the testimony of Buddhists: rarely will one see the definite article before *dukkha* (misery) or *paññā* (salvific insight wisdom), rarer still before *nibbāna*, when these terms stand alone without other accompanying, particularizing phrases. Apparently, these writers have discerned the Buddhist witness that these notions are relevant to all persons. The point is the same in the case of Dhamma.

I have continued to use the definite article before *Buddha* and *Sangha* because they both are particular proper nouns.

2. *Vin.*, I.4, referring to two male lay devotees, *upāsaka*s.

3. A reader is reminded of this early twofold formula in the commentary on the *Jātaka* (*JāA.*, I.80–81), in a thirteenth-century text, *Upāsakajanālaṅkāra*, ed. H. Saddhatissa (London: Published for the Pali Text Society, Luzac and Co., 1965), Chapter 1, p. 44; and in an eighteenth-century Sinhala text, the *Śrī Saddharmāvavāda Saṃgrahaya*, ed. Vēragoḍa Amaramoli Thera (Colombo: Ratnākara Mudraṇālayaya, 1956), p. 77. A Sinhala glossary of the *Jātaka* commentary, the *Jātaka Aṭuvā Gäṭapadaya*, ed. Mäda-Uyangoḍa Vimalakīrti Thera and Nähinnē Sominda Thera (Colombo: M. D. Gunasēna and Co., 1961), p. 47 (on *JāAg.*, I.81.1) dated possibly in the twelfth century, provides an obvious explanation for the twofold formula, "because the Sangha-gem had not arisen in the world."

4. *Vin.*, I.16–17, referring to a male lay devotee (*upāsaka*), and, ibid., p. 18, referring to a female lay devotee (*upāsikā*).

5. See, for example, *SnA.*, I.216 (on *Sn.*, v. 180); *SA.*, I.81 (on *S.*, I.215).

6. See the chapter by Edmund F. Perry and Shanta Ratnayaka, "The Sangha as Refuge in the Theravāda Buddhist Tradition," in *The Threefold Refuge in the Theravāda Buddhist Tradition*, ed. John Ross Carter (Chambersburg, Pa.: Anima Books, 1982), pp. 41–55.

7. *KhpA.*, p. 170 (on the *Ratanasutta*, see also *Sn.*, v. 224).

8. *MA.*, I.131–132. See also *AA.*, II.108–112; *DA.*, I.229–234; and *KhpA.*, pp. 16–17. I have chosen to follow the *MA.* account (which is the same as those in *AA.* and *DA.*) because it is more concise than the *KhpA.* The commentarial explanation in *MA.* has been rather freely translated into English by Nyānaponika Thera as *The Threefold Refuge* in The Wheel Series, no. 76 (Kandy, Ceylon [Sri Lanka]: Buddhist Publication Society, 1965 [first published by the Servants of the Buddha, 1949]). *KhpA.* has been reliably translated into English by Bhikkhu Ñāṇmoli as *The Minor Readings and the Illustrator of Ultimate Meaning*, Pali Text Society translation series, no. 32 (London: Luzac and Co., 1960). See George D. Bond's comparative analysis of the two modes of presentation reflected in *MA.* and *KhpA.* in his chapter, "The Buddha as Refuge in the Theravāda Buddhist Tradition," in *The Threefold Refuge in the Theravāda Buddhist Tradition*, ed. John R. Carter, pp. 16–32.

9. I am indebted to Peter Masefield for indicating, in a circulated communication, that the fear, trembling, *dukkha*, and the realization of the hindrance or impediment in one's progression along the way to freedom are not to be taken as a series in this passage, but are primarily appositional notions to be understood as being associated with a consideration of the possibility of, as well as the attainment of, a poor destination in one's rebirth. It is this fear, this trembling, this *dukkha*, this hindrance or impediment that going for refuge assuredly destroys.

10. *MA.*, I.132. So, too, *KhpA.*, p. 16. See also *Vaṃsatthappakāsinī: Commentary on the Mahāvaṃsa*, ed. G. P. Malalasekera for the Government of Ceylon (London: Published for the Pali Text Society by Humphrey Milford, Oxford University Press, 1935), vol. 1, p. 308 (on *Mahāvaṃsa*, Chapter 11, vs. 35); and *Dharmapradīpikā*, ed. Baddēgama Vimalavaṃsa Thera, 2d ed. (Colombo: M. D. Gunasēna and Co., 1967), pp. 179–183, a Sinhala version of the *MA.* passage. See also *BuA.* pp. 122–123, which makes it clear that the

commentators tended, for homiletical purposes, to take *saraṇa* as being derived from the root *śr*, "to crush," as in the following: *sarati hiṃsati vināsetī ti saraṇam*, "it crushes, slays, destroys, hence [the meaning of] *saraṇa*." The term *saraṇa* can be derived, of course, from the root *śri*, "to resort." See also George Bond's comments, "The Buddha of Refuge, p. 23.

11. As previously stated in my *Dhamma: Western Academic and Sinhalese Buddhist Interpretations—a study of a religious concept* (Tokyo: Hokuseido Press, 1978), p. 84, n.73.

12. C. A. F. Rhys Davids, *A Manual of Buddhism: For Advanced Students* (London: Sheldon Press, 1932), p. 60.

13. Wilfred Cantwell Smith, "Religious Atheism? Early Buddhist and Recent American," *Milla wa-Milla*, no. 6 (December 1966): 9. The Buddhist segment of this article has been published, with some revision, as Chapter 2, "The Buddhist Instance: Faith as Atheist?" in Wilfred Cantwell Smith, *Faith and Belief* (Princeton, N.J.: Princeton University Press, 1979); see p. 25 for the phrase quoted in the text.

14. See *MA.*, II.113 (on *M.*, I.138); *Sdpj.*, I.74 (on *Mahāniddesa* 1.I.17); and *SnA.*, I.151 (on *Sn.*, v. 80).

15. *MA.*, I.132 (on *M.*, I.24).

16. Ibid., p. 131.

17. See the discussion of the force of *śraddhā* (*saddhā*) by Wilfred Cantwell Smith in his Chapter 4 of *Faith and Belief*, pp. 59–68.

18. See, for example, the commentarial discussion at *KhpA.*, p. 183 (on *Sn.*, v. 227); *DA.*, I.181 (on *D.*, I.63), *ThagA.*, II.71 (on *Thag.*, v. 204), II.102 (on *Thag.*, v. 249), and III.41 (on *Thag.*, v. 789).

19. *MA.*, I.132.

20. Ibid.

21. Ibid., p. 133.

22. Ibid.

23. *S.*, II.220.

24. *MA.*, I.133, quoting from *Sn.*, v. 192.

25. *MA.*, I.133, quoting from *M.*, II.144.

26. *MA.*, I.133.

27. Ibid., p. 134.

28. *MA.*, I.134f.

29. One might seize on a standard polarity of *ordinary* and *extraordinary,* as has been done occasionally since the appearance of Franklin Edgerton's article, "dominant Ideas in the Formation of Indian Culture," *Journal of the American Oriental Society* 62 (September 1942): 155. The word *ordinary* has, for our purposes, an unfortunate connotation of "inferior." *Customary* tends to avoid this connotational drift and carries an additional relevance of suggesting an activity of a community.

30. An engaging discussion of the term *Christian* as noun or adjective has been offered by Wilfred Cantwell Smith in the chapter "Christian—Noun, or Adjective?" in *Questions of Religious Truth* (New York: Charles Scribner's Sons, 1967), pp. 99–123

31. *MA.*, I.134. See the brief presentation of the categories of the eight noble persons, who have attained the four paths and four fruits, given by Perry and Ratnayaka, "The Sangha as Refuge," pp. 43–44.

32. *MA.*, I.132. Note that in this *lokuttarasaraṇagamana* one "roots out what harms this going for refuge" (*saraṇagamanūpakkilesa-samuccheda*), whereas in the customary or *lokiya* going for refuge, there is only the withdrawal of support from under (*vikkhambhana*) whatever harms the process.

33. Ibid.

34. Ibid., p. 134. The quotation is from the *Dhammapada*, vv. 190–192, as translated in *The Dhammapada: A New English Translation with the Pali Text and the First English Translation of the Commentary's Explanation of the Verses with Notes Translated from Sinhala Sources and Critical Textual Comments* by John Ross Carter and Mahinda Palihawadana (New York: Oxford University Press, 1987), pp. 45, 248.

35. Compare a related passage in the *Dhammapada*, vv. 277–279. For the commentarial explanation of this *Dhp.* verse, see *The Dhammapada*, trans. Carter and Palihawadana, pp. 310–312.

36. *MA.*, I.134. The quotation is from *A.*, I.26–27.

37. I am aware that the commentary on *Dhp.* v. 27, takes *dhammā* to mean the components that constitute an individual (*khandhas*), whereas I have translated it in the text as "all things that are capable of being known." Perhaps, however, the commentary is narrowing the sense here.

38. *MA.*, I.135. *DhpA.*, III.246 (on *Dhp.*, vv. 190–192) focuses on the worship of the teachers, and so forth, as an example of how refuge, either that taken by a householder or by one who has "gone forth" into monastic life, can be disturbed or shaken; not so, however, for one who has a vision of the immovable state (*acalabhāvan*); that is, *nibbāna (dhamma/nibbāna)*.

CHAPTER 5

1. One draws attention to Wilfred Smith's reminder that we continue to be self-conscious as well of the biases found in the disciplinary approaches that have been adopted to assure something called *objectivity.* See his "Objectivity and the Humane Sciences: A New Proposal," in William G. Oxtoby, ed., *Religious Diversity: Essays by Wilfred Cantwell Smith* (New York: Harper and Row, 1976), pp. 158–180.

2. *Vin.*, I.16, 18, 19, 23, 37, 181, II.156; *D.*, I.110, II.41, 43, 44 (in the case of Vipassin, a former Buddha); *M.*, I.379–380, II.145; *A.*, IV.186, 209–210, 213. See also *Udāna*, p. 49.

3.K. R. Norman, "The Four Noble Truths: A Problem of Pāli Syntax," *Indological and Buddhist studies, Volume in Honour of Professor J. W. de Jong*, ed. L. A. Hercus, et al. (Canberra: Australian National University, 1982), pp. 377–391.

4. Ibid., p. 385.

5. In attempting to provide an interpretation of the four noble truths, one that asks the question in what sense are they true, one would want to enter a disclaimer, it seems, that one is posing as an authority on the deeper meaning of these truths and state that one is prepared to modify or reformulate one's interpretations in response to constructive criticism offered by Buddhist men and women who have lived long in light of these truths. Certainly I would not aver that all other interpretations are false merely because I have raised the question and have proffered a response. That the question is certainly worth raising and might repay reflection is partly due to the question's not having been raised

before by Western scholars. The question is also worth raising because the issues that a response will tend to generate have not been widely noted.

6. *Guide to Buddhist Religion*, ed. Frank E. Reynolds and Bardwell Smith (Boston: G. K. Hall and Co., 1981), p. 77b.

7. *Vin.*, I.10.; *S.*, V.420. One should note again the study by K. R. Norman, as indicated in note 3 to this chapter, especially his paragraphs 2.7 and 6.2. I have followed the traditional form of translation-interpretation, long anchored in the heritage, but nevertheless syntactically uneven.

8. *Vism.*, XVI.24, p. 421.

9. I continue to probe the ramifications of a superlative article by Wilfred Cantwell Smith, "A Human View of Truth," in *Truth and Dialogue: The Relationship Between World Religions*, ed. John Hick (London: Sheldon Press, 1975), pp. 20–44.

CHAPTER 6

1. *The Oxford English Dictionary* (*svv.* ethics, moral) provides examples, now several centuries old, of differentiations between ethics and moral virtues on the one hand, and orientations to theism or Christian virtues, on the other.

2. On the concept of "religion" in this matter, see the major work by Wilfred Cantwell Smith, *The Meaning and End of Religion: A New Approach to the Religious Traditions of mankind* (New York: Macmillan Company, 1963).

3. David Little and Sumner B. Twiss, *Comparative Religious Ethics* (San Francisco: Harper and Row, 1978), p. 236.

4. Ibid., p. 247. These authors write elsewhere, p. 108, "Transpersonal norms are, by definition, non-moral, although they may be religious in character."

5. Gerald James Larson, "'Conceptual resources' in South Asia for 'environmental ethics' or The fly is still alive and well in the bottle," *Philosophy East and West: A Quarterly of Asian and Comparative Thought* 37, no. 2 (April 1987): pp. 150–151. The introductory portion of this article is a revised, and refined, presentation of one of Larson's earlier studies, "Hindu and Buddhist Perspectives on the Notion of the Good," an unpublished paper delivered at

the annual meeting of the Association for Asian Studies, Chicago, April 3, 1982, pp. 9–11.

6. Larson, "Conceptual resources," p. 151. In his earlier formulation, Larson wrote, ibid., p. 10:

> The position is usually characterized as maintaining that the ultimate is "beyond good and evil" which, in my view, is simply a euphemism for what is really a much stronger moral claim, namely that there is nothing that is intrinsically good. The experience of *mokṣa, kaivalya, nirvāna,* or whatever one wishes to call it, is simply not a moral experience. It is the denial of ethics and morality, or putting the matter another way, it is the denial that moral and ethical theorizing has any value at all.

7. Larson, "'Conceptual resources," pp. 150–151; "Hindu and Buddhist Perspectives," p. 11.

8. Larson, "Hindu and Buddhist Perspectives," p. 13.

9. Ibid.

10. Little and Twiss, *Comparative Religious Ethics,* pp. 238, 241, and 246.

11. Ibid., p. 118.

12. Joanna Rogers Macy, "Dependent Co-Arising: The Distinctiveness of Buddhist Ethics," *Journal of Religious Ethics* 7, no. 1 (1979): 45.

13. Ibid.

14. Ibid., pp. 42–43.

15. See Little and Twiss, *Comparative Religious Ethics,* pp. 246–247.

16. Macy, "Dependent Co-Arising," p. 42.

17. H. Saddhatisssa, *Buddhist Ethics: Essence of Buddhism* (London: George Allen and Unwin, 1970), p. 18.

18. Ibid., pp. 18–19.

19. On the Indian scene and in the Hindu case, Franklin Edgerton writes, "But when the goal is reached, one is beyond good and evil." See his "Dominant Ideas in the Formation of Indian Culture," *Journal of the American Oriental Society* 62 (September 1942): 155. A. L. Herman modifies Edgerton's

"ordinary norm" and "extraordinary norm" thesis as it might apply to Theravāda, but continues a usage of "beyond good and evil." See his "Ethical Theory in Theravāda Buddhism," *Journal of the Bihar Research Society* 47 (January–December 1961), p. 185. See also the usage of this phrase by Gunapala Dharmasiri, *A Buddhist Critique of the Christian Concept of God* (Colombo: Lake House Investments, 1974), p. 106.

There are too many instances of the use of this phrase to note here. I have noted only these three as examples provided by (1) a recent leading Western Indologist (2) a Western philosopher writing as a graduate student, and (3) a Sinhala Buddhist layman who has studied facets of the Christian tradition.

20. C. A. F. Rhys Davids uses the expression *beyond the Good and the Bad* and notes this phrase as coming from "Nietzsche on Buddhism in 'Der Antichrist'" in her translation of the *Dhammasaṅganī, A Buddhist Manual of Psychological Ethics*, 3d ed. (London: Published by the Pali Text Society, 1974, first published by the Royal Asiatic Society, 1900; also New Delhi: Oriental Books Reprint Corporation, 1975), p. cii. For Nietzsche, the notion "bad" represents an aristocratic extension from an aristocratically originated notion of "good" whereas "evil" had as its origin resentement that constituted a part of "slave morality." A transvaluation of values occurred, Nietzsche believed, when aristocratically originated "good" became labeled as the plebeian-originated "evil" and the aristocratically originated "bad" now became the plebeian "good." See Friedrich Nietzsche, *The Geneology of Morals: A Polemic*, trans. Horace B. Samuel (Edinburgh: T. N. Foulis, 1910), especially article II, pp. 38–39.

When, with regard to analyzing Theravāda, a shift from *beyond the Good and the Bad* or *beyond good and bad* to *beyond good and evil* was made is not clear. The latter phrase is the more current. Conceivably, when persons became less familiar with Nietzsche and more conscious that Christians would form a part of the reading public, such shift occurred.

21. Stephen Crites suggests that on careful analysis one would find that the so-called three stages yield a fourfold scheme: aesthetic, ethical, religion A [knight of infinite resignation], and religion B [knight of faith]. And Crites notes that there appears to be "two intermediate stages of irony and humor," and mentions, further, a footnote by Johannes Climacus, in *Concluding Unscientific Postscript*, where a sevenfold tabulation appears; and possibly some stages appear within the aesthetic. Crites writes, "so there seems in principle no end to the exfoliation of Kierkegaardian stages." Crites still prefers to hold

to a scheme of sorts, proposing a distinction "between the aesthetic and the existential, regarding the ethical and religious spheres as existential discriminations." See Stephen Crites, "Pseudonymous Authorship as Art and as Act," *Kierkegaard: A Collection of Critical Essays,* ed. Josiah Thomson (Garden City, N.Y.: Doubleday and Company, Anchor Books, 1972), pp. 200–201.

Kierkegaard himself wrote,

> So in the pseudonymous works [where the so-called stages appear] there is not a single word which is mine, I have no opinion about these works except as third person, no knowledge of their meaning except as a reader, not the remotest private relation to them, since such a thing is impossible in the case of a doubly reflected communication. One single word of mine uttered personally in my own name would be an instance of presumptuous self-forgetfulness, and dialectically viewed it would incur with one word the guilt of annihilating the pseudonyms.

S. Kierkegaard, "A First and Last Declaration," four pages following the text of *Kierkegaard's Concluding Unscientific Postscript,* trans. from the Danish by David F. Swenson and completed with Introduction and Notes by Walter Lowrie (Princeton, N.J.: Princeton University Press, 1963 [seventh printing first published in 1941]), p. 551 (unpaginated). I am indebted to my late colleague M. Holmes Hartshorne for first drawing my attention to this passage, which is also noted by Josiah Thompson, "The Master of Irony," in *Kierkegaard,* p. 104. Hartshorne's brilliant interpretation of Kierkegaard's use of irony has appeared posthumously in his work *Kierkegaard Godly Deceiver—The Nature and Meaning of His Pseudonymous Writings* (New York: Columbia University Press, 1990).

Thompson is persuasive when he writes, "The central focus of the pseudonymous works is neither ethics nor religion nor aesthetics, but rather the dialectic of the life of imagination." Ibid., p. 113.

> For if the pseudonymous works have shown us anything, it is that *all the so called 'existential movements'* end in *failure.* If failure is the outcome of all attempts to make these movements [from the aesthetic to the ethical to the religious and through whatever intervening substages], then how can their stimulation be the aim of the authorship? It can, only if the recognition of failure and not the movements is the point. (Ibid., p. 160)

And Thompson concludes on this point, "It is failure, I submit, the necessary failure of all human projects, that is at once the central meaning of the pseudonyms, as well as the source of their deepest religious import." Ibid, pp. 160–161.

The relevance of Kierkegaard's contribution for a study of the Theravāda would hardly be that the *arahant* has gone beyond the ethical to the religious, but that without *dhamma*, one would not be able to become an *arahant.* A Theravāda Buddhist might use Thompson's words to reflect not only an understanding of the human predicatment but also the religious apperception of religious life; without *dhamma* we are confronted with "our ineradicable incapacity to pull ourselves up by our own bootstraps." Ibid., p. 162.

22. See for example, *Dhp.*, vv. 39, 267, 412; *Sn.*, vv. 547, 790; and see also *The Netti-pakaraṇa* (PTS edition; hereafter, *Netti.*), p. 96; *Petavatthu* (PTS edition; hereafter, *Pv.*), II.6.15, p. 19. For other references, see P. D. Premasiri, "Interpretations of Two Principal Ethical Terms in early Buddhism," *Sri Lanka Journal of the Humanities* 2, no. 1 (June 1976): 63–74.

23. Premasiri, ibid,

24. Premasiri's succinct observation is as follows:

> *Puñña* in its canonical use generally signified the actions etc. which conduce to a happy consequence to the agent in a future existence. The term was clearly borrowed from the earlier ethical terminology of the Brahmanic tradition. *Kusala*, on the other hand, generally signified that which conduces to spiritual bliss culminating in the attainment of the highest bliss of *nibbāna* which leaves no room for the fruition of any actions. It may be said to be a specifically Buddhist usage, perhaps because it was intended to signify a different sense of ethical value from that signified by *puñña.* When one attains *nibbāna* (the state which is equivalent to arahantship), a person is fully endowed with *kusala* qualities and is free from *akusala* as well as both *puñña* and *pāpa.* The assertion which is almost universally made by modern interpreters of Buddhist ethics that the Buddhist saint is beyond good and bad can therefore be seen to be the ressult of a terminological muddle. (ibid., p. 74)

25. The references are too many to list here. Only examples are necessary. See *DhpA.*, I.153 (on *Dhp.*, v. 18): *"katapuñño" ti nānappakārassa puññassa kattā; 'ubhayattha' ti idha 'kataṃ me kusalaṃ akataṃ pāpaṃ' ti*

nandati, parattha vipākaṃ anubhavanto nandati. "He who has done wholesome deeds [*katapuñño*] is a doer of various kinds of wholesome deeds [*puñña*]; in both places: Here he rejoices, thinking, 'Wholesome acts have been done by me, unwholesome acts have not been done'; [and] in the world beyond, he rejoices experiencing the fruits [of action done here]." *The Dhammapada*, trans. Carter and Palihawadana, p. 106. See also *DhpA.*, I.132 (on *Dhp.*, v. 16).

In the *Aṭṭhakathāsūci*, ed. Pandita Kosgoḍa Sirisumedha Thera, rev. Pandita Kosgoḍa Dhammavaṃsa Thera (Colombo: M. D. Guṇasēna, 1969), III, 754b, a detailed listing of commentarial glosses is provided: *kusale dasahupāgato* is noted as being glossed, *kusalehi dasahi samannāgato, dānādīhi dasahi puññakiriyavatthūhi dasahi kusalakammapathehi vā yutto ti attho.* (References in the *Aṭṭhakathāsūci* are to texts issued in the Hewavitarne series, to which I do not have access.) In the *Śssk.*, I.286, one notes for *kusala-dharma, pin*; for *kusala-phala, pinin läbena yahapat vipākaya*; for *kusala-vipāka, pinvalin läbena yahapat phala*; for *kusala-hetu, pinvalata hetu vana alobha adosa amoha yana tuna*; for *punya* (II.582) *sita pivituru karaṇa kuśaladharmaya*; for *pin* (II.562), *puṇyaya, kuśalaya*; for *pin pala, puṇyaphalaya, kuśalavipākaya*; for *pin daham, kuśaladharmaya*; for *pin kam, kuśalakriyāva.*

26. References to later literature provided by Premasiri are to the *Niddesa* and *DA.* See Premasiri, "Interpretations," pp. 72–73.

27. See for example *M.*, I.46–47, 489; *Vism.*, XIV.89, p. 384; *Aṭṭhakathāsūci*, III.752a; *Śssk.*, I.287a.

28. See, for example, the late, but canonical source, *Nd. 1*, I.90: *Puññam vuccati yam kiñci tedhātukam kusalābhisaṃkhāram*; *apuññam vuccati sabbam akusalam.*

29. *Vism.*, XIV.88, p. 384, *kusala* is "*Lokuttaram catumaggasampayogato catubbidhan ti.*"

30. The *Aṭṭhakathāsūci*, III.751–755, provides eight commentarial glosses presenting this interpretation.

31. See the *Aṭṭhakathāsūci*, III.754, for two occasions providing this interpretation.

32. See the *Aṭṭhakathāsūci*, III.753a, *sv. kusalassādhigamāya maggakusalassa ceva phalakusalassa ca adhigamatthāya.*

33. *Vism.*, VII.31, p. 167: *Caraṇan ti sīlasaṃvaro. . . . ariyasāvako sīlavā*

hoti ti.... caraṇena samannāgato; tena vuccati vijjācaraṇasampanno ti. See also *A.*, V.66, a reference noted also by Premasiri, "Interpretations," p. 71, n. 65.

34. *Vism.*, VIII.32, p. 167. *caraṇasampadā mahākāruṇikatam.... mahākāruṇikatāya anattham parivajjetvā atthe niyojeti....*

35. *Vism.*, VII.33, p. 167: *Sobhaṇagamanattā, sundaraṃ ṭhānaṃ gatattā, sammāgatattā....*

36. See *The Dhammapada*, trans. Carter and Palihawadana, p. 142; and *DhpA.*, I.422 (on *Dhp.*, v. 55): *Satañ ca gandho ti sappurisānam pana Buddhapaccekabuddhasāvakānam sīlagando pativātam eti.* See also *DhpA.*, I.434 (on *Dhp.*, v. 57), where the commentary glosses "those having virtues abounding" (*sampannasīlānam*) with "who are of perfect virtue" (*paripuṇṇasīlānam*), both used to refer to those in whom the influxes are extinct (*khīnāsava*); that is, *arahants*. See *The Dhammapada*, p. 144.

37. The *Aṭṭhakathāsūci*, II.458a, provides references to commentaries where *uttamattham* is taken to mean *nibbāna* or the state of arahantship (*arahattam*).

38. See *Śssk.*, I.287, *sv. kusal-daṃsapanasa.*

39. *Vism.* XXII.78, p. 589, as trans. Mahinda Palihawadana in "Is There a Theravada Buddhist Idea of Grace?" in *Christian Faith in a Religiously Plural World*, ed. Donald G. Dawe and John B. Carman (Maryknoll, N.Y.: Orbis Books, 1978), p. 183.

40. *A.*, V.2–3. The translation is Palihawadana's ibid. The passage reads in Pāli: *Sīlavato bhikkhave sīlasampannassa na cetanāya karaṇīyam 'avippaṭisāro me uppajjatū' ti. Dhammatā esā bhikkhave, yaṃ sīlavato sīlasampannassa avippaṭisāro uppajjati.* The passage continues to speak of the same process with regard to the realization of knowledge and vision of release that arises as a matter of nature without the activity of the will. See *A.*, V.3, and Palihawadana's translation, ibid., pp. 183–184.

41. Ibid., p. 191.

42. See Nyanatiloka, *Buddhist Dictionary: Manual of Buddhist Terms and Doctrines*, 3d rev. and enlarged ed., ed. Nyanaponika (Colombo: Frewin and Co. 1972), p. 88, *sv. kusala.*

43. The *Aṭṭhakathāsūci*, III.753a, notes: "When *kusala* and *akusala* are dissolved—when the *kusala* that exists because of *vipassanā* and the *akusala*

that exists because of infatuation and so forth are dissolved" (*kusalākusale niruddhe—etasmiṃ vipassanā vasena pavatte kusale sārajjanādivasena pavatte akusale ca niruddhe*).

44. Ananda W. P. Guruge, "Some Problems in Buddhist Ethics," *Añjali: Papers on Indology and Buddhism, A Felicitation Volume Presented to Oliver Hector De Alwis Wijesekera,* ed. J. Tilikasiri (Ceylon: Felicitation Volume Editorial Committee, University of Ceylon, Peradeniya, 1970), p. 5, notes the presence of the notion *kiriya-* (or *kriya*) *citta* and writes,

> according to the Buddhist concept of emancipation, the ultimate achievement is beyond ethical differentiation or evaluation. Not only is the Arahant considered to be freed of both the good and the evil (cf. *puññapāpapahīna*) [*Dhp.*, v. 39], but even his altruistic [*sic*] and otherwise meritorious deeds [*sic*] are said to be accompanied only by a functional consciousness (*kiriyacitta*) incapable of producing any reward or retribution.

P. D. Premasiri, in "Interpretations," takes issue with Guruge, and makes his (Premasiri's) point with regard to *kusala* modifying the qualities of an accomplished one during the time of "early Buddhism." However, both Guruge and Premasiri failed to lead us into a further understanding of why the tradition maintained the notion of *kiriya-citta* as an "indeterminate, unexplained action" (*avyākatakamma*) on the part of the *arahant.*

45. *Dhp.*, v. 97 and *DhpA.*, II.188. In a delightful sequence of punning, the commentary elaborates the *Dhammapada* verse as follows:

> The ungrateful one: *akataññū*
> [One is called] *akataññū* because one understands the uncreated (*akatam*)—that is, Nibbāna. The meaning is: one who has realized Nibbāna.
>
> [The man who is] a burglar: *sandhicchedo*
> [One is called] "a breaker of joints" because one has cut off the "junction" of the whirl and the "junction" of *saṃsāra.*
>
> Who has destroyed opportunities: *hatāvakāso*
> [One is said to have] "destroyed opportunities" because the seed for wholesome and unwholesome deeds has been eradicated and the opportunity for rebirth is destroyed.
>
> Ejected hope: *vantāso*
> [One is said to have] "ejected hope" because the duty that has to be

done has been done by means of the four paths and [all] wish is thereby discarded.

A person supreme: *purisuttama*
The person of this kind is said to be noble because of having reached an exalted position among persons by virtue of having penetratively understood dhamma that transcends the world. (*The Dhammapada*, trans. Carter and Palihawadana, p. 180)

46. One might argue that the phrase, "done is what had to be done" means that the *arahant* has gone beyond a sense of duty; duty is now a thing of the past, so also ethics. However, I am beginning to think that when this formula is stated it suggests not solely a person's activity that was conducive to liberation, but also, and perhaps primarily, the soteriological instrumentality of the path-process. Note *DhpA.*, II.188 (on *Dhp.*, v. 97): "because the duty that has to be done has been done by means of the four paths...[*catūhi maggehi kattabbakiccassa katattā*]." The focus would now seem to shift—that which is to be done, or that which has to be done, cannot be done by oneself alone, but, as in this case, has been done *by means of the four paths.*

CHAPTER 7

1. While writing these words, I was completing a spring term upper level seminar for a few concentrators in Religious Studies at Colgate. After a full semester focusing carefully on the notion of "faith in a religiously plural world" the participants of that seminar could write at length about expressions of faith in prose, poetry, art, behavior, community formation, and song, in the major religious traditions, how a quality of life among persons could be inferred. But all of us were unable to provide a succinct definition of that quality of human life of which we speak when we use the word *faith*.

2. All but a few translations of passages from the *Dhammapada* and commentarial literature on that text will be from *The Dhammapada*, trans. Carter and Palihawadana.

3. Ibid., v. 333.

4. Ibid.

5. Ibid., vv. 144, 303.

6. Ibid., vv. 8, 144. One notes that we have picked up several of the standard set of "spiritual faculties" or *indriyas*: (1) *saddhā* (2) *viriya* (3) "awareness," *sati* (4) "concentration," *samādhi*, and (5) *paññā*.

7. Ibid, v. 97.

8. "Nonrestraint, when it arises at that [*javana*-instant] in an unwholesome stream [of mental events] is fivefold [i.e., has five characteristic expressions]: lack of faith (*assaddhā*), impatience, sloth (*kosajjam* < *kusīta*), heedlessness, and ignorance. Restraint (*saṃvaro*), when it arises in a wholesome stream [of mental events also] is fivefold: faith, patience, energy, heedfulness, and understanding." Ibid., p. 374 (*The Commentary on the Dhammapada* [*DhpA*.], ed. H. C. Norman, vol. 4 [London: Published for the Pali Text Society by Luzac and Company, 1970; first published in 1906], p. 85 on *Dhp*. v. 360).

9. Who has no faith, the ungrateful one
The man who is a burglar,
Who has destroyed opportunities, ejected wish,
Truly he is a person supreme (ibid., v. 97, p. 179).

The commentary provides the following gloss:

Who has no faith: *assaddho*
The quality that one has attained oneself, one does not take on faith from the word of others: [one is] "not having faith" in that sense.

The ungrateful one: *akataññū*
[One is called] *akataññū* because one understands the uncreated (*akatam*)—that is, Nibbāna. The meaning is: one who has realized Nibbāna.

(The man who is) a burglar: *sandhicchedo*
[One is called] "a breaker of joints" because one has cut off the "junction" of the whirl and the "junction" of *saṃsāra*.

Who has destroyed opportunities: *hatāvakāso*
[One is said to have] "destroyed opportunities" because the seed for wholesome and unwholesome deeds has been eradicated and the opportunity for rebirth is destroyed.

Ejected hope: *vantāso*
[One is said to have] "ejected hope" because the duty that has to be done has been done by means of the four paths and [all] wish is thereby discarded.

A person supreme: *purisuttamo*
The person of this kind is said to be noble because of having reached an exalted position among persons by virtue of having penetratively understood dhamma that transcends the world. (ibid., pp. 179–180).

10. So the *DhpA.*, in ibid.

11. Ibid., pp. 454–455, n. 11. The translation is from *Dhammapada pūrāṇa sannaya (granthipada vivaraṇa sahita)*, "The Old Commentary of the Dhammapada (with a Glossary)," edited by Kamburupiṭiyē Dhammaratana Sthavira (Colombo: Maha Bodhi Press, 1926), p. 51.

12. We need to conduct much more work on this notion. The *Aṭṭhakathāsūci,* Part I, ed. Acariya Kosgoḍa Sirisumedha Thera, rev. Pandita Kosgoḍa Dhammavaṃsa Thera (Kelaniya, Sri Lanka: Vidyalankara University Press, 1960), p. 305a, gives a straightforward commentarial definition; "'having no faith' means there is no faith in it," notes our passage translated previously from the commentary on the *Dhammapada*, then provides the interesting observation:

> "Being without faith" refers to the four beginning with the ordinary person, the Stream Attainer, the Once Returner, The Non-Returner: the ordinary person indeed has not attained the faith of the Stream Attainer; the Stream Attainer is one without the faith of the Once Returner, the Once Returner is so with regard to the Non-Returner, the Non-Returner has not attained the faith of the Arahant and so is one without faith (*anāgāmī arahato saddham appato ti assaddho*).

For a general treatment of the notion of *assaddho* and several textual references, see my *Dhamma: Western Academic and Sinhalese Buddhist Interpretations,* pp. 106–108.

13. *The Dhammapada*, p. 127 (*DhpA.* I. 309–310). The *Dhampiyā-aṭuvā-gäṭapadaya,* ed. D. E. Hettiaratchi (Colombo: Published by the Press Board of the Sri Lanka University at the University Press, 1974), p. 100, elaborates: "'Such as faith, and so on'—one should take 'and so on' (*ādi*) in this phrase to include enterprise (*viriya*), mindfulness (*sati*), concentration (*samādhi*), and wisdom (*paññā*)." See *The Dhammapada*, p. 439, n. 21.

14. *S.*, V.220–222. There is an interesting parallel commentarial development: in the *Sn.*, v. 853, the phrase *not one of faith* (*na saddho*) appears. This phrase is glossed by *sāmam adhigatam dhammam na kassaci saddahati:*

"the one who has attained Dhamma oneself does not put one's faith in anyone." *SnA.*, II.549. In its elaboration of this *Sutta-nipāta* phrase, *not one of faith,* (*na saddho*), the *Mahāniddesa* quotes the passage that we are considering from the *Saṃyutta-nikāya.* See *Nd. 1,* I.235–237. The *Mahāniddesa,* in concluding its elaboration, quotes *Dhammapada,* v. 97, which includes the term *assaddho.*

15. On this usage this English translation of *saddahati* and this meaning of *saddhā* see "A Hindu Contribution," in Wilfred Cantwell Smith, *Faith and Belief,* pp. 223–225, n. 35. According to *PTSD,*, p. 674b, "lit. to put one's heart on...."

16. I have followed the *Dhammapadaṭṭhakathā*, ed. [in Sinhala script] Ambalangoda P. Buddhadatta Thera (Colombo: M. D. Gunasena and Co., 1956), p. 379, finding that it here presents fewer textual difficulties than the PTS edition (at *DhpA.*, II. 186–187 [on *Dhp.*, v. 97]).

17. The contrast between the instrumentality of one's own involvement (*attanā*) and the locus or targeted objective of this trust being placed in others (*paresam*), whether such be the Buddha or *Bhagavant* himself or unspecified "others," is a significant matter, it seems. Note Sāriputta's comment "By no means do I, sir, on this matter go on faith in the *Bhagavant*" (*na khvāham bhante ettha Bhagavato saddhāya gacchāmi*) with regard to the question about the efficacy of the five spiritual faculties (*indriyas*). Sāriputta is recorded as having also said, about others, "About that, let them go on faith in others" (*te tattha paresam saddhāya gaccheyyum*) and, further, a parallelism is introduced at the the end of the commentarial presentation, "But with regard to meditation, insight, Path and Fruits that have been attained by me, myself, I do not go on faith in others" (*eso pana attanā patiladdhesu jhānavipassanāmaggaphaladhammesu paresam saddhāya na gacchati*). So *DhpA.*, II. 186–187.

Of course *assaddhā* has been interpreted in an exclusive way, also, as in *Puggala-paññatti-aṭṭhakathā. From the Pañcappakaraṇaṭṭhakathā* (*Ascribed to Buddhaghosa*), ed. George Landsberg and Mrs. [C. A. F.] Rhys Davids, *Journal of the Pali Text Society* (1914): p. 185, where "those without faith" (*assaddhā*) are "those without faith in the Buddha, Dhamma, and Sangha." See also *MA.*, I. 152.

18. *Dhammapada* v. 38 reads:

For one of unsteady mind,
Who knows not dhamma true,

Whose serenity (*pasāda*) is adrifting,

Wisdom (*paññā*) becomes not full.

The commentary elaborates the third line: "Because of little faith (*saddhā*), or of 'drifting' faith, or of faith (*saddhā*) falling away...." *The Dhammapada,* pp. 125–126.

19. So "With faith (*saddhā*), which is twofold, namely, the customary faith and the faith that transcends the world...." *The Dhammapada,* p. 212 (*DhpA.*, [PTS] III. 86, on *Dhp.* v. 144). See also p. 329 (*DhpA.*, [PTS] III.464, on *Dhp.*, v. 303) "The faithful one: *saddho*"—"One who is endowed with faith, ordinary and transcendent,' and p. 352 (*DhpA.*, [PTS] IV. 35, on *Dhp.*, v. 333), "[A blessing is] faith, both ordinary and transcendent, unshakably established."

20. *The Dhammapada,* p. 99 (*DhpA.*, [PTS] I.76, on *Dhp.*, v. 8).

21. Morontuduvē Śrī Ñāṇeśvara Dharmānanda, *Saddharmakaumudī nam bhāvārtthavivaraṇasahita dhammapadapāliya* [The Dhammapada with a Sinhalese Translation, Commentary, and Annotation Entitled Saddharmakaumudī], finally revised and approved by Kahāvē Śrī Sumaṅgala Ratanasāra, 3d ed. (Colombo: Śrī Bhāratī Press, 1946 [first published, 1927]), p. 156. The gloss here noted from this text pertains to *DhpA.* (PTS) III.464 on *Dhp.*, v. 303. See *The Dhammapada,* pp. 329 and 490, n. 24.

22. *The Dhammapada,* p. 141 (*DhpA.* [PTS] I.419–420, on *Dhp.* v. 53).

23. These eight would be (1) stream attainer, (2) one who has realized the fruit of stream attainment, (3) once returner, (4) one who has realized the fruit of the once returner, (5) non-returner, (6) one who has realized the fruit of the non-returner, (7) *arahant,* and (8) one who has realized the fruit of arahantship.

24. For a fuller presentation of the commentarial position regarding these two dimensions of *saraṇagamana,* see the earlier discussion in Chapter 4.

25. This sense of *yes,* this notion of faith as being fundamentally an affirmation of the total personality follows the groundbreaking work of Wilfred Cantwell Smith, in *Faith and Belief.*

26. *Saddharmakaumudī,* pp. 458–459 (commenting on *DhpA.*, [PTS] III.86, on *Dhp.*, v. 144). See *The Dhammapada,* pp. 212 and 458–459, n. 9.

CHAPTER 8

1. See the fine work by Frank Reynolds, "From Philology to Anthropology: A Bibliographical Essay on Works Related to Early, Theravāda and Sinhalese Buddhism," in Bardwell L. Smith, ed., *The Two Wheels of Dhamma: Essays on the Theravāda Tradition in India and Ceylon*, American Academy of Religion Studies in Religion no. 3 (Chambersburg, Pa.: American Academy of Religion, 1972), pp. 107–121. The other essays in this volume, by Bardwell L. Smith and Gananath Obeyesekere, are also important.

2. A splendid interpretation of a comparable form of this ancient ceremony that has been passed down in Burma, the *shin byu*, has been provided by Wilfred Cantwell Smith, in "Buddhists," in *The Faith of Other Men* (New York: Harper and Row, 1972 [first published by New American Library, 1963]), pp. 39–52.

3. For an elaboration of this great notion of *saraṇa*, "refuge," see Chapter 4.

4. Jayasēkara Abēruvan, *Buddhāgama* (Colombo: M. D. Gunasēna, 1963), p. 1. We have already drawn attention to this little reader, in Chapter 2, as a signpost of a major shift in conceptualizing one's religious involvement in Sri Lanka.

5. See the discussion in the second segment of Chapter 1.

6. Abēruvan, *Buddhāgama*.

7. See Wilfred Cantwell Smith's insightful chapter, "Christian—Noun, or Adjective?" in his *Questions of Religious Truth* (New York: Charles Scribner's Sons, 1967), pp. 99–123.

8. *KhpA.*, p. 170.

9. S. F. de Silva, E. R. Eratna, and S. Vanigatunga, *Buddhadharmaya* (Colombo: Sri Lanka Prakāśaka Samagama, 1964), p. 1. This book was an approved text for upper-kindergarten children.

10. Rērukānē Chandavimala, *Pohoya Dinaya* (Colombo: Anula Press, 1966), p. 34.

CHAPTER 9

1. *Vin.*, I.83: *naccagītavāditavisūkadassanā veramanī.* This precept also occurs in a section dealing with moral virtue in *D.*, I.5. The practice of seeing

performances or shows involving dancing, singing, and instrumental music is considered a *dukkata* offense for monks (*Vin.*, II.107–108). A *dukkata* offense is a light offense. This practice is considered a *paccitiya* offense for nuns (*Vin.*, IV.267). A *paccitiya* offense is more serious in that it puts a person in a state requiring expiation or rectification before the person is again considered of proper disposition.

2. *D.*, I.6

3. *A.*, I.261.

4. *D.*, II.183.

5. *Thig.*, p. 137, v. 139. Mrs. Rhys Davids translates this verse: "Thou art fair, and life is young, beauteous Khemā! / I am young, even I, too—Come, O fairest lady! / While in our ear fivefold harmonies murmur melodious. / Seek we our pleasure." *Psalms of the Early Buddhists I.—Psalms of the Sisters* (London: Published for the Pali Text Society by Luzac and Company, 1964 [first published, 1909]), p. 83.

6. *S.*, I.131.

7. It is not yet clearly established to what degree the *vīṇā*, in the strata of texts consulted, was similar to what has evolved into the classical *vīṇā* of South India.

8. *A.*, III.375. E. M. Hare, in a note to his translation of the passage, refers to a commentarial observation: "*Satta sarā, tayo gāmā, mucchanā ekavīsati, / Thānā ekūnapaññāsaṃ, icc' ete sara-maṇḍalaṃ*" (Seven notes, three scales and one and twenty tones, / Forty-nine stops,—such is the scope of music). *The Book of the Gradual Sayings* (London: Published for the Pali Text Society by Luzac and Company, 1961 [first published in 1934]), III, p. 267, n. 1. The commentary concludes, "So he [Soṇa] was thoroughly well-versed in the art of the [heavenly] *gandhabbas*." See *AA.*, III.390.

9. See *The Jātaka* (PTS edition; hearafter, *Jā*), II.248–257.

10. *M.*, I.85.

11. *M.*, I.87.

12. *M.*, I.91–92.

13. *A.*, III.312–314.

14. *M.*, I.144.

15. *M.*, I.155.

16. *Iti-vuttaka* (PTS edition, hereafter, *Itv.*), p. 114. The references to synonyms (*adhivacana*) are listed in *PTSD.*, esp. 205b, *sv. kāma.*

17. We have mentioned this pattern of ritual expression earlier, in Chapter 8.

18. There are noteworthy differences in chanting techniques among the three monastic communities (*nikāyas*) in Sri Lanka: the Siyam-nikāya, the Ramañña-nikāya, and particularly in the case of the Amarapura-nikāya. A careful study and documentation of these differences has yet to be undertaken.

19. *Sn.*, vv. 426–427. See also *Buddha's Teachings: Being the Sutta-Nipāta or Discourse-Collection,* ed., in the original Pāli text with an English version facing it, Lord Chalmers, Harvard Oriental Series (Cambridge, Mass.: Harvard University Press, 1932), pp. 100–101.

20. *Sn.*, v. 436, *Buddha's Teachings,* p. 102.

21. *Sn.*, v. 449, *Buddha's Teachings,* p. 104. The same verse occurs also in *S.*, I.122. In that passage, Māra asks the Buddha whence has the rebirth-linking consciousness of one Godhika gone. On receiving a reply from the Buddha that such consciousness can no longer be found, Māra dropped his lute (*vīṇā*) and vanished. Of interest in this account is the notation that Māra, when he approached, was carrying a yellow-hued wood lute (*vīṇā*). The passage reads: *Atha kho Māro pāpimā beluva-paṇḍuvīṇam ādāya yena Bhagavā tenupasaṅkami.*

22. *S.*, I.122.

23. The lute (*vīṇā*) has been described in the commentarial literature. For references, see under *Beluvaṇḍuvīṇā, Dictionary of Pāli Proper Names,* by G. P. Malalasekera (London: Published for the Pali Text Society, 1960 [first published in the Indian Texts Series, 1938]), vol. 2, p. 314.

24. *SnA.*, II.393–394.

25. *D.*, II.265.

26. Ibid. *Gāthā abhāsi Buddhūpasaṃhitā dhammūpasaṃhitā arahantūpasaṃhitā kāmūpasaṃhitā.*

27. For a fine, but slightly guarded, English translation of the song, see *Dialogues of The Buddha*, trans. T. W. and C. A. F. Rhys Davids (London: Published for the Pali Text Society by Luzac and Company, 1959 [first published, 1910]), II.301–302, 303–304.

28. *D.*, II.265.

29. *D.*, II.266.

30. Mahinda Palihawadana, "Dhamma Today and Tomorrow," *Religiousness in Sri Lanka*, ed. John Ross Carter (Colombo: Marga Institute, 1979), p. 136.

31. *DhpA.*, III.225.

32. On the standard threefold formula of the Buddha, that which he taught (*dhamma*) about that of which he taught (*dhamma*), and the noble disciples (*sāvakasangha*, including but not limited to *arahants*), see *The Threefold Refuge in the Theravāda Buddhist Tradition*, ed. John Ross Carter (Chambersburg, Pa.: Anima Books, 1982).

33. A representative collection of examples of *kavi* was done by Hugh Nevill, *Sinhala Verse (Kavi), Parts 1–3*, ed. P. E. P. Deraniyagala, vols. 4–6 (Colombo: Ceylon National Museums Manuscript Series, 1954–1955). The Sinhala *kavi* are by no means limited to themes derived from the Pāli canonical and commentarial strata. The religious heritage reflected in the *kavi* is cumulative and complex. For *kavi* examples dealing with the threefold refuge (*tunsaraṇa*), see I.48; II.122, 149; Śrī Pāda or Adam's Peak, see I.37, 234.

An old "verse of the farmers" (*goyam kavi*) is often sung while working in the paddy fields and communicates an attitude of longing for the presence of the Buddha. The verse in my recording is considered old; the title is unknown, the author is anonymous, and the style is traditional.

> Is it not with an eye on the seasons
> 	That you do your plowing?
> Is it not when the blossoms have gone
> 	That the paddy matures?
> Is it not Saturn who witholds
> 	The mass of rain?
> O, when will I see
> 	the world-transcending Buddha?

The Sinhala is:

kal balā noveda govi tän karannē äṅgäṅgā
mal varā noveda kiriväda päsennē äṅgäṅgā
senasurā noveda väyipala nodunnē äṅgäṅgā
lovuturā budun kavada dakinnē äṅgäṅgā

Another example of a *kavi*, in sung chant, based on a rhythmical meter of up-country (the area around Kandy, Sri Lanka) dance patterns, tells of the coming of the revered tooth relic of the Buddha to Sri Lanka. The verses begin with an invitation of the gods Brahmā, Ganeś, Śiva, Skanda, Sumanā, and Viṣṇu (*sat at vat at tisulat haribara sumanā ēranyagarbha*), and a host of other deities, that the Buddha descend to India, there to become enlightened. The verses continue:

Having come from the heavens
  Of the thirty-[three],
He entered the womb
  Of famous Māyā and later was born.
Having sat at twenty-four auspicious
  Seats [of previous Buddhas],
Having fulfilled twenty-four
  Innumerable perfections,
Having caused twenty-four thousand
  To attain *nibbāna*,
The King of Sages, who had become the
  Buddha, passed away.

In Sinhala:

ävit pasiṅdu māyā kusa väsa bibi veminā tidāsa pura
sūvisi maṅdapayaka väḍa siṭalā
sūvisi asaṅkaya peruman puralā
sūvisi dahasak nivanaṭa häralā
vädiyayi muniraja budu vī ekalā.

On occasion dancers, while in procession, will chant these verses, and some might chant them before the tooth relic at the temple of the tooth relic, Daladā Maligawa, in Kandy. The procession of the tooth relic (*daladā perahära*), has provided a context for dance and a subject for song. The Golden Chimes, a recent "pop" group, have recorded a song with rhythmical patterns derived from the Portuguese. The song is youthful, popular, rather descriptive, but not without insight. Two verses are

The chinking sound
Of those selling beetle,
Like the sound
Of dancers' anklets,
The cracking sound
Of whips,
Tell us the *perahära* is coming nigh.
And it spreads afar the majesty
Of the venerable tooth relic.

Faintly hearing from their moving lips
Kavi-verses sung with *horaṇā*,
Up-country dancers come,
Moving feet to the rhythm of *gäṭa*-drum,
Bringing auspiciousness
To the *daladā perahära*

In Sinhala:

kiṅkiṅi nada dena
sārabulatviṭa vikuṇana ayagē sīnu hanḍayi
kasa handa pupuraṇa apahaṭa perahära
laṅga ena bava pavasayi
daladā samiňdugē teda paturayi

horaṇā nadeṭa kiyamin kavipada tolpeti maturannā
gäṭabera täleṭa tabamin pā deka uḍa raṭa naṭu ennā
daladā perahära siri ganvā.

34. An English translation of the *Jayamaṅgala Gāthā* is provided by the Venerables Nārada Mahā Thera and Kassapa Thera in *The Mirror of the Dhamma* (Colombo: Ceylon Daily News, June 1961), pp. 45–48. A recording of these verses, beautifully sung by a man, accompanied by only a *thambura*, followed by a Sinhala translation in prose, finely articulated and softly spoken by a man, was broadcast by the Sri Lanka Broadcasting Corporation—Sinhala Service, on Vesak, 1980.

35. *Sabba pāpassa akaranaṃ.*
kusalassa upasaṃpadā
sacittapariyodapanaṃ
etam buddhāna sāsanaṃ (*Dhp*., v. 183)

36. *Buddaṃ saraṇē sirasa darāgena*
dammaṃ saraṇē sita pahadāgena
sangaṃ saraṇē sivuru darāgena
iññayi tun saraṇē adahāgena.

This verse, and the second sung by the group, but with very slight modification, can be found in *Purāṇa Tun Saraṇaya,* author(s) unknown, but probably at least two centuries old (my copy; Mātara, Sri Lanka: Kānti Velando, n.d.), p. 3, vv. 16–17.

37. From my recording, the Sinhala is

saraṇayi saraṇayi buddaṃ saraṇayi
saraṇayi saraṇayi dammaṃ saraṇayi
saraṇayi saraṇayi sangaṃ saraṇayi
saraṇayi saraṇayi mē tun saraṇayi

When an idea occurs twelve times in one verse so positioned, one can hardly fail to note the significance of this idea, namely, refuge, in the Theravāda heritage.

An emeritus colleague, who had taught the Buddhist tradition at a prestigeous college for women in Massachusetts, said a few years ago, on hearing this recording of the verses sung in this manner, "I've taught the threefold refuge for over thirty years, but I think now, for the first time, I understand it."

38. The occasional critical comments or reticence to approve this new ritual form might reflect a reluctance to break with tradition. It might also reflect a sense that monks do well to refrain from composing verses for the laity. So, *D.*, I.11, regarding *kavi,* and the *Dambadeṇi Katikāvata* (thirteenth century) paragraph 49 in *The Katikāvatas; Laws of the Buddhist Order of Ceylon from the 12th century to the 18th century,* critically ed. trans. and annotated by Nandasena Ratnapala, "Münchener Studien zur Sprachwissenschaft" (Munich: Mikrokopie GmbH., 1971), p. 55, regarding *slokas.*

39. My recorded copy was taken from a recording made by Dr. B. Sirisena, who worked with me in July 1981 as we both searched for relevant recordings by listening to our tape holdings.

40. The Sinhala of the verse:

häma sitakama pin situvili vēvā
metta karunā diyaren näha vēvā

samagiya sāmaya mehi pätirēvā
siyaludenā lova suvapat vēvā.

41. The passage can be found in *S.*, I.43: *rūpam jīrati maccānam nāmagottaṃ na jīrati.*

42. *lassana säma dē mohotaka suva dē*
ehi kelavara duka vē
ehi kelavara duka vē

Compare *Dhp.*, vv. 186–187.

43. *deneta penēnaṃ suvaňda dänēnaṃ*
savana bihiri näti naṃ
säpata vāsi vī vipataṭa vī
kimada säpeka paskam.

44. *dälvena atarē sadaham dīpē*
maňda gilennē andurē pāpē
bududahamin tora säpak nätē
parama suvaya ēkayi.

45. *ataraturē nomäri märe*
dasa dahas varē
nisala nätē sasala vetē
notira sasara sāgarē.

46. *kuṇu kaya nisaruyi näta pavatinnē*
kala hoňda pamaṇayi melova räňdennē
näti bärikama leda duk äti vannē
apaṭayi minisunē
äyi meya nositannē notira sasara sāgarē.

Compare *Dhp.*, vv. 146–148.

47. *sambuddha saddharma anuhasin*
gōvinda śrī skanda śāntiyen
kamalāsanārūdha sarasvatī āsirvādayen
rasika oba milanayen
ānanda janakavū
mē soňduru rātri yāmayē
suvahasak savan yuga
prītiyen udam vēvā
prītiyen udam vēvā.

48. *sahasak domnas duk gini atarē*
dävena mahada situvili gini andurē
samiňda obe piḷiruva duṭu pamaṇin
nivī nivī yayī arumaya kimadō.

49. *pirī tirī yana maha vaturak sē*
galā hälena sihiläl gangulak sē
giman nivālana mē bava katarē
nivan sadālana budu guna mahimē
maha mevuna uyanē
samādhi budu pilimē
samādhi budu pilimē

aḍavan vū denetin galanā
met muditā karuṇā dhārā
aḍvan vū denetin galanā
met muditā karuṇā dhārā.

The English translation appearing in the text was jointly made with Mahinda Palihawadana in Kandy, Sri Lanka, 1971.

50. Omitting the refrains, the Sinhala is

muni siripā piyumē lovuturu haňda pävarē
pavan hamā ē giman nivālana
nivī pahan vī laya sänahē.

51. *Vin.*, II.108. These five disadvantages are also given in *A.*, III.251. However, there, the irritation of the householders is explained with reference to the third disadvantage in the sequence of the five by the observation, "these recluse Sakya-sons sing just like we sing."

52. In fact the Pāli term that stands behind the usual English rendering of "council" is *sangīti*; a word meaning a "song" or "chorus" and was used to refer to the early convocations because the texts were chanted and through this means of comparing memories an established memorized canon took shape.

53. There is some discussion in Sri Lanka, not yet widely conducted or available in published form, about whether devotional music or singing (*bhakti-gī*) is indigenous to the Theravāda heritage. A frequently met opinion is that this genre of religious music in the tradition is a recently reconstructed

borrowing or response to religious music of Western and Christian origin. Such appears to be the case especially at Vesak, the festive occasion of celebrating the birth, enlightenment, and the complete, final *nibbāna/nirvāna* of the Buddha, on a parallel with Christmas carols and hymns of Christmastide. But the degree to which this opinion represents a comprehensive statement of the case remains to a considerable degree based on an argument from silence: there has been no tradition of preserving in written documents a musical heritage. It is entirely plausible that religious songs were sung by the laity in the villages or while on pilgrimage, although musical scores remained unwritten.

In a tradition that has long excelled in the literary mode of versification in superb poetry in Pāli and Sinhala, it appears that, at this initial stage of inquiry into this facet of this complex cumulative tradition, one might withold the opinion that religious music, whether appropriately labeled *bhakti-gī* or otherwise designated, is not indigenous to the history of Buddhist men and women in Sri Lanka.

54. See W. S. Karunatillake, "The Religiousness of Buddhists in Sri Lanka Through Belief and Practice," pp. 3–5, and L. P. N. Perera, "The Significance of the Sangha for the Laity," pp. 79–100, both in *Religiousness in Sri Lanka*, ed. John Ross Carter (Colombo: Marga Institute, 1979).

55. This point was made by M. Palihawadana when he wrote, "The 'creative passivity' at the end of the field of possible action serves as the ground for the emergence of salvific change...." "Is There a Theravada Buddhist Idea of Grace?" in *Christian Faith in a Religiously Plural World*, ed. Donald G. Dawe and John B. Carman (Maryknoll, N.Y.: Orbis Press, 1978), p. 190.

56. See Edmund Perry and Shanta Ratnayaka, "The Sangha as Refuge in the Theravāda Buddhist Tradition," in *The Threefold Refuge in the Theravāda Buddhist Tradition*, pp. 41–55, where the recurrent observation is recently made again, that the soteriological process does not require entry into the monastic order.

57. *Thag.*, 43, v. 398.

58. *Thag.*, 49, v. 467.

59. *The Dhammapada*, translated by Carter and Palihawadana, pp. 370–371.

60. Palihawadana, "Is There a Theravada Buddhist Idea of Grace?" p. 191.

CHAPTER 10

1. Apart from some revision, this chapter was presented as a paper at a conference held on June 16, 1979, in honor of Wilfred Cantwell Smith, arranged by his former students, at the Center for the Study of World Religions, Harvard University. I broached some of the points elaborated here in a lecture at Northwestern University on February 15, 1979.

2. On the inadequacy of notions like "objective/objectivity" and "subjective/subjectivity" to suggest how we should set about our comparative studies of humankind's religiousness or to represent what we are attempting to do in the Humanities and, further, on the conceptual limitations imposed by the notion of "discipline," see Wilfred Cantwell Smith, "Methodology and the Study of Religion: Some Misgivings," in *Methodological Issues in Religious Studies*, ed. Robert D. Baird (Chico, Calif.: New Horizons Press, 1975), pp. 1–30; and "Objectivity and the Humane Sciences: A New Proposal," in *Religious Diversity: Essays by Wilfred Cantwell Smith,* ed. W. Oxtoby (New York: Harper and Row, 1976), pp. 160–180.

3. Gerardus van der Leeuw, "Some Recent Achievements Of Psychological Research and Their Application to History, in Particular the History of Religion," in *Classical Approaches to the Study of Religion: Aims, Methods and Theories of Research*, ed. Jacques Waardenburg (The Hague: Mouton, 1973), vol. 1, *Introduction and Anthology,* pp. 399–406.

4. Wilfred Cantwell Smith, "Objectivity and the Humane Sciences," in *Religious Diversity*, p. 166.

5. Ibid. See, further, Wilfred Cantwell Smith, *Belief and History* (Charlottesville: University Press of Virginia, 1977), p. 6, where a similar point is made, but with a significant addition: "An individual becomes a person in society; and a society becomes a community by being personal."

6. Heinz Bechert, *Buddhismus, Staat und Gesellschaft in den Ländern des Theravāda-Buddhismus*, vol. 1, *Grundlagen, Ceylon* (Frankfurt am Main: Alfred Metzner Verlag, 1966), p. 37.

7. Ibid.

8. Ibid., p. 38.

9. Michael Ames, "Magical-animism and Buddhism: A Structural Analysis of the Sinhalese Religious System," *Journal of Asian Studies* 23, Special

Issue: 22. Hans-Dieter Evers, in *Monks, Priests and Peasants: A Study of Buddhism and Social Structure in Central Ceylon* (Leiden: E. J. Brill, 1972), pp. 104–105, 107, picks up on Ames's definition and carries on with it rather uncritically. Incidently, Ames has recorded a peculiar interpretation of *saraṇagänīma.* "In Sinhalese," Ames wrote, "it is *lokottara saraṇagänīma,* versus *laukika saraṇagänīma,* i.e., 'taking refuge in the supramundane' (Buddhism) as opposed to 'taking refuge in the worldly' (magical-animism)." Michael Ames, "Ritual Prestations and the Structure of the Sinhalese Pantheon," Cultural Report Series no. 13, Southeast Asia Studies, Yale University, 1966, p. 37. I remain puzzled about the extent to which the evidence Ames uncovered penetrates Sinhala Buddhist self-understanding.

10. Chapter 4.

11. Ernst Troeltsch, *The Social Teachings of the Christian Churches,* trans. Olive Wyon (N.Y.: Harper Torchbooks, 1960), vol. 1, pp. 107–108.

12. Max Weber, *The Sociology of Religion,* trans. Ephriam Fischoff (Boston: Beacon Press, 1964), p. 266.

13. Ibid., p. 267. Heinz Bechert picks up on this terminology in "Contradictions in Sinhalese Buddhism," *Tradition and Change in Theravāda Buddhism,* ed. Bardwell L. Smith (Leiden: E. J. Brill, 1973), p. 11.

14. The standard Pāli forms are *nikkhamati, abhinikkhamati,* with, of course, the ideal paradigm being the act of Gotama, *mahābhinikkhamati.*

15. The standard Pāli expression is "one goes forth [one who has gone forth] from home to homelessness" (*agārasmā anagariyam pabbajati* (*pabbajita*) and "one goes forth into the order" (*sāsane pabbajati*). Related to this notion, Victor Turner has written,

> A further aspect of pilgrimage is suggested by the Buddhist concept of such sacred journeys. It seems that Buddhist usage derived first from Hindu practices. This makes it interesting that the Pāli form of the Sanskrit word for pilgrimage (*pravrajya*: Pali, *pabbajja,* literally, "a going forth," "retirement from the world") should be the technical term for admission or "ordination" to the first grade of the Buddhist monkhood. Some Buddhists, as well as Hindu holymen, like the "palmers" of medieval Europe, spent their whole lives visiting pilgrimage centers. But the point I wish to make is that there is a *rite de passage,* even an initiatory ritual character about pilgrimage.

Victor Turner, "The Center out There: Pilgrim's Goal," *History of Religions* 12, no. 3 (February 1973): 204.

By the time the Sanskrit term could have developed a technical usage, meaning "pilgrimage," in a Hindu sense (*pravrajya* means basically "to wander abroad"), the Buddhist term *pabbajja* was already formalized as a technical term denoting "going forth" into the *sāsana* or *sangha*. The very early usage of *pravrajya* suggests an activity of wandering about as a mendicant, a part of which conduct or behavior, conceivably, would entail visiting religiously significant places.

Buddhists have used other words to describe what Turner and some others tend to call *pilgrimage*. One of the earliest references to this Buddhist activity (*D.* II.141) mentions "those wandering along the route of the *ceityas*" or "those engaged in the *cetiya* journey" (*cetiyacārikam ahindantā*). Sinhala Buddhists speak of "a going for worship" (*vandanāvata yāma*) and especially with regard to Śrī Pāda, "performing compassion" (*karuṇā] karanavā*), where some tend to speak of *pilgrimage*.

16. At a glance one can discern the inappropriateness of interpreting *lokiya/laukika* in an analysis of the religious system as meaning "secular, profane," even though there is evidence of a recently coined Sinhala term, *lōkāyata*, being used for the English notion of *secular*. Incidently, *lōkāyata* traditionally meant "having to do with the mundane, the world (only)" and has designated the Cārvāka school of materialistic thought.

17. I think we should note that this modern paradigm is itself another variable to place alongside the concepts "Buddhism," "religion," and "secular," to enable one to analyze primarily a modernization/Westernization process that has been developing and secondarily to consider the relationship of currently developing religious understanding and social ethics among Sinhala Buddhists. See also Bardwell L. Smith, "Introduction," *The Two Wheels of Dhamma: Essays on the Theravāda Tradition in India and Ceylon*, ed. B. L. Smith (Chambersburg, Pa.: American Academy of Religion, 1972), pp. 1–2; and also his "Introduction," *Tradition and Change in Theravāda Buddhism*, p. 5.

18. On this way of viewing a cumulative tradition, I refer again to W. C. Smith, *The Meaning and End of Religion: A New Approach to the Religious Traditions of Mankind* (New York: Macmillan Company, 1963).

19. The process of adopting a chronological calendar sequence utilizing *Before Christ* and *Anno Domini* is not automatic. Note the attempts to provide

parallel dating procedures in some books published in Sri Lanka, and attempts, by some, to use the abbreviations, B.C.E., Before the Common Era, and C.E., the Common Era; or *Śrī Bu. Va.* (*Śrī Buddha varṣa*) in contrast with *Kri. Va.* (*Kristu varṣa*). This might suggest that a reflective Sinhala Buddhist could be more aware of religioius implications in the dating procedure than, perhaps, his or her foreign field researcher.

20. We might want to be alert not to allow an aspect of this cultural heritage, a kind of syllogistic exclusivity, in the West to give rise to a reader's possible misinterpretation of the religious practices of Sinhala men and women. Consider the following potentially misleading statement: "In making the *dēvāla pūjāva*, the individual customarily visits a Buddha shrine first to pay homage to Buddha (*vandanā*). With the merit thus earned, and a tray of flowers and vegetables, *he turns his back on Buddha* [italics mine] and goes to the *dēvalāya* to propitiate the *deviyā*." Michael Ames, "Ritual Prestations and the Structure of the Sinhalese Pantheon," Cultural Report Series no. 13 (Southeast Asia Studies, Yale University, 1966), p. 41.

21. Michael Ames, "Ideological and Social Change in Ceylon," *Human Organization* 22, no. 1 (Spring 1963): 46.

22. The three quoted statements are taken from one paragraph written by Gananath Obeyesekere, "The Great Tradition and the Little in the Perspective of Sinhalese Buddhism," *Journal of Asian Studies* 22, no. 2 (February 1963): 148.

23. Ibid.

24. Obeyesekere's advance was mainly within anthropological studies of persons in Sri Lanka. W. Brede Kristensen has placed this perspective before students of comparative religious studies. He wrote, "Every religion ought to be understood from its own standpoint, for that is how it is understood by its own adherents." *The Meaning of Religion: Lectures in the Phenomenology of Religion*, trans. John B. Carman (The Hague: Martinus Nijhoff, 1960), p. 6.

25. See, for example, Etienne Lamotte, *Histoire du bouddhisme indien* (Louvain: Bibliotheque du Museon, vol. 43, 1958), pp. 71–89.

26. Robert McAfee Brown, *Is Faith Obsolete?* (Philadelphia: The Westminster Press, 1976), pp. 28ff. Although Brown is writing as a self-conscious Christian theologian for a Western reading public (and makes some serious oversights in a few asides about the Buddhist case), his phrasing, pertaining to the notion of faith, might dispose us to consider an ongoning process by Sin-

hala Buddhists of finding new meaning, or discerning meaning anew, in their heritage as possibly also, conceivably primarily, an expression of faith rather than "modernization."

27. Paul Tillich, *Dynamics of Faith* (N.Y.: Harper and Brothers, 1957), p. 100. M. Holmes Hartshorne, my late colleague at Colgate, has indicated the familiarity with doubt in the religious life of some of us in his work, *The Faith to Doubt: A Protestant Response to Criticisms of Religion* (Englewood Cliffs, N.J.: Prentice-Hall, 1963).

28. Robert N. Bellah, "Epilogue," in *Religion and Progress in Modern Asia*, ed. Robert N. Bellah (N.Y.: The Free Press, 1965), p. 224.

29. Ibid., p. 193.

30. Ibid., p. 194.

31. The Theravāda tradition has interpreted *sangha* in the threefold refuge not as *bhikkhusangha*, the order of mendicants or the monastic order, although this Pāli term occurred in a very early formulation of "refuge," but, rather, the *sāvakasangha*, those persons who have made the breakthrough into *dhamma*, interpreted as the four paths and four fruits together with *nibbāna*. See Chapter 4; and Edmund F. Perry and Shanta Ratnayaka, "The Sangha as Refuge in the Theravāda Buddhist Tradition,"in *The Threefold Refuge in the Theravāda Buddhist Tradition*, ed. John Ross Carter (Chambersburg, Pa.: Anima Books, 1982), pp. 41–55.

32. We might well learn a great deal about the soteriological process and its sociological relevance by adding to our information the interpretations provided by parents of their son's or sons' "going forth."

33. *Mahāvaṃsa* (PTS edition), 5.196–197. The commentary on the *Mahāvaṃsa*, the *Vaṃsatthappakāsinī* (PTS edition), I.228, notes for this passage, "No others do as the mothers and fathers of *bhikkhus*, having undertaken the weighty task to be done for the *sāsana*, having demonstrated reverence—the elder (*thera*) spoke of 'heirs of the *sāsana*' in connection with this meaning."

34. See the relevant considerations in E. F. Shumacher, "Buddhist Economics," in his *Small Is Beautiful: Economics as If People Mattered* (N.Y.: Harper and Row, 1975), pp. 53–62.

35. I have not considered one who might have refrained from entering the monastic order because he judged it to be corrupt. Such person is main-

taining that his *idea of the bhikkhu* is not what he understands others to have taken it to mean.

36. Of course, there are other methods of discussing the symbiotic relationship between the Sangha and laity; the laity gives material support to the Sangha and the Sangha gives spiritual support to the laity; the laity, by giving, acquires *puñña/pin* (a word, I continue to sense, is becoming increasingly more difficult to translate adequately—ordinarily translated as "merit"). Two esteemed colleagues in Sri Lanka have responded to requests to provide interpretations of the relationship between the Sangha and the laity. See L. P. N. Perera, "The Significance of the Sangha for the Laity," pp. 79–100, and Ven. Havanpola Ratanasara, "'Reaching Out' as an Expression of 'Going Forth,'" pp. 101–111, both in *Religiousness in Sri Lanka,* ed. John Ross Carter (Colombo: Marg Institute, 1979).

37. Gananath Obeyesekere, "Religious Symbolism and Political Change in Ceylon," *The Two Wheels of Dhamma*, pp. 58–78.

38. Ibid., pp. 64ff.

39. Ibid., pp. 63–64. Obeyesekere also notes the relevance of the monk's vestments in this context. On this matter of "spatial separation" one might add that Theravāda Buddhists have not been in complete agreement about how to establish a precise distance between village and monastery. See *Vism.*, II.48–51, pp. 58–59, where the opinions of the experts of the *Vinaya* differ from the *Suttanta* experts, and a method in the *Abhidhamma* for measuring this distance does not coincide with either a *Vinaya* method or *Suttanta* method. A "rule of thumb" appears to have been a standard phrase, "which is neither too far nor too near this village" (*yam assa gāmato n'eva avidūre na accāsanne*), *Vin.*, I.39; II.158. This standard phrase, I should think, strikingly reflects how the "spatial separation of monk and temple from the peasant and the village," which Obeyesekere notes, is to be interpreted as a manifestation of "ideal doctrinal postulation." The soteriological process is not utterly unrelated to society nor is it to be identified with ordinary societal patterns.

40. Obeyesekere, ibid., p. 64.

41. In brief, let me reiterate here, that what some have meant by "this worldy and other worldly" Buddhists have called *lokiya*, or "pertaining to this world," or "customary." For Sinhala Buddhists, there is also *lokuttara*, meaning "*other* than 'this worldly' *and* 'other worldly'," "transcending *both* 'this worldly *and* other worldly'." So, I do not think this particular paradigm is adequate.

42. One might add this definitional element to Obeyesekere's consideration of what he terms *Buddhism* in "Religious Symbolism," p. 62.

43. I seize on Victor Turner's suggestive title, "The Center Out There: Pilgrim's Goal," *History of Religions* 12, no. 3 (February 1973): 204.

44. Obeyesekere, "The Great Tradition and the Little," pp. 147–148.

45. Michael Ames, "Buddha and the Dancing Goblins: A Theory of Magic and Religion," *American Anthropologist* 66, no. 1 (February 1964): 78.

46. See my brief lexical study, "Traditional Definitions of the Term *Dhamma*," *Philosophy East and West* 26, no. 3 (July 1976): 329–337. The more thorough study can be found in my *Dhamma: Western Academic and Sinhalese Buddhist Interpretations* (Tokyo: Hokuseido Press, 1978).

47. See the brilliant essay by Mahinda Palihawadana, "Is There a Theravada Buddhist Idea of Grace?" in *Christian Faith in a Religiously Plural World,* ed. Donald G. Dawe and John B. Carman (Maryknoll, N.Y.: Orbis Press, 1978), p. 191.

CHAPTER 11

1. See the related observations by Wilfred Cantwell Smith in "Participation: The Changing Christian Role in Other Cultures," in *Religious Diversity: Essays by Wilfred Cantwell Smith* (New York: Harper and Row, 1976), pp. 117–137.

2. See Wilfred Cantwell Smith, "Mankind's Religiously Divided History Approaches Self-Consciousness," in ibid., pp. 96-114.

INDEX